WHOSE PROPERTY?
THE DEEPENING CONFLICT BETWEEN PRIVATE
PROPERTY AND DEMOCRACY IN CANADA

According to Roy Vogt, questions about property rights lie at the heart of some of the most contentious debates in Canadian society. In this book, Vogt shows how the key problems confronting Canadian democracy – issues of state power, Aboriginal entitlement, environmental protection, and the distribution of rights in the family and the workplace – turn on the question of how property rights should be defined and distributed.

Vogt contends that conventional definitions of property are unhelpful and even detrimental in the context of the profound social changes under way in Canada. He argues for a more flexible understanding of property, one that can better accommodate the needs of an increasingly complex democratic society.

This broad-ranging study introduces a new way of thinking about the distribution of rights and power in society. It will be of interest to anyone who is concerned with the current and future state of Canadian democracy.

ROY VOGT (deceased) was associate professor of economics at the University of Manitoba and wrote widely about economic planning, business ethics, and workplace democracy.

ROY VOGT

Whose Property?
The Deepening Conflict between Private Property and Democracy in Canada

UNIVERSITY OF TORONTO PRESS
Toronto Buffalo London

© University of Toronto Press Incorporated 1999
Toronto Buffalo London
Printed in Canada

ISBN 0-8020-4364-x (cloth)
ISBN 0-8020-8186-x (paper)

Printed on acid-free paper

Canadian Cataloguing in Publication Data

Vogt, Roy

   Whose property? : the deepening conflict between private property and democracy in Canada

   Includes bibliographical references and index.
   ISBN 0-8020-4364-x (bound)   ISBN 0-8020-8186-x (pbk.)

   1. Right of property – Canada.   I. Title.

JC605.v63 1999   323.4′6′0971   c98-932589-x

University of Toronto Press acknowledges the financial assistance to its publishing program of the Canada Council for the Arts and the Ontario Arts Council.

This book has been published with the help of a grant from the Humanities and Social Sciences Federation of Canada, using funds provided by the Social Sciences and Humanities Research Council of Canada.

Contents

ACKNOWLEDGMENTS   vii

Introduction: Rethinking Property Rights   3

Part One: Property Rights in History
1 The Evolution of Property Rights   13
2 State versus Private Property   35

Part Two: Property Rights in Transition
3 Family Law and Family Property   67
4 Aboriginal Property Rights   83
5 Citizen Property Rights   109

Part Three: New Property
6 New Property Rights in the Workplace   143
7 New Property in Jobs and Social Investments   173

Conclusion: Restructuring Property Rights   197

NOTES   209
REFERENCES   213
NAME INDEX   231
SUBJECT INDEX   237

Acknowledgments

Roy Vogt completed the manuscript for this book prior to his death in 1997. It was the culmination of many years of research and of many more years spent thinking and talking about the way in which basic economic institutions – including the institution of property – affect the lives of citizens.

Vogt shared his thoughts on this subject with many people, and special thanks go to his family, to his students, and to his colleagues in St Paul's College and the Economics Department at the University of Manitoba. One of his colleagues, John Loxley, generously gave up time from his own sabbatical research to help prepare the manuscript for publication. Many others contributed comments and editorial advice on earlier drafts. We wish particularly to acknowledge the contributions of David Blair, Gerald Friesen, Paul Phillips, Al Reimer, and James Urry.

Thanks also to Virgil Duff and the editorial staff at the University of Toronto Press, who were consistently helpful and supportive, and to John Parry, who did an excellent job on the final editing of the manuscript.

Roy Vogt would have given his fullest acknowledgment to the contributions of his wife, Ruth, his partner in all things, with whom he shared his work and his commitments. Typically, Ruth Vogt was involved with every stage of this work, from discussing and editing the first drafts to preparing the final index. The book is dedicated to her.

Paul Vogt
Winnipeg, Manitoba
December 1998

WHOSE PROPERTY?
THE DEEPENING CONFLICT BETWEEN PRIVATE
PROPERTY AND DEMOCRACY IN CANADA

Introduction:
Rethinking Property Rights

We are in the midst of a major transformation in which property rights are being fundamentally redefined.

Joseph Sax 1983, 481

Property has been at the core of most social upheavals in human history, including those of the recent past. The many wars of this rather bloody century have been inspired for the most part by dreams of territorial conquest or by grievances over the seizure of territory. The major social revolutions of this century – the Russian of 1917 and the Chinese of 1949 – had as one of their primary goals the abolition of a particular form of property – private property. The recent undoing of the socialist experiments spawned by the Russian revolution involves above all the re-establishment of private property.

In a world of finite resources and a rapidly growing population it is not surprising that people everywhere are concerned about both the extent and the means of their control over property. The concern is pervasive as well as potentially explosive. As one student of the history of property relations has observed, 'Persons who are consistently on the short end of what they consider to be unfair [property] bargains ... may eventually wonder why it is that they afford others the position of rightful owners [of property]' (Schmid 1978, 30).

It is one of the prime duties of a state, and probably its most difficult one, to define, allocate, and protect property rights within its boundaries. The stability of any political order, whether democratic or dictatorial, depends very largely on its success in establishing satisfactory rules of property ownership. The problem is compounded by dynamic social forces that destabilize existing property relationships and also by the fact that what might be considered a satisfactory set of arrangements by one generation seems quite inadequate and even grossly unfair to another.

One of the main arguments of this study is that Canada, along with many other democratic, capitalist countries, is undergoing a significant re-evaluation of its property system and is experiencing profound social changes that are challenging existing property rules. Many Canadians no longer find the rules satisfactory and are demanding change. This discontent has already contributed to some of Canada's major economic and social problems and threatens, in the absence of reform, to create even more difficulties. The dynamics of change are likely to increase rather than diminish.

A Gallup poll taken in August 1987 found that Canadians thought that it was more important to entrench property rights in the new Canadian constitution than other rights that have taken centre stage in the ongoing constitutional debates, such as Native rights or the range of Quebec's powers. Of those polled, over 80 per cent thought it important to change Canada's constitution in order to protect their property rights (*Winnipeg Free Press*, 8 Oct. 1987, 8).

Many of the challenges to Canada's current property system that are examined in this study appear to result from a basic and growing conflict between two of the main forces that have shaped our society: capitalism and democracy. It may seem strange to suggest any opposition between these two; numerous scholars argue that there is a positive, symbiotic relationship between the development of capitalism and democracy. Milton Friedman's (1962) classic statement of this relationship, *Capitalism and Freedom*, is only one of many linking the growth of democratic freedoms to the development of capitalist institutions. It appears indisputable that the greater protection granted to private property under capitalism, and the spirit of individualism unleashed by capitalism's unrestricted pursuit of personal gain, have contributed significantly to the growth of individual freedom and democratic political institutions in the industrialized West. Capitalism is clearly not a sufficient condition for the triumph of democracy – witness the dictatorial capitalist states of this century in prewar Europe and postwar Latin America – but it appears at least to be a necessary condition.

To grant that basic elements of capitalism are necessary precursors of democracy does not, however, rule out the possibility of deep and growing conflicts between the two as each becomes a dominant feature of a given society. A recent study by Jerry Adelman (1994) of the relationship between property rights and frontier development in Argentina and Canada suggests ways in which underlying conflicts may develop between capitalist institutions and democratic conditions. On the Canadian prairies the growth of democracy was initially supported through a Jeffersonian strategy of creating independent labour through private property ownership. The widespread diffusion of independently owned farms, cheaply obtained, boded well for what Adelman calls a 'socially healthy' society (Adelman 1994, 269). However, the drive by prairie farmers to obtain more land and capital in order to satisfy a growing world market, which was a rational response to capitalist market signals, ultimately raised the cost of owning land to the point where a majority of farmers ceased to be independent labourers working on their own property. If private ownership of property – especially productive property – is a sine qua non of democracy, as most proponents argue, then the experience of the Canadian prairies poses a troubling dilemma.

Capitalism appears to thrive on the institution of private property, but like some animals (including humans) that devour their young, it creates forces in its wake that destroy the property rights of large segments of the population. It does so partly, as the prairie example suggests, and as modern industry in general demonstrates, by promoting the creation of large production units that are owned by a small portion of the population. It also does so by steamrolling over the rights of those not attuned to its aggressive pursuit of economic gain and to its peculiar, legalistic notions of how property ownership is legitimately established. The experience of Canada's aboriginal peoples testifies to this, as does that of most women in Canada. As long as property rights could be obtained only by means of money purchase, many women stood little chance of achieving property rights in marriage. This meant therefore that the rules of capitalism, as interpreted by the courts until recently, prevented half of the population from obtaining the property rights that capitalists consider so important.

The tendencies ascribed above to capitalism seriously erode the property base that is considered essential for the maturing of a democratic society. They arise, however, after democratic aspirations and democratic political institutions have already taken deep root. All adults have been given the franchise and see it as their indisputable right to elect their political representatives. Various groups in society have learned how to obtain favourable laws and benefits through the political process, partly offsetting their loss of control over private resources. A maturing democracy produces what has been termed 'an expansionary logic of personal rights' (Bowles and Gintis 1986). The result is a profound, ever-widening conflict within democratic-capitalist societies. On the one hand the expansionary, property-eroding forces of capitalism are reducing the democratic base that free people require. On the other hand, a population long exposed to democratic freedoms seeks to enlarge that base.

The so-called Keynesian accommodation of the postwar period, which involved some political management of the economy and substantial efforts to implement programs of income security and redistribution, helped for a time to placate those whose well-being is most endangered by the loss of effective property rights. However, that accommodation no longer seems to work. The twin problems of inflation and unemployment have recently eluded successful solutions by government. At the same time, the intrinsic conflicts in Canadian society have deepened. The business community, strongly encouraged by business-oriented governments, exposes workers to greater job insecurity by promoting global strategies that increase mobility of capital and jobs but not of labour (unlike the European Union, which has made greater labour mobility a major objective). Simultaneously, social benefits financed through the state, which can in effect be considered to have created important new property rights for Canadians, are threatened by concerted efforts to reduce the scope of government activity. Further, the growing interest of Canadians in protecting their environment, which this study characterizes as the exercise of citizens' property rights, is thwarted by the aggressive exploitation of natural resources, which the new global economy appears to exacerbate.

The evidence suggests that Canada's relatively successful economic system continues relentlessly to follow its own inner logic: to pursue profits wherever they may be found, with strategies that pay lip service to property rights but actually erode the rights of the majority of citizens who do not own productive resources. As two American scholars observe, 'Wealth, particularly the ownership of the productive apparatus, confers powers that are relatively resilient in the face of populist assault' (Bowles and Gintis 1986, 3).

At the same time, however, the attempts of many citizens to enlarge their control over resources – in effect, to expand their property rights – should not be seen as an ephemeral phenomenon that can easily be swept away. Even strong business–government alliances, responding primarily to the market signals of a global capitalist economy, cannot simply dismiss the numerous democratic initiatives through which citizens have sought to expand their property rights in the postwar period. The language of rights will not go away. Canadian women, for example, have fought hard to increase their property rights, and the courts have now entrenched these rights so firmly that they cannot be taken away. Aboriginal peoples in Canada will increase, rather than diminish, their efforts to gain legal support for property claims that Canadian governments and courts have slighted for a long time. Canadians have shown that they will not easily give up such basic social benefits as health care and education, or retirement and unemployment benefits, in which they have made major investments and which they correctly perceive as constituting an essential element of their property rights. Canadian workers have gained some control over their workplaces through collective bargaining, but they are now pursuing strategies that may restore even more of the property rights that working men and women lost with the advent of industrial capitalism. Canadian citizens concerned about the environment will continue to press their right, against the logic of capitalist expansion, to have a major say in the way that resources affecting their communities are used. Finally, a majority of Canadians continue to believe that the state represents an important and legitimate avenue through which they can safeguard and expand their rights, again in defiance of the current economic logic that sees the nation-state primarily as an impediment to the global pursuit of profit.

This study focuses on conflicts that are intrinsic to Canadian society and extremely serious in their consequences. At the same time, it emphasizes that Canada has traditions and institutions, both capitalist and democratic in nature, which, if properly understood and used, bode well for the eventual resolution of some conflicts. There is, for example, a legal system that, on the basis of its common law background and its highly respected courts, has both the flexibility and the legitimacy to support new citizens' initiatives in property creation. For example, what is significant about the recent gains by women of property rights through their participation in a spousal relationship is not only the extent of property that has effectively changed hands but the legal and legislative decisions that produced the change. These may, as the study suggests, have positive repercussions in other areas where property rights are being challenged.

Consider also the example of property ownership that has emerged in our capitalist system. There still lingers in conventional wisdom an illusion that the modern corporation represents a form of private ownership in which production is managed efficiently because the resources are directed by private owners. We know, of course, that this is not true. The shareholders who own the corporation[1] have little direct impact on the management of the company's resources, and the actual managers generally have few or no ownership stakes. More important, however, is another illusion that lurks behind this conception: that property rights exist, and must exist, in a unitary package, controlled by one group of persons, to the exclusion of all others. In its actual workings, the modern corporation demonstrates the opposite: that property rights can be, and are, shared among different groups and individuals; usually among shareholders, managers, and workers. This means, in effect, that significant changes in the distribution of property rights can be achieved without destroying the corporation itself.

The illusion of unitary ownership has been promoted by critics as well as defenders of capitalism. Karl Marx thought that the only way to transfer significant property rights from capitalists to workers was to destroy the capitalist class. He was convinced that property could not be shared between workers and capitalists. The capitalists agreed with his insight and have done their best to ensure that workers would not overthrow them through the revolutions that Marx advocated. What our analysis shows, in contrast, is that property rights within most corporations are being redistributed, or transferred, all the time. A number of European countries have already demonstrated that a significant redistribution of rights to particular groups such as workers can occur without destroying the corporation or even reducing its efficiency. In the United States shareholders have a comparatively big role in the running of their enterprises, while workers, who are for the most part weakly unionized, have much less influence. In Japan, shareholders have traditionally played no significant role in the operations of their companies. Shareholders in Canada have less influence than their American counterparts, while workers appear to have slightly more.

A basic conclusion of this study, which is supported by the work of many other scholars, is that property rights in any society are changing all the time. A state that is genuinely concerned to address the conflicts that arise from disputes over property will accordingly use its unique powers to alter as well as to protect the rights of its citizens. Governments that legitimize only those forms of property that favour groups with which they have formed a special alliance for the purpose of achieving and holding on to power will soon enough face conflicts of the kind described in this study.

In exploring the contested terrain of property rights in Canada, I have made every effort to keep the analysis as objective as possible. However, it proved impossible to observe a convention prevalent in the academic world, of separating a scholarly from a personal approach to the issues being examined. The discussion inevitably involves questions of fairness and justice, and it touches on matters that deeply affect the life of every Canadian. Personal judgments therefore come into play at many points, and these I offer without apology. I have made a serious attempt, however, to support the judgments with the best available evidence and to express them with humility as well as with conviction.

Before economics became a highly specialized field, creating its own language and borrowing a more sophisticated scientific method, it was frequently called political economy. Those who practised political economy believed that the study of most economic phenomena required careful consideration of the social and political conditions in which they occur. Such a belief has shaped this study's examination of property. This is not, therefore, a work of economics, or of sociology, or of law. It is instead an attempt to mine and apply insights from these fields in order to clarify a major feature of our society, which, I believe, can be understood in no other way.

In this study, I attempt to analyse and clarify the intrinsic conflicts in the contested terrain of Canadian property rights. Part I defines property explicitly and describes how property rights have evolved in Canada (chapter 1). It also shows how, during this evolution, conflicts between state and private property have been, and continue to be, central issues (chapter 2). Part II focuses on new property rights achieved in the postwar period in the family (chapter 3) and on rights that are quite advanced but still some distance from completion, such as Aboriginal rights (chapter 4) and citizens' rights (chapter 5). I describe these last two types as property rights in transition. Chapters 6 and 7, in part III, deal with new forms of property, such as social benefits, intellectual property, and workers' control over jobs and the workplace, which are being seriously threatened at the present time or are relatively underdeveloped in Canada. The main problem addressed in these cases is general lack of recognition that the rights that citizens and workers are trying to defend and enlarge are indeed property rights. In other words, they are the kind of rights to which states have traditionally accorded the protection of property, but for reasons that are explored here, these rights are not receiving property protection at the present time. Finally, the conclusion summarizes the major findings of the study and suggests ways in which some of the conflicts described throughout the study might be ameliorated.

PART ONE
PROPERTY RIGHTS IN HISTORY

1
The Evolution of Property Rights

The meaning of property is not constant. The actual institution and the way people see it, and hence the meaning they give to the word, all change over time.

C.B. Macpherson 1978, 1

Canada has an abundance of things that people need for survival and personal enjoyment. This natural abundance has attracted immigrants from all over the world, driven by the hope that they might own and cultivate at least a small part of this vast, relatively unpopulated country. This chapter examines how successive waves of immigrants laid claim to the lands they settled: how, for example, early hunting and fishing rights were established and allocated, and under what kinds of property rules and traditions individuals obtained the right to farm particular plots of land or to exploit mineral, forest, and water resources.

Going back over the evolution of property rights in Canada one discovers a great mélange of rules and practices coexisting in a system that has been constantly changing. The volatile process through which Canadian property rights emerged reflects the very different traditions that the immigrants brought with them, as well as the unique demands that the development of this country imposed on them and their successors. It is also symptomatic of the complex and elusive nature of property itself. Therefore in order to understand how property rights evolved in Canada it is necessary first to examine the nature of property more closely. Next I look at the kinds of property concepts that immigrants brought to Canada with them, beginning with the ancestors of Canada's Inuit and

Indian populations. Finally, I consider how property concepts have evolved in Canada as an economic system has developed.

The Nature of Property

While property has to do with things, modern property theory focuses not on the things themselves but on the kinds of rights required to control their use. It therefore defines property as a bundle of rights pertaining to the use of things (cf. Bazelon 1970, 53; Wiles 1977, 35; Parkin 1981, 50, Reeve 1986, 11). The 'things' over which property rights are sought include productive resources, such as land, labour, and capital, and personal goods, such as food, clothing, and shelter. This study deals primarily with rights to productive resources.

Dozens of different rights pertaining to the use of productive resources have been identified by scholars in law and philosophy (see, for example, Honoré 1961 and Snare 1972). For our purposes, we can reduce these to three basic rights. *User rights* are the rights to determine how a productive resource will be used in the production process (for example, what to produce, the hiring and firing of labour, the amount of labour time to be used, and the amount of capital investment). In modern businesses these are commonly termed 'management rights.' *Income or enjoyment rights* involve the right to determine and appropriate the income arising from the use of resources (which also implies the assumption of responsibility for losses). *Disposal rights* consist of the right to buy and sell resources and facilities or to transfer them to someone else.

'Ownership' is tied closely to the exercise of such rights. Owners of property are assumed to have all or most of these rights. In a single business proprietorship or partnership, and in a typical family farm, all these rights may be exercised by a single person or a tightly knit group. This can be called a unitary type of ownership. In most large business organizations today the property rights described above are shared between different participants in the organization. A question then arises: who is the real 'owner' of the resources being used? In a typical corporation the shareholders may be thought of as the owners because they exercise some enjoyment rights and the basic disposal rights. The corporation is created through shareholders' investments. The distribution of profit, as well as the decision to close or sell the company, requires their approval. However, in that same corporation, user or management rights are exercised not by shareholders but by a management group, which usually has only a very small financial stake in the company (though shareholders may have some indirect management rights through their control over the appointment and dismissal of managers). Simultaneously, in corporations that bargain collectively with their workers, some basic income rights, and sometimes even users' rights, are shared between workers and managers.

As noted in the introduction, the actual pattern of property sharing varies from one corporation to another and from one country to another. General corporate practices may also change significantly over time without altering the outward appearance of the organization. Thus significant reforms may be possible without changing the basic character of the corporation. Confusion on this score seems widespread, as illustrated in an experience recorded by Lee Iacocca, former head of the (U.S.) Chrysler corporation. As part of a desperate, and successful, attempt to save the firm from bankruptcy, Iacocca proposed that the head of the Auto Workers Union, Douglas Fraser, be given a seat on the board of directors. The intention was to secure the cooperation of employees for a wage-reduction program. What Iacocca had not anticipated was the violent reaction of other business leaders to his suggestion. He was accused by many of them of undermining the American corporate system, of selling out to the creeping forces of socialism. As Iacocca ruefully observed, 'The business community went wild ... Until then, no representative of labor had ever sat on the board of a major American corporation. And in Japan they do it all the time. So what's the problem? It's that the average American CEO is a prisoner of ideology ... He still believes that labor has to be the natural, mortal enemy' (Iacocca and Novak 1984, 236–7). The proposal, which Chrysler adopted, did nothing to increase the company's socialist character. What it did, however slightly, was to change the distribution of property rights within the company. Labour's rights may have increased marginally at the expense of management and shareholders.

So who owns the modern corporation? There is no simple answer to the question. An accurate response would require a careful weighing of the different rights exercised by each of the participants in a particular corporate enterprise.

The major theoretical point illustrated by these examples is that property rights are often shared. Whenever a splitting of such rights among different parties occurs, it will be referred to in this study as 'shared property.' When they are not split, they are termed 'unitary property.'

Another feature of property rights is that they can be exercised exclusively or inclusively. 'Private property' is characterized by the exclusive exercise of such property rights by one party or more. Those persons in possession of private property have the right not only to use, enjoy, and dispose of the resources in their possession, but also to exclude others from the exercise of such rights with respect to those resources. 'Common property,' in contrast, refers to more inclusive use of resources. A fishery in which fishers cannot prevent others from harvesting in the same area is an example of common property.

To summarize: property consists of a bundle of rights with respect to the use, enjoyment, and disposal of resources. 'Unitary property' refers to a comprehensive control of property rights by a single person or a tightly knit group. 'Shared property' involves the sharing of property rights among several groups or individuals. 'Private property' refers to the exclusive exercise of such rights, while 'common property' involves a more inclusive exercise of rights.

Another characteristic of property essential for understanding its historical evolution is that it is very much a human creation, dependent on political institutions and laws. Jeremy Bentham observed, 'Property and law are born together and must die together. Before the laws there was no property; take away the laws, all property ceases' (quoted in Bazelon 1970, 55). Property rights cannot exist without legitimation and enforcement by a higher authority. Bentham was responding to a 'natural-rights theory,' identified with the seventeenth-century philosopher John Locke, which postulated a 'natural' right to property derived from the labour of the individual. It seemed to suggest that property rights in society could exist prior to and independent of the support of a state. However, even Locke acknowledged that property in society must be recognized and protected by the state (Bazelon 1970, 55; Tully 1980, 98–101; and Waterman 1982, 103). Through the state, or through another recognized higher authority, society grants property rights to some kinds of labour and not to others. Otherwise there would be no theft, because the labour of the thief would not be distinguished from anyone else's labour. As Schmid observes, 'The labour that is regarded as imparting a right is always a socially selective thing' (Schmid 1978, 24). At any time one is entitled to ask why only certain kinds of rights are legally admissible; for example, why managers are protected by the state in their right to fire workers, but workers are not protected by the state in holding on to their jobs. As one scholar observes, 'Although the law may treat the rights of ownership in true universalistic fashion it is silent in the manner by which only some "expectations" are successfully converted to the status of property rights and others not' (Parkin 1981, 50). The result of the selective creation of property by the state is the existence of property and propertyless classes.

In referring to the U.S. Supreme Court's defence of private property prior to 1937, the author of the article on 'Property' in the *Encyclopaedia of the Social Science* concluded: 'It is incorrect to say that the judiciary protected property; rather they called that property to which they accorded protection' (quoted in Bazelon 1970, 59).

All these writers emphasize that property rights depend ultimately on the laws and protection of a governing authority. This body decides, inevitably in a selective way, what kinds of rights sought by members of society will be recognized as property rights and accorded appropriate protection. Several implications follow from this insight. First, property rights may vary considerably from one society to another, and in a particular society from one period to another, because they are historically determined. Second, the property rights selected by a particular authority will invariably favour certain groups or individuals and certain types of rights over others. Third, conflicts over property rights are therefore virtually inevitable in every society. The history of property rights in Canada provides ample proof of all these propositions.

The Origins of Canadian Property Concepts

The earliest settlers who arrived on the North American continent thousands of years ago, following the last glaciation, established property rights in accordance with their main activities: hunting, gathering, and fishing. For the most part, the Indian and Inuit groups were non-agricultural. The first agricultural revolution, characterized by subsistence farming, began about 10,000 years ago but reached the area of what is now southern Ontario only about AD 500. The agriculture practised there after this period was a simple one, based on a narrow range of crops and lacking domestic livestock. It was combined with, but did not replace, hunting and gathering and often took place under transient conditions. Nevertheless, it supported quite large local populations and flourished until the mid-1660s, when conflict between agricultural and non-agricultural Indian nations led to the dispersal of the former and the reversion of cleared land to bush (Troughton 1991, 64; see also Heidenreich 1971). However, even in their non-agricultural activities, Canada's Aboriginal peoples developed strong regional specialization and self-sufficient economies in an ecologically sustainable manner. The Plains Indians, for example, concentrated on the buffalo, and the Inuit, on sea mammals and caribou.

18 Property Rights in History

In conjunction with their economic activities, these early settlers developed their own unique property system. A statement by the Yukon Native Brotherhood issued in 1973 describes some of its basic elements:

For many years before we heard about the Whiteman our people who lived in what is now the Yukon lived a different way. We lived in small groups and moved from one place to another at different times of the year. Certain families had boundaries which they could not cross to hunt, because that area was used by other Indians ... We had our own God and our own Religion which taught us how to live together in peace. This Religion also taught us how to live as a part of the land. We learned how to practice what is now called multiple land use, conservation, and resource management ... People were busy supplying the needs of the community. All possessions belonged to the group and individuals did not suffer unless the whole group was in need. This required planning, organization and leadership. These three were carried out without a formal organized system, which is one of the reasons why we are finding it difficult to adopt the Whiteman's way. (Quoted in Elliott 1985, 49)

This quotation is consistent with recent findings of historical scholarship – that Native groups had established a system of laws and traditions governing use of land long before the Europeans arrived. The concept of 'title to land' was alien to them. The emphasis was on use of land, not formal possession. As a spokesperson, Leroy Little Bear, observed in 1976, 'Indian property concepts are holistic. Ownership does not rest in any one individual but belongs to the tribe as a whole, as an entity' (cited in Elliott 1985, 49). Comparing Indian concepts to modern non-Aboriginal concepts, he noted that 'communal Indian ownership is akin to a joint tenancy, and, by virtue of its restriction to Indian people, somewhat less than a fee simple interest' (49).

Aboriginal property was essentially what I term 'common property'; individuals within a nation could not lay claim to a particular piece of land so as to exclude others from its use. However, on a temporary basis, in conjunction with a particular hunting or fishing expedition, individuals received exclusive rights to certain woods or portions of a river. Such 'private' rights were always temporary, however, and were restricted to user and enjoyment rights. In the absence of a 'fee simple interest' – meaning a secure title to the land or stream – no individual possessed disposal rights. At the same time, as the statement from the Yukon Native Brotherhood reveals, the rights of one nation excluded the rights of others; property boundaries were established between them. Thus a common form of property was modified through the granting of limited and temporary exclusive rights to individuals in the group and by the fact that one group's rights could negate those of other groups.

It was this system of property that the new European settlers encountered in the sixteenth century. They in turn brought their own system with them, in which exclusive individual rights were much more significant than common rights.

Canada's non-Aboriginal property law outside Quebec traces its roots to English common law, which had its beginnings in medieval England. Quebec's property law is rooted in the French civil law, as codified by Napoleon in 1804. The latter combined a considerable amount of Roman law, as codified by the Emperor Justinian in 528, with French custom and legislation. The common law and civil law systems have developed many similarities but differ substantially in their approach to the law. A Canadian legal scholar has summarized these differences as follows: 'The civil law system begins with an accepted set of principles. These principles are set out in the civil code. Individual cases are then decided in accordance with these basic tenets. In contrast, the common law approach is to scrutinize the judgements of previous cases and extract general principles to be applied to particular problems at hand' (Gall 1977, 39). Yet, in practice, the property laws resulting from these two approaches do not differ significantly.

The development of English common law as it pertains to property rights falls into two periods: the medieval (roughly pre-seventeenth century) and the modern (seventeenth century and later). Medieval property law developed within a system of feudalism that emerged slowly from the ruins of the Roman Empire after the sixth century AD. During several centuries of near anarchy, both in England and in continental Europe, numerous people and families seized control, often temporarily, over roughly demarcated tracts of land. Makeshift justice was achieved through the operation of local courts, but without the guidance of a carefully worked-out legal code. Though no single ruler was strong enough to impose a uniform system of landholding on English soil, over the centuries a unique, complex system emerged. The emerging property rules, based on precedent, were consolidated after the Norman invasion of 1066, with the establishment of a more centralized political and economic system.

William, the Norman conqueror, systematized and extended the existing feudal system by claiming the whole of England as his by right of conquest. He then granted 'tenures' in land to a selected group of aristocrats, who numbered about fifteen hundred at the time of the Domesday Book (1086 – see Gillese 1990, 6:2). These direct tenants, or 'tenants in chief,' 'paid' for the land granted to them through specified continuing services to the king. Apart from the land kept by the king, known as crown land, the whole of England was divided among these direct tenants. Then a process of subinfeudation began. The tenants in chief sublet parts of their land to other tenants, in return for specified services. These second-layer tenants in turn sublet parts of their land to still others. 'Thence there arose a series of lords of the same lands, the first called the chief lords, holding immediately of the sovereign; the next grade holding of them, and so on, each alienation creating another lord and another tenant' (quoted by Gillese 1990, 6:2).

In this complex way the relations of human beings both to each other and to the soil were firmly established, which is the essence of a feudal system. Individuals and families on each rung of the property pyramid had tenants' rights, for which they rendered services. Those in the upper rungs demanded political, economic, and military allegiance from the next rung down, and so on down the line. The peasant serfs constituted the lowest rung and had no one to serve them. They had no personal autonomy because their 'persons' were owed to those above them.

The basic production unit was the manor – 'an organically complete brotherhood of associates whose proprietory and personal rights were inextricably blended together' (Noyes 1936, 232). In exchange for a vow of allegiance to a secular or religious lord, and the payment of taxes and some services, the peasant received an assured right to the use of the land.[1] By the time of the Norman invasion most peasant-tenants had achieved a perpetual and heritable right to the land on which they worked. There was no concept of 'ownership,' however, and no word for it in medieval England (Noyes 1936, 265). Only the crown could claim absolute ownership. The most that others could have was a possessory 'interest' in land.

Therefore English common law developed what has been called 'an assorted lot of possessory rights' (Noyes 1936, 283). On a single piece of land there were a large number of different interests. This interdependence protected the rights of all property owners, including the lowest serf. Though the lot of the medieval English serf was by no means easy, and some of the claims made on his services by the lord were extremely onerous, he was more than a mere lessee of land. He was tied to the land and to his lord through his feudal obligations, but the land was also tied to him. He had user and enjoyment rights, without disposal rights. The serf could not sell the land he worked, but neither could the lord sell it from under him.

Medieval property rights were seldom based on a formal document signifying that the person had actually purchased the land. Rights were based on custom, substantiated by long-term occupancy. Proof of possession and participation, not purchase, formed the basis for most property claims. Later, as a market economy developed based on money exchange, such non-monetary claims to property lost much of their legal standing. However, there remains in English common law an underlying strand of rights based on occupancy and participation, and this has had, as can be seen below in the discussion of family law (chapter 3) and Aboriginal land claims (chapter 4), profound implications for later property contestations in Canada.

The main features of medieval English property laws still form the basis of Canadian law. First, only the crown had absolute property rights, and ultimately all property belonged to the crown; everyone else's rights were tenant rights, consisting of an 'estate' in property. Second, property rights under feudalism were shared rights, reflecting the interdependent nature of property relations. Use of land, distribution of benefits, and disposal of land required joint decisions of peasants and lords. Third, though there was much that was 'communal' about the medieval manor – sharing of the common fields, celebration of feast days, and common use of the lord's capital equipment – the property rights exercised within it were basically private rights. The strips of land cultivated by each peasant were usually clearly demarcated and restricted to that person's use. Even the village common, in which peasants collectively grazed their animals and cut firewood, was open only to members of the village (see Dahlman 1980). The missing element, from a private-property perspective, was privately held disposal rights. Neither the peasant proprietor nor the lord could unilaterally transfer 'ownership' to someone else. For that reason there was no concept of 'ownership' in legal discourse. Fourth, property rights were not purchased rights, but were based on prior possession and active participation.

Between the thirteenth and seventeenth centuries profound changes occurred to this system. In the thirteenth and fourteenth centuries, as trade between England and the continent increased and land became increasingly a source of profit as well as a means of subsistence, lords tried harder to gain control of manorial property rights. To produce the goods that were in greatest demand in the expanding markets and to work the land more efficiently they required greater control over use and disposal rights. Increasingly they sought ways of reducing or eliminating the rights of the peasants and acquiring the full range of property rights for themselves – a process referred to as 'alienation.' The lords were willing to sacrifice control over the person to gain individual control of land. However, common law tradition, enforced by the king's courts, prevented rapid or wholesale alienation. For some time a compromise was reached: what was identified as the 'ancient inheritance' of a peasant family could not be alienated, but more recent acquisitions could (Noyes 1936, 262).

Over the following centuries the lords at various levels of the feudal pyramid used numerous stratagems to weaken the control of the crown over land and to increase their own control over it. The most direct route was through political action. The protestations of the lords against the rule of an absolute monarch, which began in this period, are often interpreted from a modern perspective as a struggle for parliamentary democracy. However, they can be characterized more accurately as a series of attempts on the part of economically ambitious nobles and landlords to gain more control over their substantial estates. The revolt of the barons against King John, which produced the Magna Carta in 1215, as well as the much later rebellion of Oliver Cromwell and his fellow landlords against Charles I were sparked by a variety of grievances, but underlying all of these was a desire to enhance the property rights of the landlord class. For this purpose the rights of the monarch had to be curbed. The rebellions were part of a general movement among the landholding class to obtain unfettered control of land. By means of a Parliament open only to members of the landed class, political power eventually shifted from the monarch to that class, enabling it to enact laws furthering its economic interests.

As early as 1290 the landholding class was able to pressure the monarch into passing the Statute of Quia Emptores, which for the first time permitted land in England to be sold without the transfer of feudal relationships. After this, individual familial holdings more and more replaced feudal tenures, permitting sale and purchase of land and thereby also greater use of land for commercial purposes. Land came increasingly to be regarded as a marketable commodity; it supported individual ambitions rather than communal concerns. In the seventeenth century, the new system of individual rights, favouring the alienation of land by the landholding class, gained the political base that it previously lacked.

There was some opposition to the exclusive control of Parliament by the landholding class even among members of that class. For example, among those who supported Oliver Cromwell was a general, Thomas Rainsborough, who felt that Parliament should represent the interests of everyone and include representatives from the whole population. He proclaimed, 'I think that the poorest he that is in England hath a life to live as the greatest he; and therefore, every man that is to live under a government ought first by his own consent to put himself under that government.'

However, one of Cromwell's closest associates, Henry Ireton, reacted to this proposal in horror. 'I think that no person hath a right to an interest or share in the disposing of the affairs of the kingdom ... that have not a permanent fixed interest in this kingdom' (quoted in Bowles and Gintis 1986, 28). By a 'fixed interest' he meant, of course, a substantial permanent holding of land. Following this line of reasoning the new system of private property was firmly secured by a Parliament dominated by landholders.

The shift to a more private, autonomous view of property, which C.B. Macpherson claims was completed in the seventeenth and eighteenth centuries (cited in Held 1980, 211), was supported not only by political reforms but by profound changes in ideology. A number of philosophical works appeared promoting individualism in general and justifying private property in particular. These 'justification' theories I examine more closely below in chapter 2, where I discuss both the virtues and the problems of private property more fully. Essentially, a two-fold change occurred. There was a shift in the perception of the individual's goals and role in society and a corresponding alteration in the understanding of property. C.B. Macpherson (1962) has characterized the first change as the development of a 'possessive individualism.' The individual was now thought of as 'essentially the proprietor of his own person or capacities, owing nothing to society for them ... The human essence is freedom from dependence on the will of others, and freedom is a function of possession' (3). This stress on individualism was linked to new 'possessive' goals: 'All individuals seek rationally to maximize their utilities ... Some individuals want a higher level of utilities or power than they have' (54). O'Brien quotes John Cunningham, the noted British economic historian, on this change. Whereas in medieval society 'relations of persons were all important,' in the new society of the seventeenth century 'the exchange of things is the dominant factor' (O'Brien 1968, 10). Things had to be exchanged easily in order to satisfy new personal economic goals. The new private rights attached to land accomplished this end.

As noted above, medieval property was private in that it permitted existing users of land to exclude others from it. What was missing was easy, unilateral purchase and sale of land. First, sale required that land be tied more closely to specific individuals, not to communities of shared interests, and it had to be perceived as a marketable commodity. As one scholar has put it: according to the new ideology property must, by the nature of things, 'belong' somewhere and to someone, and moreover, 'under a sort of Euclidean axiom, it cannot "belong" in different respects to two persons or in two groupings at the same time' (Noyes 1936, 517). What happened in fact was that property came to belong to a relatively few members of society. Second, previously unsaleable rights to land were now saleable (Macpherson 1978, 7–8). In summary, as of the seventeenth century, land and resources were owned by individuals and were alienable.

The growth of private property in land did not, however, extinguish the property rights of the crown. First, the king himself, though greatly diminished in power by the growth of Parliament, retained holdings to a considerable amount of land and to special tax revenues (LaForest 1969, 2–6). Second, and more important, the crown's primary ownership of property, with the power to shift or modify ownership rights now residing in Parliament, received effective force in law through the doctrine of eminent domain. Parliament retained the right to many primary resources, such as minerals, forest, and waterways, and reserved the right to expropriate privately held property for the public good. However, the transition from absolute to parliamentary monarchy brought a significant change in application of this doctrine. The monarch, standing alone at the top of the feudal pyramid, had used the doctrine to support his or her own property ambitions. At the same time, however, he or she had stood above class divisions and, as noted, frequently used his or her power to curb the ambitions of one class in order to protect the rights of another.

Parliament was class-based and therefore used the doctrine of eminent domain to further its own interests. Meadow and forest lands, for example, which in many areas of England had been owned in common, under the protection of the king, were now seized by the state and sold to merchants, landowners, and other wealthy persons for their private use. Not until parliamentary government became parliamentary democracy in the twentieth century could one envisage, at least in theory, that the property rights of the crown would be exercised in the interests of the general public. (In practice, of course, class interests continue to find expression in parliamentary decision-making.) Therefore, although the doctrine of eminent domain remained, in theory, a check on the unilateral exercise of private-property rights after the seventeenth century, in practice it was often used by Parliament to strengthen rather than weaken the growth of private property. Nevertheless, in Canada as well as in England the doctrine of eminent domain remains in force and provides a strong legal basis for government control of property.

While the shift to private property occurred gradually in England over several centuries, in France it was introduced abruptly in 1804, with adoption of a new Civil Law. The French Civil Code explicitly defined private property rights and protected them, following a legal tradition going back to Roman times. However, while the English and French systems differed in numerous respects, their main features were, and are, quite similar. First, both give strong support to private property, with respect to both personal goods and productive resources. Second, both ground property rights on possession of formal legal title, obtained through purchase or inheritance. Third, in both systems the crown has primary property rights, giving it ultimate control over use of resources.

Property Creation in Canada

These European traditions shaped the development of property rights in Canada. The basic legal foundation outside Quebec has been English common law; in Quebec, both before and after adoption of the Napoleonic Code, it has been French civil law.[2] The application of these laws in Canada was profoundly affected, however, by three factors: the prior existence in Canada of Aboriginal peoples adhering to neither system, the conquest of Quebec by Britain, and local conditions.

A detailed discussion of the first dimension – reconciling the property demands of new European settlers with the rights of the Aboriginal inhabitants – appears in chapter 4. Suffice it to say here that much of the land was obtained from the Aboriginals through treaties that, despite their unfairness in many cases, implicitly acknowledged the sovereign status of the Aboriginal peoples.

The second dimension – Britain's conquest of Quebec – also complicated development of property laws in Canada. By the proclamation of 7 October 1763, George III imposed his rule on the inhabitants of Quebec, declaring that courts be set up which would adhere 'as near as may be agreeble to the laws of England' (LaForest 1969, 7). Subsequently, after numerous protests from Quebec, English criminal law remained, but French civil law was reinstated through the Quebec Act of 1774 (Gall 1977, 45). This meant that when thousands of Loyalists fled to Canada from the United States during and after the American Revolution, and entered a region that was part of Quebec, they encountered a seigneurial landholding system which was strange and unacceptable to them. They proceeded to ignore the system, buying and selling land as though it were held in fee simple, even though it was under seigneurial tenure (Norrie and Owram 1991, 165). Problems of this kind ultimately led to the creation of two separate provinces, Upper and Lower Canada, in 1791. Upper Canada then passed a statute providing that 'in all matters of controversy relative to property and civil rights resort shall be had to the laws of England' (LaForest 1969, 7). So French civil law prevailed in Lower Canada, and English common law in Upper Canada, and in the British territories east and west of Quebec. When, after 1867, Lower and Upper Canada became respectively the provinces of Quebec and Ontario, the separate legal traditions were maintained. This bifurcated system has presented few legal problems since.

The major problem in both regions of Canada has been how to establish property rights to the vast resources found in Canada. About 10 to 15 per cent of the country has agricultural capability (Troughton 1991, 64); nearly half is forested, representing 24 billion cubic metres of wood, capable now of supplying one-fifth of the world's annual timber demand (Dufour 1991, 87); about 7.6 per cent is covered by lakes, representing the largest area of water of any country, and Canada has about 9 per cent of global river flow (Kreutzwisser 1991, 154). In addition, both energy and minerals are found widely throughout the land, and Canada is currently self-sufficient or has a positive trade balance in all the major fuel sources: oil, gas, coal, hydroelectricity, and uranium (Harker 1991, 185).

Though much of this potential was not perceived by the early settlers, most were drawn to Canada by its immense promise. Their prime objective was to gain ownership of some of these resources. The first Europeans to arrive had little more need than the indigenous people to establish private property rights. Fish, timber, water, and other resources were present in such abundance that individuals could satisfy their needs without restricting the rights of others. As Demsetz (1967) has argued, and as the discussion above of medieval European rights shows, individual private rights seem necessary only when resources become scarce and valuable (see also Pearse 1988, 308).

From 1600 to 1780 European settlement was confined to the Maritime periphery and the St Lawrence Valley; the total population remained below 300,000, with only a tiny fraction of the land base occupied (Harris and Warkentin 1991; Troughton 1991, 66). In the early British colonies the crown gave land to settlers on the basis of common law. The 'crown grants' usually carried with them the full range of freehold rights, including unrestricted rights to use the surface of the land, whatever lay beneath the surface, the water and timber on it, the wildlife, and so on (Pearse 1988, 309). Later provincial governments placed more restrictions on their land grants.

In the French settlements along the St Lawrence, where fur trading more than development of land drew the first settlers, the Company of New France established a feudal system of landholding, based on the seigneurial system of France (similar in organization to the earlier manorial system of England). By the end of the seventeenth century some one hundred and fifty *seigneuries* (large blocs of land under the jurisdiction of *seigneurs*, who constituted the local aristocracy) were available for rural settlement (Harris and Warkentin 1991, 36). The land in turn was subdivided, via the long-lot survey, and sublet to *censitaires*, or *habitants*, as they came to be known in New France, under a system of mutual obligations. The *seigneur* was expected to provide a grist mill and protection for the *habitants*, and they in turn had to pay rent to him, undertake labour for a fixed number of days on roads and bridges, grind their grain at his mill, and pay a fee to the seigneur on sale of their property (Norrie and Owram 1991, 77). Because many of the *habitants* had only a marginal commitment to farming, and land was plentiful, they led a much more independent existence than their counterparts in France. 'Many men were as much at home in a canoe on Lake Superior or the Ohio River as on a farm lot along the lower St Lawrence' (Harris and Warkentin 1991, 61). When the seigneurial system was legally abolished in 1854, many of the feudal dues had long been extinguished, and much of the land had been organized on a more-or-less private basis. Because many of the *habitants* could not reimburse their *seigneur* for the value of their strips of land, they contined to pay rent after abolition, so that not much seemed to change. Nevertheless, abolition of the system opened the door to further commercialization and privatization of agriculture in what was then Lower Canada.

In southern Ontario, meanwhile, a very different settlement pattern and property system emerged, based on township survey and individual farm lots. The basic objective was to promote individual family farms producing for the market (Troughton 1991, 68). Most Ontarians held ideas similar to those that had developed in England in the seventeenth century, stressing individual freedom and self-reliance (Harris and Warkentin 1991, 112). This, plus the growing scarcity of land, furthered the growth of strong private property rights.

In 1867 the British North America Act made the dominion government responsible for regulation of trade and commerce, the postal system, defence, navigation, shipping, currency, and coinage, but it granted all matters of civil rights and property to the provinces. Though the national government received the right to intervene in use of Canadian resources for 'the general advantage of Canada,' thus potentially enabling it to share in some degree the responsibility for property assigned to the provinces, in practice the courts have supported provincial responsibility against Ottawa's challenges (LaForest 1969, and Nelles 1974).

The constitutional provision granting responsibility for property to the provinces applied initially, of course, only to Ontario, Quebec, Nova Scotia, and New Brunswick, but it was extended to British Columbia (1871) and Prince Edward Island (1873) when they subsequently joined Canada. When, however, Manitoba (1870), Saskatchewan (1905), and Alberta (1905) became provinces, specific provisions reserved the natural resources of those provinces to the dominion (LaForest 1969, 75). These prairie provinces had resource rights transferred to them only in 1930. Newfoundland later received the same rights.

The crown rights assigned to the provinces gave them far-reaching control of property. Before Confederation, in the early stages of settlement, most of the land had belonged to the crown. However, as land grants were given to settlers, in areas where English common law prevailed, the crown at first surrendered most of its rights to the land and its attached resources. After Confederation the provinces continued this policy for most urban and agricultural land. However, for reasons to be explored further, more restrictive rights were applied by the end of the nineteenth century to other resources – notably timber, minerals, and water (Pearse 1988, 309). Lands obtained by private persons primarily for the purpose of extracting the benefits of such resources were increasingly leased rather than sold. Title therefore remained in the crown.

This practice has persisted in Canada. For example, 80 per cent of commercial forests currently belong to the provinces, 11 per cent to the federal government, and 9 per cent to the private sector (Dufour 1991, 88). Some of the leases, like those applying to timberland and minerals, were long term and granted rights to leaseholders that were virtually equivalent to those of private property. Others, such as water rights, granted licences for specific use for a shorter period. Still others conveyed only a right of access to the resource in company with others, notably in the fisheries. Fisheries, in other words, were treated as common property, where the right of one fisher could not exclude the rights of others. In the case of hydroelectric power, provincial governments, beginning with the creation of Ontario Hydro in 1906, set up government enterprises both to produce and to distribute the product. Thus, as Pearse observes, by the turn of the century Canada's property system was characterized by 'a spectrum of property rights, ranging in duration, comprehensiveness, exclusiveness, and transferability' (Pearse 1988, 309).

The development of a broad spectrum of property rights seems to coincide with the historical pattern of settlement in Canada. The earliest settlements in the east received the most comprehensive private rights. There is generally a reduction in the extent of private rights attached to many resources as one moves westward. Even today in British Columbia private ownership of resources is insignificant, and in the northern territories it is almost non-existent (Pearse 1988, 309). By the turn of the century, governments increasingly asserted formal ownership over natural resources, conceding user and enjoyment rights, but not disposal rights, to private individuals and companies. As Pearse observes, 'Our reliance on the private sector to exploit natural resources is as entrenched as our commitment to public ownership of them' (Pearse 1988, 310).

Not only were more natural-resource lands retained in government hands as settlement moved west, but the bundle of rights granted to private owners of land diminished. Increasingly the crown reserved the rights to minerals under private land, water flowing over it, wildlife, and so on. Statutes altered the rights assigned under common law. The changes made to water rights, legally known as riparian rights, provide a good example. Common-law riparian rights grant owners of land along streams user rights to the water, subject to certain conditions. For a while, in the late eighteenth and early nineteenth centuries, the crown used statute law to keep for itself the riparian rights to several key Upper Canadian water-powers, in order to prevent them from falling into the hands of speculators. However, in the course of the nineteenth century, as population grew, the government retreated from this position and let use of streams be governed only by the common law of riparian ownership. Then, later in the century, when technological change greatly increased the importance of water-power, provincial governments created new statutes that gave them control of riparian rights (Nelles 1974, 7–8). The result has been that in most parts of Canada, though more so in the west, private ownership of land has generally entailed only the right to use the surface of the land (Pearse 1988, 309–10).

In moving towards greater government control of resources, Canada departed from the English tradition. It also differed substantially from the system being developed by its neighbour to the south. What Nelles observes about Ontario might be said about most of Canada: 'The principles of reservation, crown ownership and leasehold tenure which characterized Ontario resource policy stood in bold contrast to their nineteenth-century American counterparts. Americans placed a premium upon the rapid transfer of the public domain ... into unrestricted private ownership, and the retention of property rights by the state for the welfare of the community became an increasingly un-American notion' (Nelles 1974, 39). Why was the mix of government and private rights so different in Canada?

H.V. Nelles's case study (1974) of the politics of development in Ontario between 1849 and 1941 throws some light on this question. When he embarked on his research he was struck by the power that the state exercised over resource development in Ontario. He asked, 'Where had this statist tradition originated? How and why had it survived an era of laissez-faire liberalism?' (viii). He subsequently arrived at several answers. First, in comparing developments in Canada with those in the United States he noted significant differences in geography. Americans moving westward set their beliefs 'against a physical backdrop of seemingly endless fertile land.' This fortified the image of the yeoman farmer and the conviction that land ownership brought with it status and self-respect. The result was that 'the primary intent of American land policy by mid-century was the western extension of a "fee simple" empire' (43). In Ontario, in contrast, the Canadian Shield 'laid down a definite and undeniable boundary to the limits of prime arable land, it frustrated the application in Ontario of a unitary socio-political conception of the environment similar to the agrarian homestead myth which so radically affected American ... policies' (42). The landscape did not permit one conception of land use to dominate the entire framework of resource allocation.

Another reason for the larger role played by the state lies in the growth of a populist spirit in central Canada, fostered by a highly decentralized political system. As we saw above, crown ownership of natural wealth was a joint legacy of the French and British legal systems. From both came the distinction between possession of surface rights and ownership of the minerals underground. This political-legal legacy was maintained in Canada and even strengthened at the end of the nineteenth century. When, in 1854, committee hearings were held in Upper Canada to reform the method of disposing of crown lands, several participants called for an

American-type land-sales system. A Michigan businessman, Jonathan R. White, recommended 'adoption of the American procedure of selling clear title to the land which carried full rights to both the minerals and the timber found on the land' (Nelles 1974, 15). However, Canadian lumbermen and timber administrators disagreed sharply. Some feared that sales would favour the wealthy and permit a few people to buy up all the best lands for speculative purposes (15). Upper Canada maintained crown ownership and licensing.

This kind of populist sentiment may have remained effective in Canada because the British North America Act, 1867 (in 1982 renamed the Constitution Act, 1867), created a very decentralized state. In their study of private property in Ontario, Armstrong and Nelles (1973) argue that the granting of control over property rights to the provinces rather than to Ottawa, placed responsibility for property in the hands of political units that were more sensitive to populist sentiments at the local level and more inclined to assert their ownership rights on behalf of the general population. Large business corporations wished to increase their control over resource development and hoped that the national government, to which they had better access than other groups, would assist them in this quest.[3] Provincial and municipal governments were asked by smaller business groups to protect them from monopolistic practices of large business and were therefore under pressure to exercise their proprietary rights.

This decentralized control contrasted sharply with developments in the United States. There, the Fourteenth Amendment to the constitution was used by the Supreme Court in 1898 to rule that states could not violate the sacred rights of private property in any 'unreasonable' way (Armstrong and Nelles 1973, 21–2). This meant that individual states would find it difficult to enlarge their property rights and that when confiscation did occur the state was required to compensate the private owner.

In Canada, in contrast, the highest courts consistently ruled in favour of provincial property rights, and in 1898, in the *Fisheries reference*, they even exempted the provinces from any legal obligations if they abused their rights with regard to the takeover of previous private property rights. According to the ruling, 'The supreme legislative power in relation to any subject-matter is always capable of abuse, but it is not to be assumed that it will be abused; if it is, the only remedy is an appeal to those by whom the legislature is elected' (quoted in Armstrong and Nelles 1973, 21).

In 1906, when a silver-mining boom occurred in the Cobalt region of Ontario, the provincial government introduced legislation reserving the rights to the bed of Cobalt Lake. A private concern, the Florence Mining Co., claimed to be the legitimate owner of the lakebed under existing legislation. Business leaders such as E.R. Wood of Dominion Securities Corp. appealed to Ottawa to intervene against the Ontario government, arguing that it had veto power under the constitution to safeguard private property. The dominion government decided reluctantly not to do so, keeping in mind a number of recent court rulings favouring provincial rights. When the Florence Mining Co. appealed to the courts, Justice W.R. Riddell remarked in dismissing the case: 'If it be that the plaintiffs acquired any rights – which I am far from finding – the Legislature has the power to take them away. The prohibition "Thou shalt not steal" has no legal force upon a sovereign body, and there would be no necessity for compensation to be given' (Armstrong and Nelles 1973, 33).

This extreme interpretation of provincial power over private rights raises issues that are discussed further in chapter 2, but it serves to indicate how provinces were able to act effectively to control the use of property. 'By establishing control over mineral resources ... the government of Ontario consciously strove towards a balance between private rights and public responsibilities like that already struck with the forest industry' (Nelles 1974, 3). However, a government effort to go even further in the silver-mining case, by operating its own mine, ended in failure. The land was auctioned to private interests in 1909.

Only in the field of hydroelectric power did a combination of populist sentiment and provincial ambition result in creation of a long-lasting government enterprise. In 1888 a 'Report on the Lakes and Rivers, Water and Water-powers of the Province of Ontario' had stressed that because of the potential of electricity for farmers, manufacturers, miners, employers, employees, and all classes of society a franchise in hydroelectric power was 'one consequently, in which the rights of the crown, or in other words of the people, are to be most jealously and carefully guarded' (Nelles 1974, 36–7). This led to the Waterpower Reservations Act of 1898, which incorporated the principle of leasing rather than selling waterpower for the production of electricity. Already, in 1892, the Ontario government had leased exclusive rights to the use of Niagara Falls to the Canadian Niagara Power Co., a wholly owned subsidiary of an American firm across the river. Subsequently, companies dependent on hydro complained of erratic delivery and high prices from firms exploiting the water resources. The government initially got into the transmission business to supply municipalities with hydro, but reluctantly it also built up production facilities as complaints from consumers mounted. Finally, in 1906, over the objections of powerful groups within the business community, 'fearful of a general assault upon the rights of private property' (Armstrong and Nelles 1973, 21), Ottawa set up a publicly owned hydroelectric system. It was promoted particularly by Adam Beck, a determined small manufacturer from London, Ontario. During the First World War, with planned construction of the world's largest generating station, Ontario Hydro developed into a fully integrated generation, transmission, and distribution organization. Most of the other provinces created similar provincial hydroelectric companies. Canada's decentralized political system thereby produced a type of state property unique in North America.

Finally, Armstrong and Nelles suggest that growing state control of property around the turn of the century was a response to the wishes of sizeable segments of the business community, even if some of the larger companies protested actual state ownership. In fact, reflecting on the results of his research, Nelles elsewhere concludes: 'The positive state survived the nineteenth century primarily because businessmen found it useful ... The province received substantial revenue from the development process and enjoyed the appearance of control over it, while industrialists used the government – as had the nineteenth century commercial class before – to provide key services at public expense, promote and protect vested interests, and confer the status of law upon private decisions' (Nelles 1974, ix). Most firms favoured development of a hydroelectric system that delivered electricity reliably at low prices. They also favoured leasehold rights to timber and mineral land: they could harvest the resource without large capital outlays for the land and without paying for the resources before they were sold. 'Lumbermen never seriously challenged the principle of crown ownership of the forests partly because they were primarily interested in timber rather than land, but, more important, because they were able to use the licence system – which deferred payment for the timber until it could be sold – as yet another means of lengthening their lines of credit' (Nelles 1974, 12).

In the first few decades of this century, government policy responded primarily to the interests of the business community, which largely shaped property policies. Nelles (1974) observes that 'frequent discussions between businessmen and politicians necessarily exalted business opinions and discouraged the views and claims of other groups within society' (427). In 1926, for example, the premier of Ontario, Howard Ferguson, spelled out the intimate relationship between his government and the province's pulp and paper industry, which the government regulated. 'There must be co-operation between the contracting parties. In a sense we are just as deeply interested in the success of your company [i.e., the Spruce Falls Pulp and Paper Company to which he was speaking] as its shareholders. In fact, we are in a way the largest shareholders because we contribute the power and the timber at very reasonable prices' (384).

As other groups in society developed greater political consciousness, they pressed governments to respond to a broader set of demands, though business interests never receded far into the background. The shift in government involvement in the economy from the early part of the century to the later years has been termed a shift from promotion to intervention (Traves 1985, 9). Instead of primarily promoting business development, governments were asked to use their revenue, spending, and regulatory powers to redistribute income and to provide assistance to farmers and workers as well as to business people. Accordingly, a system of old-age pensions, shared between national and provincial governments, came in in 1927, national unemployment insurance in 1941, family allowances in 1944, government-supported hospital care in the late 1940s, and medical care in the 1960s. The Natural Products Marketing Act, 1934, established the first of many marketing and regulatory agencies created to assist farmers. During the Second World War, Ottawa created some twenty-eight crown corporations, passed legislation favouring establishment of labour unions, and greatly increased its spending on social and economic programs. As Norrie and Owram (1991) observe, 'It was really only in the 1940s that Canadians experienced Big Government for the first time' (517). In the late 1980s and early 1990s this direction was partly reversed, and the proper mix of private and government property became a major concern of many Canadians.

Property rights in Canada have evolved through several stages and have resulted in a wide spectrum of different kinds of rights, ranging from virtually absolute private rights to personal things, through exclusive but less comprehensive private rights to urban and agricultural land, through common rights in resources such as fishing and hunting, to limited leasehold rights to water, mineral, and timber resources.

A problem that has been solved in different ways, and will have to go on being solved, is the proper mix of private and government control of resources. As Sylvia Ostry has commented, 'The mark of a democracy is that the "big" choices that allocate scarce resources between public and private activities are ultimately made at the ballot box' (Ostry 1985, 21). And, we ought to add, in the courts. The next chapter deals with this problem of balance as it has re-emerged in the last few decades.

2

State versus Private Property

Property rights matter. The effects of alternative systems of property rights on behaviour and welfare are substantial and pervasive.

Louis De Alessi 1980, 40

Two political legacies of the 1980s color and constrain the economic policies of the 1990s. One is a renewed enthusiasm for private enterprise. The other is an enduring, deficit-induced imperative to limit government spending. The confluence of these two trends has led to great hopes and claims for 'privatization.'

John D. Donahue 1989, 3

One of the great property debates of the 1990s has centred on the issue of state versus private property. Though the quotation above from John Donahue emanates from the United States, it applies equally well to Canada and to many other Western industrialized nations. A concerted effort is being made to enlarge the private business sector at the expense of the government sector and to reduce government spending. Behind this endeavour there is an implicit assumption that, to repeat the words of Louis De Alessi, property rights matter, and different forms of property produce different types of behaviour and results.

What accounts for this late-twentieth-century attack on state property and the renewed, vigorous defence of private property? To answer this question it is necessary to examine not only the growth of the government sector in the last few decades but also how, and why, this growth is perceived to threaten private property rights. The perception of such a threat is rooted in turn in how Canadians understand private and state property and how they have come to attribute appropriate roles to each. This ideological background I therefore examine first in this chapter, followed by an analysis of the current debate about the relative merits and defects of the two types of property.

How do state property and private property differ from each other? In the previous chapter I define 'private property' as a legally sanctioned relationship between persons and things in which individuals and groups of individuals may not only use, enjoy, and dispose of particular things but also exclude others from exercising the same rights over those things. The main feature that seems to distinguish private property from other forms of property, such as common property and state property, is its exclusiveness. The things 'owned' by the state, such as highways, libraries, schools, and hospitals, are generally made available to all, while things owned privately are not. 'The organizing idea of a private property system,' argues Jeremy Waldron, 'is that, in principle, each resource belongs to some individual,' and the resource is therefore used for the benefit of that individual, to the exclusion of others (Waldron 1985, 327). Behind state property, in contrast, lies a collective organizing principle. The government lays claim to society's resources in the name of the people, and it appropriates particular resources so that they can be used for the benefit of society as a whole. So private property is individual property used for individual benefit, while state property is collective property used for collective benefits.

The Merits of State and Private Property

Of more interest than these distinctions are the various virtues that have been attributed to these two types of property. The current debate over the relative merits of state and private property is simply the most recent in a long series of attempts to determine why, and to what extent, one type of property ought to be preferred to another.

From a historical perspective, private property is a fairly recent phenomenon. It has taken many centuries for its defenders to establish a strong case for it, let alone a preferred status. The problem in earlier societies was not to defend private property against state property but to justify the placing of rights to basic productive resources in the hands of specific persons, to the exclusion of others. Why, as many Native people in Canada still ask, should individuals be able to claim land for themselves when the earth's resources were presumably created for the use of everyone?

The question that Canada's Aboriginal peoples, and many other people around the world, ask about private property arises from a particular understanding of justice. One of the arguments in favour of private property is that it promotes individual autonomy and freedom. Individuals, so the argument runs, must have secure access to resources – free from interference by others or the state – in order freely to pursue their interests. However, there is a paradox here: the freedom that private property guarantees to some invariably restricts the freedom of others. As one scholar notes, and as many others have have argued over the centuries, if private property is really an essential condition of freedom, then all must have a right to it (Ginsberg 1965, 100). The trouble is that in a world of finite resources, where things are invariably distributed unequally, the private rights of some inevitably limit or eliminate the property rights of others.[1]

The problem alluded to here applies particularly to productive resources and is most acute when, as happens inevitably, they are not apportioned equitably. An unequal distribution of property rights to such resources gives power not only over things but, through things, over persons. Ginsberg concludes: 'Any form of property which gives man power over man is not an instrument of freedom but of servitude' (Ginsberg 1965, 101).

Unfortunately, as modern socialist states have shown, the problem of power is not resolved by transferring ownership of productive resources from private individuals to the state. This 'adds political power to economic power, rendering the individual more helpless than in capitalist systems, in which power and responsibility are more widely diffused' (Ginsberg 1965, 101). Nevertheless, the paradox of private property should remind us that it is not only state property that potentially limits the rights and freedoms of individuals. The private property of some individuals limits the rights of others.

Despite this paradox, a strong tradition in its defence developed in Western industrialized countries as earlier suspicions subsided. Early Christian philosophers – men such as Ambrose of Milan and Augustine of Hippo – had attacked the very notion of private property, arguing that property was meant to be held communally. In their view, men and women in community had a natural right to the earth's resources, but individual persons did not. The theft of nature's bounty by usurping owners, they maintained, was even worse than the robbery of a plough or an ox because the latter type of theft ceases with the act, but the former is 'a continuous plunder, fresh every day' (Avila 1983, 10; also O'Brien 1968, 66, who notes some exceptions to this patristic tradition). However, as commerce expanded in parts of medieval Europe and land became not only a means of subsistence but a source of profit, a system of private ownership gradually developed. It was promoted largely by a powerful landholding class, but it also got support from a number of leading thinkers who gave it ideological justification.

Numerous 'justification theories' for private property sought to answer this basic question: why, and under what conditions, is it desirable to grant private property rights to individuals? The answers are an integral part of the private property system that Canada inherited from England and form a basis for the current debate regarding the relative merits of private and state property.

There is a considerable literature on these justification theories (see, for example, Becker 1977; Ryan 1984; and P. Vogt 1985). The summary given here follows a typology developed by Morris Ginsberg (see Ginsberg 1965, particularly chapter 1). He describes three separate, though not mutually exclusive types of theory: natural-right theories, acquisition theories, and utilitarian theories.

Natural-Right Theories

The natural-right theory grants pre-political sanction to individual private property. It is found, for example, in the *Summa theologiae* (vols. 37 and 38) of Thomas Aquinas. This masterpiece of late-medieval thought presents a serious attempt to understand the growth of private property and to assess both its positive and its negative features. While cognizant of the earlier warnings against private property, Aquinas reached back to the ideas of Aristotle and to the *Digest of Roman Law*, which was rediscovered in Bologna in the twelfth century, to produce a qualified defence of property (Waterman 1982, 100). Like most of his Christian predecessors, Aquinas asserted that primary property rights belong to people in general, as part of the human community. However, he accorded to individual persons a 'secondary natural right.' This right arises from a human's natural condition, which is a sinful one. Because of sin, human beings desire more and more goods, and because of this desire they work harder and take better care of the earth's resources if they can lay personal claim to them (see Ginsberg 1965, 96; Grunebaum 1987, 47–8). What Aquinas does is to take an essentially utilitarian argument, emphasizing the benefits to be derived from private property, to produce a natural-rights justification of such property. However, he was not entirely satisfied with this stance and continued to stress that private property could be justified only if it were used for the benefit of the whole community. For example, if too much poverty existed, he said, the poor were justified in taking resources forcefully from the rich' (O'Brien 1968, 84).

Though Thomas Aquinas placed limits on private property, the sanction that he gave to it as a natural human right had a profound effect on later thought. In the seventeenth century the English philosopher John Locke gave vivid expression to the natural-right theory in his *Two Treatises of Government* (1690). He argued that humanity has a natural right to the goods of the earth because of the requirement of self-preservation. He added to this a theory of acquisition: that man has a natural right in his own person and to that with which he 'mixes his labour' (see Macpherson 1962; Tully 1980; Oliverima 1974; and Waterman 1982). However, Locke also acknowledged that property rights cannot exist without the sanction of the state. He observed, for example, that those who have private property must be prevented by the state from using it to harm others (Grunebaum 1987, 9). Therefore, strictly speaking, the natural right that he supported was not pre-political.

By the eighteenth and early nineteenth centuries leading figures in Britain and France, most notably Adam Smith and Jean Bodin, helped to ensure that private property was regarded almost universally as a natural human right (Dietz 1971, 65). By the end of the nineteenth century even the Catholic church, through the famous encyclical of Pope Leo XIII (*Rerum novarum*, 1891) endorsed the view that private property rights exist prior to the institution of government and rest on natural law. The encyclical argued that private property was 'inviolable' and that the chief function of the state was 'the safeguarding of private property by legal enactment and public policy' (Waterman 1982, 104–5). However, it added a proviso: because private property is a natural right it should be distributed as widely as possible. Unfortunately, it did not explain how wide distribution was to be accomplished. Catholic teaching in the twentieth century has departed quite radically from this extreme natural-right theory of private property. However, the theory itself has had a profound influence on Western thought.

Acquisition Theories

Acquisition theories of private property have also given support to natural-right arguments. According to this theory, men and women have a right to own those things that are products of their labour. In pre-industrial societies, private property rights were usually granted to consumable goods, which were obtained in hunting or fishing. They were obtained, in other words, through acquisition. Philosophers such as Locke, Jean-Jacques Rousseau, and Immanuel Kant went further. They sought to justify the rights of individuals to own basic resources such as land and capital acquired through their labour (see Grunebaum 1987, 67–80). They initially envisaged humans in a 'state of nature,' with enough resources available for everyone. Under such conditions property rights could be assigned without difficulty on the basis of 'first appropriation.' However, when they extended their analysis to societies in which resources are scarce, and most have already been allocated, they confronted more difficult problems. First, there are bound to be conflicting claims. Second, some persons who work will obtain no property because of the prior appropriations of others. Rousseau felt that most of these problems could be solved if personal ownership of productive resources were limited to an amount needed for subsistence, reinforced through a social contract. Karl Marx, for one, rejected as utopian any suggestion that a system of private property could be constrained in this way. It was foolish to think, he argued, that those with property will ever agree to the kind of social compact recommended by Rousseau, which would seriously diminish their holdings.

Despite serious problems associated with acquisition theories, Canadian law bases property rights to some extent on first appropriation and on labour expended. However, it is also clear that the labour of some has led to their ownership of productive resources, while that of others has not. For example, most women have only recently established property rights to resources accumulated in marriage; previously their labour did not count nearly as much as that of their spouses in the attainment of rights. Canada's Aboriginal peoples, as chapter 4 shows, are still trying to establish property rights on the basis of first appropriation and labour. Canada's laws have generally granted greater legal support to the property acquired by European settlers and later immigrants. Most workers in Canada apply their labour to resources owned by others; they have not been able to establish property rights based on their labour. In contrast, as is shown in chapter 6, several industrial nations have found ways of enlarging the property rights of workers on the basis of their work participation. What is required is political will and consistent application of existing legal principles.

Utilitarian Theories

Critical ideological support for enlarging property rights of workers in this way also comes from utilitarian theories of private property, which are cited widely today. These theories argue that a system of private property promotes the well-being of society more than does any other system.

There are three types of utilitarian theories – idealist, republican, and efficiency. They differ in terms of the benefits they attribute to private property. First, the so-called idealist theory stresses the contribution of individually owned property to the development of human personality. This theory was articulated well by the English philosopher T.H. Green (1882) in his *Lectures on the Principles of Political Obligation*. He maintained that private property is essential 'because it is the external means of realizing and expressing that inner, free, and rational will which is the distinguishing mark of man vis-a-vis other animal beings' (quoted in Forsyth 1971, 3). Private property is a condition of the individual's freedom to act and therefore of his or her self-fulfilment.

Similar arguments occur in the writing of such diverse thinkers as Plato, Aristotle, Kant, and Hegel. The Greek philosophers examined property in terms of its contribution to the cultivation of three basic virtues: 'knowing oneself,' 'moderation,' and the ability to do that for which one is most suited. For the last especially, individual control of resources was necessary. To Hegel is attributed the comment, 'In his property a person exists for the first time as reason' (Parkin 1981, 49). The noted sociologist Emil Durkheim argued that personal rights to property are part of a general line of development whereby the individual emerges as a distinct and separate entity from out of the shadow of the group (Parkin 1981, 49). James O. Grunebaum, in *Private Ownership* (1987), relates ownership of property to personal autonomy. Similarly, three Canadian scholars have argued that 'the justification of the rights of property resides in its enhancement of the freedom to act. Without property rights we are radically diminished as agents' (Coval, Smith, and Coval 1986, 467).

While exponents of the 'idealist' utilitarian theory of property rights stress the need to give all persons individual rights to property, some are notably hesitant to imbue such rights with the restrictive features of private property. Green emphasizes that the state must actively intervene to ensure a fair distribution of rights. Grunebaum and C.B. Macpherson favour common property (see Grunebaum 1987, 25; Macpherson 1962).

What all 'idealists' have in common is the conviction that human beings depend on the earth's resources to develop their full personalities. Some, including Durkheim, Hegel, and Kant, conclude that private property rights are essential for this (Coval, Smith, and Coval 1986) while others do not. So, strictly speaking, idealist theory has been used to support private property, but it has also been applied against it.

A second utilitarian theory supporting private property we may call the 'civic' or 'republican' theory (see Becker 1977; P. Vogt 1985; and Cribbet 1986 for fuller treatments). This theory was developed by the English social philosopher Thomas Hobbes (1983) in his *De cive* of 1647 and was later supported by Locke, Rousseau, and David Hume, among many others. Some, such as Hobbes and Hume, argued primarily that property rights are a necessity in any civil society, in order to prevent chaos and conflict (see Hume 1955).

In a similar vein other Western thinkers, going back to Tocqueville and Jefferson, link private property to political freedom. An American scholar suggests that the dominant U.S. political tradition holds that 'private property is essential to individual freedom and to democratic government, and that government interference with private property rights is suspect as a step toward despotism' (Barton 1983, 915–16). The recent contribution of Milton Friedman to this debate was noted in the introduction (see also Friedrich von Hayek 1944). I also observed that there are some problems with the notion that democracy and a capitalism based on private property are harmoniously linked. However, the claims for an underlying link seem well established. Even critics of the U.S. system acknowledge: 'The discourse of individual rights, the near-universal spread of literacy, the extension of social interaction to ever-wider circles of contact, the consequent destruction of many forms of patriarchy, parochialism, and political deference are all integral to democratic culture and at least in some measure they are promoted by the extension of the capitalist economy' (Bowles and Gintis 1986, 132). Two Canadian scholars claim that most Canadians regard private property as a necessary foundation for individual liberty. 'If an individual has property it is more difficult for the state or society to deprive him of his liberty ... Democracy and capitalism are held to be mutually reinforcing' (Rea and McLeod 1976, 4).

A third type of utilitarian justification invokes the notion of economic efficiency. As early as Aristotle, strong arguments have been made that private property promotes the most efficient use of productive resources and therefore produces the highest possible standard of living. In *The Wealth of Nations* of 1776, Adam Smith (1937) attributed higher rates of economic growth to a market system based on private property. Since then the link between private property and better economic performance has been defended in several ways: private property encourages people to produce more by allowing them to appropriate the results of their work; it encourages initiative and responsibility; and it creates certainty and order for producers (for a summary of the arguments see John Van Doren 1985).

This type of utilitarian defence was stated most clearly at the beginning of the industrial revolution by Thomas Malthus, a young contemporary of Adam Smith. Like Aquinas earlier, Malthus was impressed by the sinful, slothful nature of humankind and felt that private property was an essential spur to human initiative. In his own words of 1798: 'There can be no well-founded hope of obtaining a large produce from the soil but under a system of private property. It seems perfectly visionary to suppose that any stimulus short of that which is excited in man by providing for himself and family and of bettering his condition of life should operate on the mass of society with sufficient force and constancy to overcome the natural indolence of mankind' (Malthus 1960, 33–4).

In the last few decades a controversial but influential body of economic work has developed which gives new impetus to this efficiency-based defence. 'Property-rights' theory focuses on the performance of managers in private and non-private enterprises. It maintains that the former is greatly superior to the latter. To understand the concerns of these theorists it is necessary first to look at the historical context. The inspiration for the theory appears to flow from a perception that in most Western countries the state has been growing much too rapidly and threatens the exercise of private property rights. I examine the validity of this perception for Canada, noting developments first in the private and then in the state sectors, including the attack on government and the push for constitutional protection of property rights. In my opinion, the new theorists generally ignore developments that might qualify their conclusions. After that I return to the property-rights theory.

Recent Developments in Canada's Private Sector

There have been at least four influential developments in Canada's private business sector that property theorists must consider. First, over the whole century there has been a marked shift to larger production units, spurred on by economies of scale[2] and by the benefits derived from the exercise of market power. This has increased the concentration of business ownership, both in industry and in agriculture. In the pulp and paper industry, for example, the number of firms declined from twenty-six in 1902 to five in 1931. The several dozen companies in the iron and steel industry in 1900 were reduced to four by the end of the First World War. The number of banks declined from thirty-six to five between 1900 and 1990 (Niosi 1981). Even the most ardent defenders of private property, going all the way back to Adam Smith, acknowledge that vigorous competition among businesses is absolutely essential if the potential virtues of private property are to be realized. Perhaps one of the most troubling aspects of larger firm size and increased concentration is the power that business obtains in the political realm. As one Canadian business scholar observes, 'To appreciate the centrality of corporate decision-making in the economy is to appreciate the special place that corporate executives have in government, a place that no other interest-group can begin to approach' (Beck 1985, 184).

Second, the growing importance of the corporate form of business has meant that in the operation of many Canadian businesses there is a large gulf between those who 'own' the company's resources and those who manage them. When economists evaluate the performance of private firms relative to state enterprises, they emphasize the relative ability of private owners to influence resource use. What they often miss is the separation of ownership from management in most corporations.[3] Canadian company law stipulates that a board of directors elected by the shareholders shall manage the business of a corporation. However, as the Royal Commission on Corporate Concentration (1978) noted: 'The directors of most large Canadian companies are selected by senior management ... Shareholders at the annual meeting invariably ratify that selection ... The directors then re-appoint the senior management of the company and, of course, it is the senior management and its staff that supervise day-to-day business operations' (292).

It is clear from the above description that the owners of the corporation – the shareholders – have little control over its operation. Control instead rests with managers, who are only loosely monitored by representatives of the shareholders. In fact, they largely determine who the monitors will be. Under these conditions managers are fairly free to pursue objectives quite different from those that might be favoured by shareholders. Stan Stewart of Strategic Associates Inc. of Toronto has observed: 'Corporate governance in Canada is at best mediocre. The landscape is littered with companies who evidence no real direction, little sensitivity to emerging opportunities, and real myopia when it comes to management competence' (cited in McQueen 1996, S14). William Mackenzie, vice-president of Fairvest Securities Corp., a Toronto brokerage firm specializing in shareholders' rights, has remarked that directors who are supposed to be watchdogs protecting the interests of shareholders compromise their independence by approving incentive packages that benefit management and can also line their own pockets. 'Everybody scratches each others' backs' (McQueen 1995, 2). Some corporations have belatedly sought to make directors more responsive to shareholders, instructing them to exercise greater control over management. The Toronto Stock Exchange adopted guidelines for corporations in May 1995 calling on boards of directors to watch more carefully that managers make decisions that favour shareholders (see McQueen 1996). A special Senate committee is also studying ways of increasing corporate responsibility to shareholders as well as to other stakeholders, including workers.

Third, foreign ownership has grown in major segments of Canadian industry. Since the 1930s, and especially since 1945, many firms operate as subsidiaries of foreign companies, primarily American. Foreign concerns control the assets of about 25 per cent of all non-financial industries in Canada, a ratio that is higher than that of any other Western industrialized nation (Statistics Canada, various years). Many companies doing business in Canada are therefore pursuing objectives that may not be those of their Canadian shareholders or of the regions in which they operate.

Fourth, the development of global strategies by Canadian multinational firms has greatly increased their international orientation. More and more, companies plan their location and their business strategies on a global basis. Though it is not new, the practice of global corporate planning seems to be accelerating, fuelled by dramatic improvements in world-wide communication networks, internationally integrated financial markets, and by 'free trade' initiatives such as the North American Free Trade Agreement (NAFTA). Global corporations are unlikely to accept responsibility for the local, social consequences of their decisions.

Recent Developments in Canada's State Sector

It is not only the private business sector that has changed profoundly in the last century. The state sector, whose initial growth I described in chapter 1, has also been altered significantly. Historically, Canadians have granted to governments a major economic and social role and have accepted fairly uncritically the creation of state property that accompanies such a role. For several decades after Confederation the state played what has been called a promotional role. It facilitated capital accumulation and the building of a substantial infrastructure. Gradually, in response to growing business concentration and new demands from a wider range of interest groups for government assistance and protection, a regulatory state emerged. Both national and provincial governments began to intervene more directly in such matters as private business behaviour, income distribution, labour–management relations, and health and education.

After the Second World War the role of the state continued to expand in several ways. First, government expenditures increased much more rapidly than gross domestic product (GDP). At the end of the Second World War total annual government purchases of goods and services averaged about 10 per cent of GDP; by 1970 this ratio had increased to 20 per cent, after which it levelled off. Meanwhile, government transfer payments to the provinces in support of health, education, and welfare also grew rapidly, so that by 1990 government purchases plus transfer payments amounted to about 45 per cent of GDP. Employment and income generated in the public sector grew at similar rates; the proportion of total salaries and wages originating in the public sector increased from 10.1 per cent in 1926 to 11.7 per cent in 1950 and to 24.2 per cent in 1980. Total government employment, including health and education, grew to 20.3 per cent of the labour force in 1975, falling to 17.2 per cent in 1982 (Royal Commission on the Economic Union 1985, vol. II, Part III, chapter 7, 39–41).

Government regulation also increased. As Sylvia Ostry, a leading Canadian economist, has observed: 'During the 1960s and early 1970s governments ... introduced an enormous and bewildering flow of rules and regulations intended to protect us from unsafe goods and hazardous products, to make us more informed consumers, to reduce pollution, to help preserve our scarce environmental resources, and to deal with a range of related concerns' (Ostry 1985, 30–1). By the end of the 1970s a considerable proportion (29 per cent) of the goods and services produced in Canada were subject to some form of direct regulation – meaning some control over price and/or supply (Rea and McLeod 1976, 155; see also Stanbury 1986).

What is perhaps most noteworthy, however, is the growth of state enterprises involved in production. Beginning with the creation of Ontario Hydro in 1906, governments across the country created crown corporations to provide certain types of goods and services, including energy, transportation, and communications goods and services. Some leading examples prior to the Second World War were the Canadian National Railways (1919), the Canadian Wheat Board (1935), the Canadian Broadcasting Corporation (1936), and Air Canada (1937). After the war few new ones were established until the 1960s and 1970s. However, in those two decades both federal and provincial governments rapidly expanded the number of crown corporations carrying out business functions. By 1982 the federal government had about forty such crown corporations, with one hundred and thirty subsidiaries, and the prime minister could boast that 'Government corporations are vital participants in economic development through their actions across major industrial, financial, and service sectors, deployment of some $440 billion in assets, receipt of annual revenues in excess of $7 billion and employment of more than 200,000 Canadians in all regions of the country' (quoted in Laux and Molot 1988, 63). The corporate holdings of provincial governments greatly exceeded those of Ottawa. A comprehensive survey carried out in the early 1980s identified some two hundred and thirty-three provincial state enterprises, with dozens of subsidiaries. In eight of Canada's ten provinces the assets of state enterprises exceeded 20 per cent of GDP (Laux and Molot 1988, 63-4).[4]

What is most striking about this development is that some 72 per cent of provincially owned corporations and 58 per cent of federal enterprises were created after 1960. These included on the federal level PetroCanada (1975), Canadair (1976), and VIA Rail (1978). New provincial enterprises included Sidbec (Quebec, 1964), Potash Corporation of Saskatchewan (1975), and Quebec's Société nationale de l'amiante (1978). In addition, Ottawa and several provinces, most notably Alberta and Quebec, invested revenues in numerous private businesses, partly as a form of government saving and partly to influence economic development (Laux and Molot 1988, Part III; Brooks 1987).

In establishing separate state enterprises with outside boards, governments tended to follow principles laid down by Sir Herbert Morrison in Britain. In his view, concerns that operated at arm's length from the government promised 'a combination of public ownership, public accountability, and business management for public ends' (Laux and Molot 1988, 67). The difficulty, of course, was to achieve a proper balance between managerial initiative and political control, so as to achieve both economic efficiency and desired public goals.

Much of the growth in the number and size of state corporations may have resulted from changing conditions within the economy, supported by an ideology that was not hostile to government. The leader of one of the banks described the economic system at that time as 'one with free enterprise, private ownership of property, and the predominant role of government' (quoted in Rea and McLeod 1976, 346). National Conservative leader Robert Stanfield characterized his party's position as follows:

Conservatives attached importance to the economy and to enterprise and to property, but private enterprise was not the central principle of traditional British conservatism. Indeed, the supreme importance of private enterprise and the undesirability of government initiative and interference was liberal 19th century doctrine. It was inherited from Adam Smith and was given its boldest political statement by such liberals as Cobden and Bright ... The conservative concept of order encouraged Conservative governments to impose restrictions on private enterprise where this was considered desirable ... Traditonal liberalism started with the individual, emphasizing liberty of the individual and calling for a minimum of government interference with the individual. Conservatives, on the other hand, emphasized the nation, society, stability, and order. (Quoted in Rea and McLeod 1976, 380 and 382)

Canadian attitudes of this kind provided fertile soil for the growth of government. However, they do not explain the sharp increase in the number of government enterprises established in the 1960s and 1970s. One of Canada's most astute social critics, Jorge Niosi, has suggested that this expansion was primarily an extension – albeit rather vigorous – of Canada's longstanding support for government initiatives. He has characterized the 1970s as a period that ushered in a decline in American hegemony and the renaissance of Canadian nationalism (Niosi 1981, 24). Other scholars, such as Laux and Molot, take a different view. They interpret the spurt of government activity as part of an accommodation to new conditions in the world economy. Government buyouts of weak Canadian companies, such as Sidbec and Canadair, and the creation of new companies such as PetroCanada, reflected problems arising from growing exposure to foreign trade, a relatively weak industrial structure, reliance on foreign capital and technology, and uneven regional development (Laux and Molot 1988, 59–60). Nationalism experienced an upsurge in the period around Canada's centennial celebrations, lending credibility to Niosi's interpretation. However, the brief outburst was hardly a 'renaissance,' and without the special conditions alluded to by Laux and Molot it appears unlikely that government involvement in the economy would have increased as much as it did.

In an international context Canada's nationalization drive does not seem extreme. Its state-owned sector falls in the middle of the pack, with a level of government ownership greater than the United States and Japan but much less than, for example, that of Austria, Britain, and France (Tupper and Doern 1988, 6). Public opinion data on general impressions of crown corporations do not reveal any strong dissatisfaction with their overall role or size (see Johnston 1985, 181-4, as cited in Tupper and Doern 1988, 9).

The Attack on Government

What few foresaw in the early 1980s was the emergence of a strong negative attitude to government participation in the Canadian economy. It seemed to begin quietly, but strongly, as a business-led protest against regulation, taxation, and other government incursions on private property. This in turn was provoked partly by the constitutional debates in Canada and the growing interest in a Charter of Rights. It produced in its wake widespread demand for constitutional protection of private property, similar to what is contained in the U.S. constitution. Almost simultaneously there were growing demands for the 'downsizing' of government, centred on calls for deregulation of key industries and privatization of government-owned corporations.

Surprisingly, in light of the views articulated by Conservative leaders such as Robert Stanfield, the election of the Conservatives in 1984 brought to power the first federal government since the Second World War committed to a reduction of the public sector. Its position reflected a neo-liberal movement that was gaining momentum in several other countries, particularly in Britain under Margaret Thatcher and in the United States under Ronald Reagan.[5] It was spearheaded in Canada by the business community and by academics in tune with it. They criticized government not only for being excessive but for being the fundamental cause of what was perceived as a growing economic and social malaise. They therefore promoted government downsizing under several banners: freer trade, deregulation, tax reduction, expenditure restraint, and privatization. These issues came to dominate political debate.

In general the increased attacks on government embodied two major concerns. The first was worry that the growth of the state directly threatened property rights in the private sector. This perception produced a demand for the constitutional protection of property. The second concern was that government involvement in the economy, by way of regula-

50   Property Rights in History

tions, taxes, and its own production facilities, made Canada increasingly uncompetitive in the world economy. This produced a broad set of proposals to reduce the size and role of the state. I examine each of these concerns in turn.

Demands for Constitutional Protection of Private Property

I noted in the introduction to this study that a 1987 Gallup poll found that Canadians thought it more important to entrench property rights in the constitution than Native rights or Quebec's powers. Of those polled across Canada, 81 per cent thought it fairly or very important to obtain constitutional protection for property. Who was threatening their property? Unfortunately the poll did not ask that question, but it is quite safe to say that most Canadians saw the threat as coming from the state. In most public discourse, state property is seen as the sole alternative to private property and therefore the main threat to it.

The concern expressed in the poll had first been articulated less than a decade earlier, in the debates leading up to patriation of the constitution in 1982. Participants paid considerable attention to insertion of a clause that would explicitly protect private property. Quite early on it was agreed that a number of rights, such as the right to life, liberty, and the security of the person, would be given protection in the Charter of Rights and Freedoms, which eventually became a part of the constitution. However, no similar protection was initially contemplated for property. The federal Conservative party decided to fight for a property clause in the Charter, and in January 1981 this proposal briefly received the support of the Liberal government and seemed assured of passage. However, in the end the opposition of several provincial governments, disturbed by the prospects of greater limits being placed on their ability to regulate property, combined with the opposition of the New Democratic party, persuaded the government to change its mind. The result is that Canada does not have a clause in its constitution guaranteeing a right to private property.[6]

Those who fought for a property clause stressed that several dozen nations, including the United States, West Germany, Australia, and New Zealand, had such clauses in their constitutions. Furthermore, the Canadian Bill of Rights passed by Parliament in 1960 affirmed the right of private citizens to the 'enjoyment of property' and continues in force today, though applying only to the federal order of government and its legislation. Even earlier (1948), Canada was a signatory to the Universal Declaration of Human Rights, which affirms the right of everyone to 'own property alone as well as in association with others.' That declaration also states that 'no one shall be arbitrarily deprived of property.' In addition to all this support, the Canadian Bar Association officially endorsed constitutional protection of private property, as did the BC legislature.

In January 1986, several years after defeat of the clause, the BC minister of intergovernmental relations Garde Gardom, received assurances from Prime Minister Brian Mulroney that 'it is governmental policy to include a discussion on a property rights amendment in the next round of constitutional talks' (*Financial Post*, 22 March 1986, 8). Such an amendment was later presented, as part of a package of constitutional proposals distributed by the federal government in the autumn of 1991. However, because of provincial opposition the amendment did not go forward as part of the Charlottetown Accord, which was submitted to the Canadian public for approval in 1992. Though Mulroney's assurance was unfulfilled, it is quite likely that demands for protection of private property will resurface.

It is important to understand what it is that those wishing to insert a property-protection clause in the constitution really hope to accomplish. The amendment proposed by the Conservative opposition in January 1981 provides some clues. It reads: 'Everyone has the right to life, liberty, security of the person, and enjoyment of property and the right not to be deprived thereof except in accordance with the principles of natural justice' (Canada, Parliament, 1981).

Two concerns are clear in this proposed amendment: that persons should have a guaranteed right to enjoy property and that they should be protected against unjust confiscation. The first protection – that of enjoyment – expressed a vague but nevertheless strong and seemingly widespread belief that government actions were threatening the use of property by private persons. This may have been a reference to growing government regulations and taxation and perhaps also to a belief that government growth threatens the very existence of private property. The second concern was that the state could confiscate property without following principles of natural justice. Because the crown has a primary claim to property, based on the doctrine of eminent domain, and because therefore all private rights are held, in effect, at the pleasure of the state, the property of private holders is always vulnerable to seizure by the state. The proposed amendment did not challenge this basic right. What it hoped to ensure was that state expropriation of private property would be carried out in a fair way, in accordance with natural justice. The framers of the amendment probably had in mind three related obligations that the U.S. constitution, for example, imposes on government: that compulsory takings follow fair procedures, include fair compensation, and can be carried out only for a public purpose. Currently none of these requirements has constitutional support in Canada.

Canadian jurisprudence is marked by judgments such as those of Justice W.R. Riddell who, as noted above, declared that '"Thou shalt not steal" has no legal force upon a sovereign body,' and therefore governments in Canada are not even obligated to compensate owners for the taking of their property. In fact, governments have tended to provide compensation, but they have not always done so (Nepon 1983, 22; Augustine 1986, 59). Those demanding compensation for government confiscation of their property have had to rely on the goodwill of the government or on court decisions. Under the protection of a 'natural justice' clause, property holders could appeal to a standard above legislative laws, which would be easily enforceable by the courts.

The second concern – to provide protection against confiscation without proper procedures and compensation – seems to have considerable merit. It seems only fair that owners of private property be adequately protected against government 'takings.'

The first concern – that the expansion of the government sector unduly restricts the freedom of owners of private property and possibly threatens the very existence of private property – is more difficult to assess. Everyone is aware, of course, that governments often impose bureaucratic and tax burdens on property owners that may be wasteful and unnecessarily onerous. Canada's goods and service tax (GST) provides a case in point. Yet Canadians by and large expect their governments to protect them from shoddy business practices, including pollution of the environment. What business firms therefore see as a state threat to their freedom may frequently be a legitimate action on behalf of society at large.

It seems clear none the less that by the mid-1980s a sizeable number of Canadians felt that governments had intruded too much into their lives. Does the growth of government pose a serious threat to the very existence of private property? Those who raise this spectre usually have in mind the complete displacement of private property by state property in Soviet-type economies. They fear that what was accomplished there very quickly through revolution will eventually happen here through gradual but inexorable government growth. Aside from the fact that the world seldom behaves in a domino fashion (few of the children who shoplift at ages eleven or twelve become thieves later; a little bit of inflation is not necessarily followed by a lot), there are several basic problems with this concern. First, it focuses too exclusively on the threat of state property to private property. Surely one can argue that in the past century and more the private property rights of many Canadians have been eroded as much by the property acquisitions of private citizens as by the state. Hundreds of thousands of farmers and business people have lost their small holdings not to the state but to a relatively small group of private corporate owners.

Second, government property often – though not always – enhances the actual control of resources by private citizens, because few restrictions are attached to it. In the constitutional debates of 1981, several members of Parliament suggested that an attempt to protect the property rights of Canadian citizens must necessarily involve the protection of government-provided goods and services that the private sector would not make as readily available to all citizens. This argument receives fuller attention below in chapter 7. Canadians clearly feel that some services, such as health and education, are on the whole provided more effectively by the state than by the private sector.

Third, one can put a strong case that government spending plays an important role in a capitalist economy and that it does so in two principal ways. It underpins and subsidizes, directly or indirectly, the activities of the private business sector through provision of financial assistance, physical infrastructure, and an educated workforce. And it provides services such as unemployment insurance and social welfare to those hurt by the operations of the private sector. Looked at from this standpoint, the state facilitates both accumulation and legitimation of private capital (O'Connor 1973).

Of course, government agencies, like some private corporations, may on occasion display a rapacious appetite for resources quite unrelated to any good purposes that they might serve. Empire builders are found in all walks of life. Nevertheless, many Canadians continue to believe that government property enhances rather than diminishes their access to some resources. At the same time a significant number are fearful of too much government interference in their lives.

Broader Initiatives to Reduce the Size and Role of Government

Since the early 1980s those persons who see a significant threat to private property in the state sector have chosen to play down the constitutional protection of private property. Instead, they have vigorously attempted, with considerable success, to reduce the size of the government sector. The downsizing of government has taken place on a number of fronts: deregulation, reduced government spending and taxation, and privatization.

The growing criticism of the state sector in Canada in the 1980s and 1990s had several causes. Among them was the perception, promulgated by the business community and the conservative media, that public expenditure on social programs had been growing too rapidly in previous decades, leading to large and increasingly unmanageable budget deficits, public debt, and public debt charges. In fact, this perception was false, as a 1991 study by Statistics Canada (Mimoto and Cross 1991) showed that almost all the increase in federal debt between 1975 and 1981 was the result not of excessive program spending but of shrinking tax revenues resulting from tax breaks for business and the wealthy and high costs of borrowing caused by tight monetary policies. Whatever the causation, however, there could be no doubt that Canada was facing what O'Connor (1973) would call a 'fiscal crisis of the state.' Business leaders and a number of academics also fostered the perception that many goods and services produced in the government sector could be produced more efficiently by private firms. The last concern has led to a major privatization program.

In response to pressures from the business community and to arguments advanced by a number of economists, governments have seized on privatization as a way of reducing their debt while simultaneously encouraging a more competitive and efficient economy. Between 1985 and 1992 Western governments realized revenues of U.S.$328 billion from the sale of government assets (*Economist*, 21 Aug. 1993, 18). Canada was in seventh place among twenty major privatizing nations, with sales of $5.7 billion (*Economist*, 19 June 1993, 112).

In 1993 and 1994 the federal government was involved in twenty-eight privatization transactions, fifteen of which exceeded $100 million in nominal value. During those same years provincial governments undertook seventy-four privatizations, twenty of which were crown corporations. Of these twenty, eight exceeded $100 million (Stanbury 1994, 5). In terms of annual revenues, the largest federal corporations sold whole or in part were PetroCanada, Air Canada, Teleglobe Canada, and Canadair. While many transactions failed to generate large revenues to apply to government debts, this does not mean that debt reduction was not one of the reasons for their sale. In several cases governments were saving money by ridding themselves of perpetual money losers. Full-time employment in federal crown corporations fell from 183,000 in 1986–7 to 135,000 in 1990–1. About 58 per cent of this reduction was attributed to privatization, and 42 per cent to efficiency gains (Stanbury 1994, 26).

Privatization has involved not only the sale of corporate assets but the contracting out (or 'outsourcing') of activities. Governments have traditionally contracted out projects that occur at irregular intervals, such as construction of buildings and of sewer and water lines and some highly specialized professional services. However, in the last decade the list of contracted services has grown to include a wide range of regular services, such as waste management, social and cultural services (libraries, day-care centres, home care), and public transport (see McDavid 1988; Harry Kitchen 1994, 11–12).

In the sale of government corporations and in the contracting out of government services, efficiency arguments have been particularly important justifications. One of the more active scholars in the field concludes that 'the activities that have been privatized have generally been those that the public sector is not well suited to handle in the first place' (Stanbury 1994, 23). This opinion, as noted above, is in keeping with centuries-old views regarding the relative efficiency of private and government ownership. The reasoning behind it has been reinforced in recent years by a relatively new school of economic thought – property rights theory, referred to above. Without this strong, new ideological underpinning, it is doubtful that the privatization movement and the broader agenda of government downsizing would have gained the momentum that they have. It is time now to assess the validity of the efficiency argument, particularly the case made for it by recent theoretical work in economics.

Property-Rights Theory and the Attack on Government

For a long time economics did not consider 'property' a significant determinant of economic behaviour. It was one of those things that economists held constant as they built their models. They assumed, either explicitly or implicitly, that all rights to resources were fully allocated, privately held, and voluntarily exchanged at zero information and transactions costs.[7]

Beginning in the 1960s this neglect of property came under increasing attack, particularly from economists who began to point out that alternative institutional arrangements – especially alternative systems of property rights – could affect the way decision makers use the resources at their disposal. A new 'property-rights' school gradually emerged and has become an important branch of economics (see Dragun 1987, 859).

Initially much of the interest in property rights centred on the issue of private versus common property. It was argued, for instance, that when resources are held in common, individuals have little incentive to conserve resources because no one exercises full rights to the output of an individual investment. Therefore commonly owned pasturelands, fisheries, hunting grounds, and forests are frequently used more intensely and exhausted more quickly than they would be under private ownership (see Hardin [1968] 1993; De Alessi 1973; 1980; H. Gordon Scott 1993).

More recently interest has grown in the nature of modern business organizations, and observers are comparing private and state ownership. The question asked is: which type of ownership results in the most efficient use of resources? It is assumed that the main internal tasks of any business organization, state or private, are to determine the productivity of each input and to create appropriate incentives to achieve the highest possible productivity. This assumption puts the emphasis on proper goal setting, communication between goal setters and managers, and effective monitoring of the results.

Further development of this theory has led to the identification of a fundamental business dilemma known as the 'principal–agent' problem (see Oliver Williamson 1970 – a pioneer in this type of analysis). Most business organizations, government or private, have layers of decision making, made up of individuals with unique goals. It is useful, however, to divide the decision makers into two groups – principals, who are the owners and goal setters, and agents, who are the managers hired to achieve the goals of the principals. The basic problem is that of ensuring that the principal is faithfully served and that the agent is fairly compensated.

Property-rights theorists acknowledge that the problem of communicating and executing the principal's goals and providing appropriate rewards for agents' performance is present in both private and state corporations. One of the leading exponents of this approach, Svetozar Pejovich, notes, for example, that the separation of ownership from management in both types of corporations leads to a serious attenuation of ownership rights (Pejovich 1979, 235). The principals (shareholders in private corporations, taxpayers in public corporations) have limited ability to control the decisions made by their agents (managers, politicians). As we saw above, a manager may arrange for generous personal rewards at the expense of shareholders' profits. While Pejovich and other exponents of this theory admit that such problems exist in all types of corporations, most believe that they are more pervasive in, and do more harm to, state corporations than private enterprises. Market forces shape the behaviour of private firms but are largely absent from government corporations.

In theory, there are three features of the market that prompt managers of private corporations to act efficiently, in keeping with the profit goals of shareholders. First, through the stock market the investing community is constantly judging managerial decisions. If the judgment is negative, the price of stock will fall, imposing a direct cost on poor managerial performance. Second, the managers' future earnings depend on present performance, in terms of pay and bonuses from shareholders and attractive offers from other firms. Third, managers of private firms are not a monolithic group; there is competition within management ranks, and if some managers perform inefficiently others hurt by such behaviour have an incentive to eliminate it (see Pejovich 1979, 241–3).

A government corporation allegedly has a radically different ownership structure and is subject to fewer outside forces. Consequently, so the theorists hold, it performs less efficiently. First, in the absence of shares traded in the stock market, taxpayers as shareholders in government firms have no easy way of obtaining information about corporate performance or of signalling their concerns to management. Second, the cost of monitoring, supervising, and controlling government corporations involves political processes and is thought to be higher than doing the same things through capital markets. Canadian economist Thomas Courchene adds that government managers tend to cut into potential profits in order to maximize political support and routinely use too low discount rates when planning investment (Courchene 1987, 16–17; Tupper and Doern 1988, 18).

In general, property-rights theorists hold extremely negative views about the willingness of government agents (politicians and civil servants) to fulfull the goals of their principals. One of their most prestigious spokesmen, Nobel Prize–winning economist James Buchanan, attacks particularly the notion that governments consist of individuals who, as elected representatives of the people, unselfishly spend money to improve the welfare of society. What they do instead is maximize their election chances by spending money where it will do the most good politically.

The conclusions reached by these theorists are by no means accepted by all economists, and they frequently do not correspond with empirical studies of business behaviour. Tupper and Doern (1988) observe that property-rights theory is hotly contested (19). Many economists and political scientists reject the assumption, for example, that managers of private corporations are effectively disciplined by the stock market or that they are effectively monitored in other ways. Stock prices fluctuate for all kinds of reasons other than an accurate reading of how managers are doing, and, as noted above, the directors who are to act as watchdogs for shareholders seem to fail quite miserably at their job. A study initiated by Industry Canada (1995), called *Corporate Decision-Making in Canada*, stresses the need for the empowerment of shareholders and outside directors. The study is particularly critical of conglomerates. By controlling the dividends of various firms within a conglomerate, managers are able to shuffle profits from firms in which they have few shares to firms in which they have more. They are thus able to enrich themselves at the expense of shareholders.

An alternative school of business behaviour, sometimes referred to as the 'managerial school,' emphasizes the effective role often played by government managers. Many are quite apolitical in their approach and behave very much like managers in private corporations (see, for example, Aharoni 1981 and Anastassopoulos 1985). These researchers do not conclude, therefore, that government corporations are less efficient than their private counterparts.

What do empirical studies show? Those who have examined the relative performance of private and state firms have found it to be an extremely complex undertaking. D.G. McFetridge (1985), a Canadian analyst of corporate behaviour, points out that the notion of efficiency is itself complex. Government firms, for example, may deliver goods and services in a more satisfactory way than private firms (for example, serving more areas with telephones, buses, and electricity), but at a higher cost. Basically a different product is being delivered, so cost comparisons are hardly valid. Even when one assumes that the product is the same, studies of such goods and services as rail and air transport, telecommunications, and electrical generation indicate that commercially oriented government corporations, particularly competitive ones, are generally as efficient as private corporations (these studies are summarized in Borins and Boothman 1985; see also McFetridge 1985; Tupper and Doern 1988). These same studies suggest that the environment in which a firm operates has more influence on efficiency than does the form of ownership. The environment in this case includes the degree of competition in the industry and the internal management of the company.

Though the data on the relative efficiency of public and private firms are limited and contradictory, and therefore inconclusive, this does not deter those economists who favour private firms from creating the impression that their judgments are scientifically founded. Tupper and Doern (1988) cite a number of Canadian economists with biases of this kind (24). They also note that the Economic Council of Canada often recommended privatization of particular firms even though no assessment had been undertaken of the benefits to be derived from such action.

In the past few decades, several major research projects have sought to measure the relative efficiency of services traditionally carried out by governments but now often contracted out to the private sector. Several studies show that when contracting out is done in such areas as refuse collection, it results in substantial savings (see McDavid 1988; Harry Kitchen 1994, 12, 13). McDavid found that public-sector provision was 51 per cent more costly than privately contracted operations. In municipalities where public agencies operated in competition with private agencies, cost differentials were much smaller.

John D. Donahue (1989) has produced one of the most comprehensive reviews of research on this topic in both Canada and the United States. He cites two projects in particular whose results are enlightening. The first one, a U.S. study of trash collection in 1,378 communities, examined the effects of four different ways of organizing the collection: (1) public monopoly; (2) private contractors bidding for contracts from a public body and paid by the public body; (3) private monopolies with exclusive, long-term franchises, paid by consumers; and (4) private, competitive firms each enrolling their own customers. It was found that method 1, was about 9 per cent more costly than method 2, but method 3 was more efficient than method 1. The least efficient method was no. 4 (62). Other researchers, Donahue says, have discovered a similar pattern: contractors are cheapest, followed by public agencies, and last by open competition (64).

Some basic questions arise. Why, for example, is open competition among private firms the most expensive? It would seem that private firms struggling for every customer in competition with other firms would have the strongest incentives to reduce costs. In fact, such companies face high costs of information, pick up, and administration. It is difficult to sell customers on cheaper rates. With a number of rival firms operating in the same area, each loses the 'economies of contiguity' that a single company enjoys when it picks up the garbage at each house in turn. As well, competitive firms have to bill each customer, while public monopolies and contractors bidding for rights from a public body are paid from general revenue. Finally, what appears to be competition often is not. Firms in such situations sometimes use strong-arm tactics to control particular regions. In such cases the extra information, pick-up, and administrative costs attributed to competition may actually reflect the excess profits of a company behaving like a cartel (Donahue 1989, 65–6).

What accounts for the relative efficiency of private firms contracting with a public body (such as a municipality)? The answer may be 'competition.' The competition in this case is not with rival firms in the provision of the service, which we saw above can be quite costly, but with rivals in the bidding process and with the public body that awards the contract. Though winning companies enjoy a temporary monopoly, the process itself is highly competitive. Further, it involves municipal officials with a good knowledge of actual costs. To the extent that they gained such knowledge through their previous management of a public monopoly, this competitive element will erode, the more private contractors are used. Since private contractors were slightly less than 10 per cent cheaper than public monopolies, and since some of the cost saving was due to public negotiators' knowledge of the industry, municipal authorites might very well hesitate to switch to a private system, where such knowledge would ultimately be lost.

A second study cited by Donahue (1989) involved a wider range of municipal services and has had a tremendous impact on the public's perception of the relative efficiency of private and government services. It was sponsored by the U.S. Department of Housing and Urban Development and conducted by economist Barbara J. Stevens. Stevens surveyed every community in Los Angeles, seeking out examples of public services delivered by both private contractors and city agencies. She selected eight kinds of services, from street cleaning to payroll preparation, which at least ten communities performed themselves and which ten other communities paid private for-profit firms to deliver. The study found that every service except payroll preparation (where there was no difference) was more costly when performed by city agencies (Donahue 1989, 139). The difference ranged from asphalt construction, which was 96 per cent more expensive when performed by the city, to tree maintenance, which was 37 per cent more costly. The major explanation for these differences appears to have been labour costs. The share of direct labour costs in municipal services was 60.2 per cent versus 49.0 per cent in private contracting firms. Forty-eight per cent of municipal workers were unionized, versus 20 per cent in the private sector.

Donahue (1989) summarizes the main findings thus: 'Two facts are equally evident: Delegating certain functions to private firms usually saves tax dollars, and much of these savings comes at the expense of public employees' (145). How should one weigh these conclusions? Critics of government argue that its participation in the economy is justified only if it can provide reliable services to the public at the lowest possible cost. It is not the business of government to provide workers with jobs or to give them higher salaries than they might have otherwise. However, it can be argued that governments do have a role to play in providing good jobs to people who might not otherwise get them. Government jobs have often been the gateway to economic participation for immigrants and minorities. Municipal governments have traditionally employed a disproportionate number of women and minorities (Donahue 1989). To insist that nothing matters in public delivery of services but the 'bottom line' is to adopt a needlessly narrow view of the role of government.

The following four conclusions emerge from the studies cited here plus others surveyed by Donahue (1989): First, a number of services traditionally delivered by governments can be delivered at lower cost by private firms. Second, much of the cost saving is derived from lower wages paid to workers in the private sector. Third, government agencies perform more efficiently when in competition with private firms. Fourth, many functions of government cannot be privatized with measurable benefit. Where output is not easily measured as in health and education, and reliance has to be placed on the measurement of inputs, public organizations may be as effective as, or even more effective than, private organizations. 'There are many instances of unwise privatization' (Donahue 1989, 147).[8]

Donahue (1989) provides a balanced assessment of the empirical work as follows: 'Delegating tasks to profit-seekers can make public action ... more efficient, more accountable, more firmly under the citizenry's control when contracts can be clearly written and fairly enforced ... It would be wrong and wasteful to deny the considerable potential of privatization in these cases. But it would be reckless to claim that private delivery is any sweeping remedy for the fundamental complexity of the public realm' (223).

It is difficult to determine whether the recent enthusiasm for privatization in Canada displayed by business and government alike represents a fundamental, long-term attack on government or is merely a correction to the previous sharp increase in state activities. Laux and Molot (1988, 198) concluded that the main motive was to streamline government business, not to dismantle it. In a similar vein, Stanbury noted (1994) that only a handful of the largest federal or provincial crown corporations had been sold and that therefore 'state worshippers' had reason to be comforted (26). However, the recent privatization of such major corporations as CN Railways and PetroCanada, and the election of governments in Ontario and Alberta with major plans for privatization, suggest that the drive is more sweeping than was earlier anticipated.

A Summing Up

This chapter has shown that property rights matter. The form they take can affect human lives in profound ways. The merits of two forms in particular, private and state property, have been a source of controversy ever since the emergence of market economies based on private property. It took several centuries for some of the leading minds in the Western world to produce persuasive justifications for granting exclusive property rights to individuals. The paradox of private property was not, however, forgotten. Because exclusive private rights provide autonomy, freedom, and prosperity for some, while denying them to others, many citizens continue to see the state as an avenue through which their property rights are protected and even enlarged.

Canada, like many other countries, has found it difficult to achieve a satisfactory balance between the individual rights of private property and the collective rights of government property. When too few limits are placed on the exercise of private rights, the result is inevitably severe inequality and substantial abuse of resources. When government intervention becomes too pervasive, it stifles personal initiative and reduces the productivity and therefore the welfare of society.

Canadians accepted and even welcomed the expansion of government activity after 1945. Growing prosperity was seen as a boon to society only if it was accompanied by a more comprehensive and adequate 'safety net.' This included universal health care, education, unemployment insurance, pensions, and social welfare. There was, and remains, broad support for the government provision of such services. However, the growth of the public sector brought higher taxes and more intrusion in the lives of citizens. This was widely resented. A new school of economic theorists emerged to remind us that governments expand not only in response to human needs but to satisfy the egos and ambitions of their employees. In the process, both efficiency and democratic rights may be diminished.

The evidence on the relative efficiency of private enterprise is not, however, as straightforward as property-rights theorists have led us to believe. The corporate form of business is such that both private and government corporations have difficulty solving the principal–agent problem. The spur of competition is essential for both, and it may be lacking as much in industries controlled by large private corporations as in those where government corporations predominate. In the provision of services on the municipal level, evidence indicates that neither government monopolies nor competitive private firms give the public the best deal. The best solution in some cases may be one in which knowledgeable government employees invite private firms to tender for a temporary monopoly. In large areas of the service sector, such as health and education, where output is virtually impossible to define or to monitor, government operations are likely to be more efficient and effective than private ones.

Canadian history attests to the fact that strong but not overly intrusive governments can combine with a vigorous private sector to produce a prosperous and relatively fair and free society. In view of this history, the recent strong attacks on government are surprising, and they raise the suspicion that they are driven by ideology or narrow group interests rather than by a thoughtful, historically informed notion of what is best for the public at large. In O'Connor's (1973) terms, the state is now being dismantled to promote private-sector accumulation, but in the process, the legitimation function is also being eroded, with possibly damaging consequences both for economic stability and for social harmony. There are many other major issues, including issues of property, that should concern us. Even James Buchanan, the arch-critic of large government, warned some time ago that 'the grand alternatives, laissez-faire and socialism are moribund and [their] revival is not to be predicted' (Buchanan 1975, 174). The present need, he said, was to work with both private citizens and governments to create a better social order.

The remaining chapters of this study indicate that some of the most troubling property questions of our time have little to do with the problem of state-versus-private property. What they involve instead is the control of resources within both sectors. It is ultimately, as suggested in the introduction, a question of democracy. How can more citizens gain more secure control of the country's resources, whether those resources are currently in private hands or in the hands of the state?

PART TWO
PROPERTY RIGHTS IN TRANSITION

3

Family Law and Family Property

The transition taking place in family law throughout the Western world ... is little short of a revolution. The law no longer seeks to define and enforce a particular concept of marriage and the family, but rather to tolerate a wide diversity of living arrangements and then to offer protection and adjustment when things go wrong.

Brenda Hoggett 1987, 5

Historians pay a lot of attention to property battles that involve clashes between large armies fighting for control of substantial territory. The transformation of property rights in Canada is occurring without armies and, so far, without the redrawing of national boundaries.[1] Nevertheless, major changes are taking place, and subtle but profound alterations are being made to property boundaries. This chapter deals with changes in property rights at the most basic level of society – the family.

In Canada, as in most other countries, significant property rights are exercised within the structure of the family. The ownership of homes and land and the distribution of income from jobs, stocks, bonds, social welfare, and other sources are determined largely within families. The average Canadian household's net worth – total assets such as houses and stock portfolios minus liabilities such as mortgage debt – was $261,400 at the end of 1989, compared to $115,000 at the end of 1983 (Ip 1990, 3). In addition, about 20 per cent of all households with both husband and wife had business equity in the mid-1980s (Statistics Canada 1984, 35).

Those societies that have developed a substantial body of law to protect the institution of the family have done so primarily to regulate property transactions within families. Family law, as one prominent scholar has observed, is preoccupied with property (Glendon 1981, 1 and 102). The interest of the state in preserving the marriage contract, and in prescribing the conditions of its dissolution, is largely a property interest. Conversely, as Glendon notes, 'in cultures where marriage is simply the decision of the partners to live together and raise common children, and involves no exchange of property, it tends to be dissolved simply by desertion and separation' (103).

Because families control a significant portion of property in Canada, changes within the family shape the exercise of property rights in the country. The institution of the family, and family law, have changed drastically in the last few decades, and this has transformed Canada's property system. This chapter examines the background to these changes, the reforms that began in the late 1960s, and their likely implications for social policy in Canada.

The New Family and New Family Law

In a paper on family law in Canada, Julien D. Payne observes that radical changes have taken place in recent years in the federal and provincial laws governing the rights and obligations of spouses to one another in marriage breakdown or divorce. He lists some of those changes: no-fault divorce, no-fault maintenance orders, bilateral spousal maintenance obligations, rehabilitative maintenance awards, and equitable disposition of property between spouses on marriage breakdown. Payne notes that these are 'concepts that were largely unknown in Canada prior to the late 1960s' (Payne 1985, 1).

The official basis for these changes was laid in the federal Divorce Act of 1968, with its introduction of no-fault divorce and new maintenance provisions. The result was a five-fold increase in the divorce rate (Payne 1985, 2), leading to current projections that 40 per cent of all marriages in Canada will end in divorce. By making the dissolution of marriage much easier and by altering the conditions for maintenance after divorce this act altered the property rights of marriage partners and their children. This, in turn, necessitated further legal innovations, requiring courts to re-examine previous property concepts and to develop new ones. In addition, all the common-law provinces of Canada have enacted reform legislation with significant effects on entitlement to property and support for spouses (see Mossman 1986, 46). Since 1968 no field of law in Canada has undergone such radical change as family law, and it can be argued that nowhere have property rights been so profoundly altered (3).

It would be quite wrong, however, to attribute these changes solely to the Divorce Act of 1968 or to subsequent provincial acts and court actions. The new marriage and divorce laws have given impetus to the loosening of family ties, but they are also an expression of underlying changes to the family that have been taking place for some time in many countries. In her comprehensive study of the family and family law, Mary Ann Glendon (1981) concludes that a 'new family' has emerged in most Western countries in the twentieth century, characterized by 'increasing fluidity, detachability and interchangeability of family relationships' (3-4).

Many students of the family have concluded that the 'nuclear family,' comprising a husband 'breadwinner' and a wife 'homemaker' and their dependent children, is an 'outmoded stereotype' (Payne 1985, 22), whose basic form began to crumble long before the legal changes mentioned above. Mossman (1986) observes that 'although the family as a societal institution has existed throughout history, its form and functions have changed markedly over the centuries' (44-5).

Prior to the industrial revolution the family in Western societies usually included a wide circle of people from different households related by blood ties and by a feeling that they belonged to a neighborhood, a community, or a larger political entity (Glendon 1981, 13-14). The family was part of the social and economic structure and was linked closely to the feudal tenure system. Land was the basis for wealth and status and remained intact within the family, passing from one generation to the next by way of the eldest son. During the industrial revolution, as capital increased in importance, displacing land as the primary source of wealth, and community-based economic organization gave way to individual economic initiatives, a smaller, nuclear family emerged, defined in terms of a marriage bond between husband and wife with dependent children. Glendon argues that in the twentieth century, with the growth of the modern welfare state, the basis of wealth and status in society has changed once again, altering the position of the family. The emphasis has shifted even further from the family to the individual, and the economic welfare of each spouse in a marriage relationship depends more on personal employment opportunities and personal entitlement to government benefits than on the marriage relationship itself. The 'new family,' to use Glendon's terminology, has emerged in tandem with the 'new property.'

'New property' is a term coined by a former Yale Law School professor, Charles Reich (1965a, b), who argued that for most people employment and work-related benefits, such as pensions, as well as claims against governments, have replaced land and capital as the principal forms of wealth. These changes, Glendon argues, have diminished the importance of the family in furnishing the basis of an individual's economic security and have conversely increased the importance of work (employment) and government benefits. This change in the respective roles of work, family, and government is in turn reflected in legal changes. 'Family law reflects this movement in that legal ties among family members are becoming attenuated ... (while) employment law, on the other hand, reflects the increased importance of the job, in that the network of relationships that secure an individual's job to him ... is becoming more articulated. Similarly, in social welfare law, support claims against government are made a matter of right, while ... family support claims are becoming less so' (Glendon 1981, 7).

The changing status of the family in the twentieth century is indeed reflected in major changes in family law. According to English common-law principles, which formed the basis for the pre–twentieth century family law of English-speaking Canada, husband and wife became one in marriage, and 'the one was the husband' (Mossman 1986, 45). On marriage, a husband acquired the sole right to manage and control land owned by his wife, the right to all rents and profits from the land, and the right to grant or withhold consent to its disposition. In other words, for all practical purposes the husband had sole property rights. This principle was changed with the enactment of the Married Women's Property Acts in England in 1882, which established the principle of separate spousal property (Hoggett 1987, 9). However, 'in fact, men continued to control the property of women, even if only in the capacity of advisors rather than husbands or trustees, since women were precluded from acquiring the skills thought to be needed for the proper administration of their property, such skills being locked within the male profession' (Mossman 1986, 46).

In Canada similar changes to family law occurred, with similar results. The Parliament of Canada has exclusive jurisdiction over marriage and divorce. However, it has done little to exercise its authority over marriage, and until the enactment of the Divorce Act in 1968 its divorce power had lain dormant (Payne 1985, 5). Provincial legislatures have exclusive authority to make laws in relation to property and civil rights, and their laws have had considerable impact on property transactions within marriage.

While national marriage and divorce laws in Canada generally followed English common law, the provinces eventually enacted legislation incorporating the new principles of property ownership contained in the English Married Women's Property Act of 1882. For a quarter-century after passage of the English act, the jurisdiction that was then the North-West Territories continued to follow the pre-1882 common-law principle, which effectively merged the legal personality of husband and wife into that of the husband (Keet 1990–1, 170). However, in 1907 Saskatchewan, which had been carved out of the Territories and made a province in 1905, followed the English example by passing its own Married Women's Property Act. This act, and subsequent reforms, improved the situation for women. They accorded women certain individual property rights and made them no longer subject to loss of legal personality on marriage; legally a wife could acquire, hold, and dispose of real or personal property independently of her husband and in her own name (Keet 1990–1). Other provinces developed similar legislation.

Though the property position of female spouses improved with new provincial legislation in the early part of this century, several serious problems remained. First, the new laws generally recognized only those contributions to a marriage that had received validation in the marketplace. That is, the contributions had to involve a financial outlay and legal certification. Women's more indirect, non-financial contributions were rarely recognized, and the title to land was customarily held in the man's name. Consequently wives rarely received a share of such property after marriage (Keet 1990–1, 170). The law's failure to recognize that a wife's domestic efforts assist a family's acquisition of property placed a burden on women that was not rectified for a long time. Only slowly did judges and legislators heed the wisdom contained in Lord Simon of Glaisdale's piquant observation that 'the cock bird can feather his nest precisely because he is not required to spend most of his time sitting on it' (Hoggett 1987, 10).

The new provincial laws granting separate property rights to women also failed to address the problems created by the changing character of property. As noted above, economic security and status have come to be based more on job opportunities and access to government benefits than on ownership of fixed assets such as land and capital. Thus the tradition of the nuclear family, combined with a growing emphasis on individual rather than family effort, put married women into an extremely disadvantageous position. Pursuit of good jobs, for example, required individual mobility and ongoing training, both denied to women with children if the husband is considered the breadwinner and the laws prevent easy exit from marriage. Further, the social policy underlying government benefit programs was directed to underprivileged individuals and to employed persons (mostly males), not to mothers with child-care and educational needs.

The radical reform of family law in Canada, beginning with the Divorce Act of 1968 and continuing to the present with numerous new provincial laws and court challenges, represents a belated but serious attempt to address the problems created by the 'new family' and the 'new property' in Canada. The basic elements of this reform as well as its shortcomings I describe in the next section. The last section reviews how the reforms have affected property rights in Canada and offers some observations on their implications for Canadian social policy.

The Reform of Family Law

Starting with enactment of the federal Divorce Act of 1968, Canadian laws with respect to marriage breakdown and property entitlement following a breakdown have been radically changed. The reform process has been uneven and circuitous, moving from Parliament to the courts, then through the provincial legislatures, and back to the courts again.

The Divorce Act of 1968 contained several significant reforms. First, it established uniform grounds for divorce throughout Canada. Second, it made divorce much easier for both parties by introducing 'no-fault' grounds for divorce and by increasing the number of 'offence' grounds on which divorce could be granted. Prior to the act, divorce was available only by private acts of Parliament in Quebec and Newfoundland, while in the rest of Canada it was available only on the ground of adultery (except in Nova Scotia, where cruelty was also a ground (see Payne 1985, 3). Third, the act also changed the criteria regulating spousal support following a divorce. Before the act the provinces had imposed a unilateral obligation on a guilty husband to maintain his innocent wife after a marriage breakdown. The wife's entitlement to lifelong financial support had apparently developed as a corollary to her lack of entitlement to property in marriage and to her inability to earn a living because of her sex-defined role as homemaker and child-care provider within the family (Mossman 1986, 46). The Divorce Act sought to do justice to the new understanding of sex roles by establishing 'legal' equality of rights and obligations for husband and wife. It also altered the basis for maintenance rights and obligations following divorce from the traditional fault-oriented approach to one focusing on financial need and on the ability of the spouse to pay (Payne 1985, 4).

Though the Divorce Act was a radical reform, it failed on several counts to satisfy the conflicting property claims of spouses after divorce. Given decades of legal neglect and the jurisdictional division between Parliament and provincial legislatures over marriage, divorce, and property, it is not surprising that a number of problems remained to be solved. For example, by dropping the assumption that a wife was inherently a dependent member in a marriage, entitled to lifelong support, the act created a type of legal equality without real equality. It did not ensure that maintenance and property settlements after a breakdown would leave the woman in a position equal to that of the man. It soon became apparent that because of the continuing inequality of husband and wife both at home and at work the abandonment of basic, long-term support for the wife meant a step back from equality for many women (see Hoggett 1987, 16). We return to this problem below in the discussion of social policy.

The issue of maintenance settlements has split feminists into two groups, those who dislike the whole idea of dependent women and see the concept of maintenance both during and after the marriage as both a cause and a reflection of such dependence, and those who argue that it is quite unrealistic and unjust to abandon the principle of spousal support, given the actual inequality in marriage of many women (Hoggett 1987, 16). The fact remained that most women in marriage continued to have less work experience outside the home than their husbands, suffered greater interruptions in education, and continued to have major responsibility for the raising of children. Even though the reforms initiated by the Divorce Act required maintenance to be paid according to need after a marriage breakdown and provided for 'rehabilitative' spousal support during a retraining period for the wife, salaries and pensions earned by wives still average only two-thirds those of their ex-husbands (Mossman 1986, 47). As an expert on family law in Canada noted, 'the principles of independence and equal treatment of spouses on marriage breakdown may result in real economic hardship for women because the principles do not match the reality of their lives' (Mossman 1986, 48).

Because property creation in marriage falls under provincial jurisdiction, the Divorce Act of 1968 was unable to rectify another problem noted above: to give due recognition in law to indirect, non-market contributions made by women to family property. The problem of legal jurisdiction is a complex one. Where a claim for support or custody arises in the context of divorce, the dispute is governed by the federal Divorce Act. Where, however, the claims arise during the marriage, independent of divorce, they are governed by provincial statute (see Payne 1985, 6). The problem described here involved both jurisdictions; it related to the process of property creation during marriage but actually surfaced in court cases following a breakdown. It was thus adjudicated under federal law but required that provincial property legislation be properly corrected. Legislatures continued to ignore this issue, until several court challenges forced their hand.

New property legislation recognizing indirect contributions was sparked by the famous *Murdoch case* in Alberta in 1975. Irene Murdoch was a farm wife who got nothing from her husband after the breakdown of their marriage, despite having laboured alongside him on the land for twenty years. Prior to this case no wife had disputed a divorce settlement in court (Maclean 1984, 29). In a controversial decision that aroused consternation across the country, the Supreme Court of Canada denied her claim to a share in the farm assets. (She later received a modest $65,000 in a private settlement.) The court refused to recognize the legitimacy of a property claim based on indirect contributions and unsubstantiated by a certifiable transaction.

This traditional legal position was narrowly reversed in a 1978 Saskatchewan case, *Rathwell v. Rathwell.* In a 4–3 decision, the Supreme Court of Canada gave Helen Rathwell half of the farmland she had worked on with her husband, though she received no share of the land that her husband had bought cheaply from his mother (Maclean 1984, 29). Still, this decision represents a landmark in the development of family property law in Canada. It moved the court significantly from an exclusively market-oriented view of property rights, based on money transactions certified by contract, to a view in which indirect contributions, based on a persons's participation, are also recognized. In reaching this decision, the Supreme Court went back to common-law principles of constructive trust. According to these principles, where a wife is involved in her husband's business, through expended labour or financial contributions, the assets of half that business are deemed to be held in trust for her by her husband, even though title may be in his name.

This adoption of constructive trust, which led the court to recognize indirect, non-market contributions to property in marriage, was extended in 1980 by another Supreme Court decision, which accorded the same rights to common-law relationships. In *Pettkus v. Becker* (Ontario), Rosa Becker was granted a fifty-fifty split of house, land, and a beekeeping business after an eighteen-year common-law relationship with Lothar Pettkus, despite the absence of any written or even verbal agreement between the parties. Justice Dickson wrote that the award was justified because Lothar's property creation was made possible by Rosa's contribution.

In response to these decisions, the provinces began to develop legislation granting equal property rights to spouses on the basis of indirect contributions. Saskatchewan, for example, passed the Matrimonial Property Act in 1980. Its stated premise was 'an assumed equality of spousal contribution, regardless of its nature, creating entitlement to share matrimonial property equally' (Keet 1990–1, 174–5). Section 21(1) made the explicit starting point of every case 'the assumption that each spouse contributed directly or indirectly to the acquisition of property during the marriage and so was entitled to share the property equally' (cited on 175). This act, as well as other provincial acts passed in the 1980s, established the clear principle that a claim to property on marriage breakdown no longer depended on the holding of a legal title or on a direct financial contribution. Fifty-fifty splits of property became the legal norm. Several provinces, notably Alberta, Manitoba, Quebec, and Saskatchewan, applied the principle of fifty-fifty sharing to all assets acquired during the marriage (except gifts, inheritances, and other instances where there were strong reasons for individual ownership), while the other provinces for several years applied the principle to domestic assets (such as house and car) but not to assets acquired in business. Gradually most provinces have included all assets in the property to be distributed equally after divorce.

The legislation adopted in Saskatchewan and in most other provinces went beyond the *Rathwell–Rathwell* decision of 1980. It supports the idea that participation in a marriage is in itself a contribution to the creation of property within the marriage, regardless of whether the wife has worked on the land or in the family business. This is in accordance with the observation of Lord Simon of Glaisdale that a bird sitting on the nest enables the cock bird to feather it. The Saskatchewan act of 1980, for example, assumes equality of spousal contribution 'regardless of its nature.'

It was not long before the Supreme Court of Canada began to catch up with developing legislation. In the 1982 *Leatherdale v. Leatherdale* divorce case (Ontario), it granted the wife, Barbara, half of the family assets (primarily the home) but only one-quarter of the business assets. It justified this smaller fraction of the business assets on the grounds that Barbara had been primarily a homemaker and was not directly involved in the husband's business (Payne 1985, 4). In 1984 the Supreme Court of Canada took a different approach in a case emanating from Saskatchewan. The original trial judge had ruled in *Farr v. Farr* that the wife, Eleanor Farr, should receive 50 per cent of all family assets after divorce, even though she had brought no material assets to the marriage, while her husband, Glen, had put $16,750 of seed money into ventures that were subsequently developed. Their small stake had grown to $2 million, and their life after thirty years of marriage included more than eighteen hundred acres of farmland, an aircraft, and a luxury cottage in the United States. After taxes and liabilities the amount to be distributed was $1,680,000. The trial judge granted Eleanor exactly half of this. On appeal, Saskatchewan's highest court reversed the initial decision, ruling that Glen Farr should receive more than half because of his greater direct contribution. On further appeal, the Supreme Court of Canada upheld the initial decision, splitting the family assets fifty-fifty.

This decision came as a shock to some divorce lawyers. As one observed, 'If a husband has accepted a lifestyle in which he thinks he works hard downtown while his wife looks after the home, that's an agreed equitable arrangement by inference, and she'll be after half of it all if they break up' (Maclean 1984, 29). Following this decision other provinces, such as Ontario, moved belatedly to adopt legislation incorporating the principle of fifty-fifty splitting of all assets, business as well as household, with some allowance left for individual inheritances and written agreements.

Another problem that had to be settled by the courts was the treatment of asset appreciation after the divorce settlement. This issue came to a head in a case brought before the Supreme Court of Canada in 1990. The Rawlicks of Toronto had divorced in June 1984, after twenty-nine years of marriage. They had one major asset – two pieces of land in North Toronto valued at $400,000. The land was registered in Mr Rawlick's name, but under the new property laws each partner received half of it in the divorce settlement. What actually happened was that Mr Rawlick paid Mrs Rawlick $200,000 and assumed sole ownership of the land. Once this action was taken, the case seemed closed. However, when Mr Rawlick decided to sell the land a few years later, its value had increased to more than $14 million. Mrs Rawlick took the case to court, arguing that she deserved to share equally in the increased value of the land. Her lawyer argued that Mrs Rawlick had been a full business partner with her husband and therefore remained entitled to any assets flowing from that business. This argument depended on the common-law concept of constructive trust, which granted wives special property status if they had been involved in their husband's business. However, under new provincial family law, including the law of Ontario, that principle appeared to have been superseded by a blanket, once-and-for-all award based on participation in marriage, not on specific contributions. Therefore, Mrs Rawlick's case appeared rather weak and was indeed turned down by the Ontario courts.

The Supreme Court of Canada, however, was impressed by the apparent injustice that resulted in this case from the application of the new laws. After all, one of the prime purposes of these laws was to create a fairer distribution of property for women, and yet, in this case as well as in others that had surfaced, the result was less favourable than it would have been under earlier legislation. Previously the courts could have used common-law principles to support the special case of Mrs Rawlick, who had been involved in the family business. The use of a broader principle, emphasizing participation in marriage and not a specific contribution to a family business, had seemed to promise a fairer system of property distribution. However, under initial court rulings involving appreciation of assets it seemed to do the reverse. The Supreme Court ruled in favour of Mrs Rawlick on grounds of fairness and justice, arguing that the new laws were not meant to abrogate the property rights accorded under the old laws. The court ruled that there are two kinds of asset ownership in marriage: finite ownership (finalized at the time of the divorce settlement), based simply on the existence of the marriage, and long-term ownership (continuing after the divorce, and split only at the time of sale), based on the principle of constructive trust. While this situation still appeared to discriminate against wives who could not prove participation in their husband's business (their claims to property were deemed final at the time of divorce), it restored the special rights of those who did participate, without infringing on the newly won rights of all wives.

The New Family and Social Policy

The court decisions and legislative reforms described in the previous section have revolutionized the property rights of women in Canada. When property entitlements of women are now determined in the 40 per cent of marriages that end in divorce, most women automatically receive 50 per cent of all the assets accumulated in the marriage. They do not have to prove that they participated directly in creation of the family assets – their participation as partners in a marriage or in a common-law relationship is enough, and they do not have to have legal title to the assets they claim. In most, though not all, parts of Canada virtually all assets, including those attached to the home and to the family business, are divided up on a fifty-fifty basis.

In their survey of international trends in family law, Weitzman and

Maclean (1982) show that these reforms have been adopted in virtually all Western countries. 'Today's courts are more likely to recognize the equal importance of home-making and child-rearing and to assume that marriage is an economic partnership. Under this partnership theory of marriage, it is assumed that each spouse makes an equal (but not identical) contribution to the acquisition of marital property. Thus the assets of the marital relationship are "theirs"' (Weitzman 1982, 87).

These substantial achievements, won through years of hard litigation, have been a boon to thousands of Canadian women who previously would have received little or nothing after the breakdown of their relationship with a man.

However, as has been noted, the new laws have not been an unmitigated blessing to all such women. Their generally more favourable position has at times created new and unforeseen problems. When these problems are examined it also becomes clear that they cannot be solved without some new social policies. The 'new family' and the 'new property' have created radically new situations, and new opportunities, for women, but they have also brought in their wake new problems requiring new forms of social support. When a marital or common-law relationship is dissolved today several problems are immediately present: first, the underlying problem of reconciling the independence sought by the spouses (and encouraged by the courts) and the actual dependence experienced by a majority of divorced women; second, the practical problems faced by a dependent spouse; and third, the problem of 'melding' the resources of the family and the state in response to the difficulties noted in the second problem.

Regarding the first problem, the contemporary demand for equality among the sexes, which helped to generate support for the notion of equal treatment among spouses at the time of marriage breakdown, has also led to the view that each spouse should be as independent as possible, as soon as possible, after their relationship is formally dissolved. Independence has come to mean that the break be made cleanly, that each spouse make a serious effort to obtain a reliable source of income independent of the relationship, and that any remaining dependence end as soon as possible. As Julien D. Payne observes, 'The traditional notion that marriage entitles a dependent spouse to lifelong support has been trenchantly criticized in recent years,' and new provincial legislation has emphasized that 'a financially dependent spouse is required, in law, to achieve self-sufficiency' (Payne 1985, 22; see also Patricia Evans 1988, 126 and 132).

In practice this new policy involves a balancing of the notions of independence and dependence, since the courts recognize that in many cases spousal dependence is unavoidable. Courts and legislatures have had a very difficult time achieving such a balance. In 1978 Alberta imposed a work requirement which includes single mothers with one child over the age of four months, and in 1981 British Columbia announced a policy that permitted benefit reductions to single mothers who were expected to, but were not actually, working (Patricia Evans 1988, 132).

A second problem – the state of dependence of many women after a marriage breaks down – presents society with a host of practical difficulties. Before considering some possible remedies, we should understand the reasons for the difficulties. First, most women generally remain responsible for the care of their children. Separated and divorced women become the primary custodial parent in approximately 85 per cent of all marriage breakdowns (Payne 1985, 26). Such women not only have a substantial ongoing need for income but are uniquely disadvantaged in finding and holding jobs that would provide such income. Second, despite equal sharing of family assets, such assets are seldom enough to support a divorced wife and her children. As one expert in Canada has observed, 'A court-ordered division or negotiated property settlement rarely provides sufficient capital to give a "displaced homemaking spouse" any degree of financial security for the future' (Payne 1985, 21).

The fifty-fifty rule, which sounds so fair in theory, hardly reflects the relative family responsibilities of males and females after a marriage is over. It is obviously not fair to the large numbers of single mothers who end up taking care of the children. Maintenance provisions also do not ease the problem significantly. Most divorced men remarry, and, as Kitchen has noted, 'It is quite impractical to expect men to be able to support more than one family' (B. Kitchen 1984, quoted in Mossman 1986, 60). As Julien D. Payne (1985) observes, 'The freedom to remarry that has resulted from the new divorce regime has carried in its wake increasing problems for courts as they seek to balance the competing demands of the divorced wife and children of the dissolved marriage against the demands of the divorced husband's subsequently acquired family dependents' (21).

In tackling this problem some courts have endorsed the view that the primary responsibility is to the first family, while others have asserted that the new family takes precedence because the public interest is best served by promoting the success of the present relationship (Payne 1985, 21). Partly because of these complications created by remarriage, and partly because of hostility between partners and an inadequate commitment on the part of the male spouse, about half of all maintenance awards are defaulted. Some surveys have shown that in 80 percent of the defaults the non-compliance was explained not by inability to pay but by lack of responsibility (Payne 1985, 25). Regardless of the reasons, under current practices a majority of families headed by divorced or separated wives cannot expect to receive agreed-on maintenance support from their ex-spouses.

Another reason why women find it difficult to escape dependence after a marital breakdown is the problem they face in getting a decent job, should they be in a position to seek one. They are uniquely vulnerable in society's transition from old forms of property to new. They want to, and are expected to, give up the lifelong security that marriage previously provided, even after a divorce, and they want to, and are expected to, gain access to new property in the form of jobs and fringe benefits. The trade-off, unfortunately, seldom favours them, at least at present. As Mary Ann Glendon (1981) writes, 'With the fluidity and easy detachability of family and group ties, what the liberated individual gets in return for the lost network of family and kin is the precarious security of the new property and the freedom to choose and pursue a "lifestyle" which promises the greatest self-realization' (138). However, 'women and members of certain racial and ethnic minority groups have limited access to the preferred forms of new property (good jobs and fringe benefits) that at present are important sources of security in our society' (193).

These dilemmas are compounded by the fact that they are likely to be long term. On average, marriages that are dissolved have lasted about ten years, and the average post-dissolution lifespan of the former spouses is from thirty-eight to forty-three years (Payne 1985, 24).

The sad result is that a substantial number of families headed by divorced women end up near or below the poverty line, even if the woman is able to find employment (26). Those who are most cognizant of this situation generally maintain that it will not likely be remedied by reform of spousal or child support laws or better enforcement (26). This statement may be too pessimistic with regard to more effective enforcement of maintenance obligations. It is not at all clear that enough serious effort has been made to strengthen enforcement. However, it is probably safe to say that, given the realities of the new family, with its fluidity and dispersion of responsibility, and the realities of the new property, with limited access to good jobs and fringe benefits, the situation faced by hundreds of thousands of families headed by single mothers will not improve substantially without new social policies supported by the state.

Therefore a third problem for families after breakdown is to find an appropriate mix of family and state-based support. Women have had reasons for trying to escape their dependence on male spouses; however, it would seem a poor solution to create a new and even stronger dependence on the state. Nevertheless, the state ultimately is responsible for regulating property, and it has had a major role for some time in alleviating all kinds of social dependence. Given the desperate situation of many families headed by a single mother, it seems imperative that society, through the state, assist such families.

Canada has had a dual system of income support for family dependants – family law, which regulates the obligations of members to one another, and social assistance policy, which regulates the financial responsibilities of the state (Payne 1985, 3). Unfortunately, these two systems have not always been well coordinated and sometimes in fact work at cross-purposes.

As we have seen, family law now tends to recognize the equality of family members and the independence of the spouses on divorce. Social welfare, in contrast, focuses on the family unit to determine individual need and entitlement. In the words of one expert, the unfortunate and ironic result of these two approaches is that 'in the name of protecting "the family" people are disentitled from public support on the basis of their family' (Eichler 1983, 110, quoted in Mossman 1986, 49). In brief, social-welfare law focuses on the individual's family, while family law increasingly concentrates on the individual. In most provinces, for example, a wife must bring a support action against her husband as a condition of entitlement to welfare. In most cases she will receive entitlement to welfare after she has failed in a suit of support against her former husband, but the fact that family law assumes equality and independence means that she will probably experience some delay, frustration, and hardship before the systems mesh (Mossman 1986, 50).

Madam Justice Bertha Wilson, appointed in 1982 to the Supreme Court of Canada, observed some years ago that 'we are beginning to think about the relationship between family law as administered by the courts and welfare as administered by the state. We are groping for the right principles and the right policies' (quoted in Payne 1985, 31). Frustration was expressed by another judge, Rosalie Silberman Abella, in an extra-judicial observation on a 1983 case, *Messier v. Delage*, in which the judges disagreed on the central issue of whether the wife's inability to secure employment should result in the imposition of a legal obligation on the ex-husband or on the state to subsidize her. Judge Abella declared ruefully, 'To try to find a comprehensive philosophy in the avalanche of jurisprudence which is triggered by the Divorce Act ... and the various provincial statutes is to recognize that the law in its present state is a Rubik's cube for which no one yet has written the Solution Book. The result is a patchwork of often conflicting theories and approaches' (Payne 1985, 22).

The attenuation of family ties in Canada and the emphasis on spousal equality and independence in the event of a marriage's failure has essentially individualized the participants in a modern family. It is therefore anachronistic of the state to pursue solutions based on strong, continuing family ties. As Mossman (1986) argues, 'In the long run, it is only policies that reflect and encourage individualism that will result in economic equality for women' (64).

Those spouses who find themselves in a state of extreme economic dependence after the breakdown of a marital-type relationship cannot achieve true independence and equality without state assistance. As Alva Myrdal of Sweden observed in 1971, 'Income from one's own job and the modern social insurance system are the two foundation stones upon which the security of the individual will rest in the future' (Glendon 1981, 192).

The Canadian welfare system will have to be reformed to provide at least the following: a basic guaranteed income for single mothers; better-financed retraining to ease their entry into good jobs; well-supported child care; and more stringent enforcement of child-support payments by the non-child-raising spouse. These are the kinds of property rights that citizens left destitute by family breakdown require. The new family, encouraged in its formation by state laws, has brought the destruction of old forms of property. The onus is now on the state to ease the transition to new property forms, so that the equality and independence assumed in the law can become a practical reality.

4

Aboriginal Property Rights

No federal or provincial law or agreement will ever separate us from our homelands, resources and environment. We have used and occupied our lands for centuries and we are not about to leave.

Ovide Mercredi in Mercredi and Turpel 1993, 182

The notion that First Nations lands, which we have occupied before contact, must now be held by the government on our behalf is both bizarre and insulting. It is like someone coming for dinner uninvited and then taking your house as their own: it's pretty presumptuous, and the sting does not wear off.

Mary Ellen Turpel in Mercredi and Turpel 1993, 132

In 1990 a major confrontation between Mohawk and Quebec police at the Kanesatake Reserve outside Montreal brought to world-wide attention longstanding land disputes between Canada's Aboriginals and its governments. The Oka crisis involved a dispute over the proposed expansion of a golf course on lands claimed by the Mohawk people. Though the dispute concerned a relatively small area, it brought to a head centuries-old grievances and served notice that if they are not handled satisfactorily in the near future even more violent protests are likely.

The crisis demonstrated the wide gulf that exists between Aboriginals and non-Aboriginals in Canada in their perception of their respective property rights. Aboriginal people claim the rights to much of Canada's territory on the basis that they discovered, occupied, and settled it long before anyone else. The charge they make is that late arrivals from Europe imposed a foreign system of laws and government on them and through force and cunning took most of the land from them. Many Aboriginals, however, claim that their rights to land were obtained legally by means of treaties and purchases.

We are clearly dealing here with one of the most important and contentious property-rights issues in Canada. Aboriginals have recently pressed their land claims with growing success, lending credence to a prediction that by the end of this century they will own or control a third of the Canadian land mass (Greenwood 1993, 17). Their claims to much of Quebec's territory will probably place them in a pivotal position with regard to that province's sovereignty aspirations. However, despite growing recognition of the importance and justice of their claims, the Aboriginal people continue to feel that their economic and political rights are being seriously violated. For reasons explored in this chapter they insist on their right to self-government and to greatly enlarged property rights.

In this chapter I examine legal definitions of 'Aboriginal,' Aboriginal experience with Europeans, Aboriginal and non-Aboriginal views of property, and possible future developments.

Who Is an Aboriginal?

Broadly speaking, the term 'Aboriginal people' encompasses all people who trace their ancestors in Canada to time immemorial (Morse 1985, 1). More specifically, as defined in section 35 of the Constitution Act, 1982, it refers to the Indian, Inuit, and Metis of Canada. These three peoples have traditionally been known as 'Native people,' but in recent years, both in common parlance and in legal discourse, the term 'Aboriginal people' has become more widespread.

According to the 1991 census, slightly more than 1 million individuals, or about 4 per cent of the Canadian population, identified themselves as members of this collectivity. Of this number, 783,980 individuals listed their origins as Indian, 212,650 as Metis, and 49,260 as Inuit.

Unfortunately, it is extremely difficult, on the basis of past legal definitions and practices, to determine precisely who is an Indian or a Metis. The Inuit are easier to identify. Until recently they were known as Eskimos, and though they are legally included within the meaning of the word 'Indian' they constitute a fairly distinct and homogeneous cultural and linguistic entity, 85 per cent of whom live in the Arctic.

When the government of Canada assumed the authority under section

91 (24) of the Constitution Act, 1867, to legislate in relation to 'Indians and Lands reserved for the Indians' it immediately faced the problem of determining who was an Indian. The Indian Act of 1868, which officially made Indians wards of the national government, set up a complex system for registering Indians, administering their lands, and regulating their lives. Government agents were sent to the various Indian nations to enumerate persons in order to develop treaty payment lists or band lists. Many Indians were undoubtedly missed in this registration, because their band was in a remote area or they were away hunting or fishing. Subsequently, many were deregistered, some voluntarily because they wanted to attain the full benefits of Canadian citizenship, such as the right to vote (which was otherwise denied to them until 1960), to send their children to public schools, or to join a profession such as law. To obtain these rights they had to be 'enfranchised,' which meant giving up their status as Indians under the Indian Act. Many more Indians were enfranchised against their will, as an unintended consequence of serving in the military or obtaining a university degree. Also, many Indian women, but not men, lost their status by marrying non-registered persons. In this and other ways thousands of people who considered themselves 'Indian' in terms of ancestry, culture, and religion lost their legal status as Indians, becoming what are termed 'non-status Indians.' Consequently, most scholars consider the census estimates of the Aboriginal population to be seriously understated.

An amendment to the Indian Act in 1985, Bill C-31, granted status to Indian women who married non-registered persons. It also defined seventeen categories of Indian, thereby enlarging the number of persons granted status. Yet many in the Indian community remain upset by the very idea that a government body assumes the right to say who is an Indian and who is not (Mercredi and Turpel 1993, 88–9; Mercredi himself 'achieved' status as a Cree Indian with the 1985 amendment, but his daughter did not). The expression 'First Nations' has come to be used increasingly to designate Canada's Indian population. The word 'nation' signifies a distinct political and cultural community. The emphasis is on common culture, not race (Mercredi and Turpel 1993, 6–7).

Estimates of the Metis population are similarly inexact. The term is often used to describe all those people who have mixed Native and non-Native ancestry. Historically the Metis represented a unique cultural group located in the Canadian prairies, blending the culture of the French *coureur de bois* and the Indian. Today they reside throughout Canada. Separate estimates by the federal Secretary of State office after the 1981 census suggested that the actual number of Metis together with non-registered or non-status Indians was possibly about 350,000 more than the census recorded. This means that the total Native or Aboriginal population may be around one and a half million, or about 5 per cent of the Canadian population, making it the fourth largest ancestral-origin group in the country, behind the British, French, and Germans. Mercredi and Turpel (1993, 19 and 197) several times refer to 'about' two million Aboriginals but do not indicate how they arrived at this number. Even accepting their estimate of slightly less than one million First Nations people, it seems unlikely that the total Aboriginal population would be close to two million.

Aboriginal Experience

The Cultural Roots of Discrimination

Though the Aboriginal peoples were the first to inhabit this country, and still constitute a significant part of the population, their historic rights to their religion, land, and culture have constantly been threatened by the new settlers who began to arrive from Europe five centuries ago.

Our particular concern is with their property rights. As this chapter shows, the Aboriginal peoples' struggle for recognition of these rights has been extremely trying, and it is far from over. Their difficulties illustrate not only the deep-seated prejudices and arrogance of those who presumed to bring a 'higher order' of civilization to this country but also the very different property concepts they brought with them. Even when courts and legislatures have attempted to deal fairly with Aboriginal property claims, by adjudicating such claims according to accepted legal criteria, they have often failed to achieve a fair result because they have been unable or unwilling to rethink and reformulate their legal criteria so as to accommodate Aboriginal concepts of property and Aboriginal ideas of what constitutes fairness and justice. That there is something inherently unjust about the imposition of laws based on concepts understood and agreed to only by those who are in a position to impose them seems to escape most judges and legislators. A leading legal adviser to the Assembly of First Nations, Mary Ellen Turpel, makes this case very forcefully. She maintains that by ignoring the difference in 'knowledge structures' between cultural groups, and by presuming to judge in a universally valid way, the Canadian legal system has demonstrated not its fairness or objectivity but merely the 'power of the dominant culture to impose its knowledge-structure and cultural system' on others. In brief, 'The denial of difference is a political tool of cultural hegemony' (Turpel 1989–90, 25). As seen below, this problem surfaces particularly in the treatment by Canadian legislatures and courts of Aboriginal property concepts.

This chapter deals not with instances of blatant prejudice and cupidity in Canada's treatment of Aboriginal property rights, of which there appear to be many, but with the property concepts used by Canadian courts and legislatures to adjudicate such rights.

The Historical Background

Almost five centuries ago the Micmac Indians of what is now Nova Scotia were among the first Native North Americans to encounter Europeans. It is estimated that between 10,000 and 35,000 Micmac lived on the east coast. They migrated between the ocean and inland lakes, making their living from hunting and fishing. They appear to have been healthier than many Europeans at the time. Evidence suggests that they had an average life expectancy of thirty-four to forty years – a lifespan that the average European did not achieve until the nineteenth century (York 1989, 55).

The Micmac had their own political structures, boundaries, and laws and a sophisticated culture and language. Tragically, European settlers respected neither their culture nor their prior claim to the resources of the eastern coastland. When they defended themselves against the encroachment of English settlers on their territory the Micmac were ruthlessly repulsed. In 1749, Nova Scotia's English governor, Colonel Edward Cornwallis, ordered his troops to 'annoy, distress, take or destroy the Savages commonly called Mic-macks, wherever they are found' (York 1989, 56). Hundreds of Micmac were subsequently massacred in a campaign of genocide that lasted more than a decade.

In the early 1760s the English softened their approach and entered into peace agreements. However, they made no attempt to compensate the Indians for the land that was taken. It was not until the early nineteenth century that small reserves of land, mostly unsuitable for agriculture, were set aside for the Micmac. Unfortunately, by that time less than fifteen hundred were still alive.

As French and English settlers spread across eastern Canada they treated the Natives they encountered in a fashion similar to that of the Micmac. In New France, Indian policy was placed into the hands of the church by 1700. The church created reserves for some of the Indian bands but never entered into official treaties with them and therefore never spelled out their political and economic rights. This was similar to the situation in the Maritimes, where political treaties and alliances were made but nothing was done to settle land issues (Wildsmith 1985, 216–17).

In southern Ontario a new pattern of dealing with the Natives emerged. Because of more extensive white settlement and the discovery of valuable minerals on some lands, it became necessary to regulate property rights more systematically. Between 1764 and 1850 a complex series of treaties and surrenders, often covering very small areas, were entered into over most of southern Ontario (Wildsmith 1985, 217). Unfortunately, many of these treaties left significant details, such as boundary lines and distribution of property rights, so imprecise that they could not be upheld as legal documents. Many private individuals also took advantage of confusion among Native people to take sole possession of lands that the Natives felt they were merely sharing.

Following the British conquest of Quebec in 1759, which was confirmed by the Treaty of Paris in 1763, King George III issued a Royal Proclamation which, among other things, spelled out the ways in which Indian rights were to be treated in British North America. This proclamation had the force of statute, for the king had power to legislate for a newly conquered territory by virtue of the royal prerogative (LaForest 1969, 109). This document had two purposes: first, to correct past abuses of land acquisition from native people and to prevent future abuses, and second, to identify regions of Canada in which lands were to be reserved for the Native people.

The proclamation notes that

> whereas great Frauds and abuses have been committed in purchasing Lands of the Indians, to the Prejudice of our Interests, and to the great Dissatisfaction of the said Indians; In order, therefore, to prevent such Irregularities for the future, and to the end that the Indians may be convinced of our Justice and determined Resolution to remove all reasonable Cause of Discontent, We do ... strictly enjoin and require, that no Private Person do presume to make any purchase from the said Indians of any Lands reserved to the said Indians ... but that, if at any time any of the said Indians should be inclined to dispose of the said Land, the same shall be purchased only for Us [i.e., the crown], in our Name, at some public Meeting or Assembly of the said Indians. (Zlotkin 1985, 272)

In brief, the proclamation specifies that the Indians are not to be molested or disturbed in their possession of the lands reserved for them, private individuals are not to purchase land from them, and if any have settled on such lands they are to vacate them. Further, Indian lands can be surrendered to the crown's representatives only at public meetings of the peoples in question.

Vast tracts of land were deemed to be held in reserve for the Indians. While excluding specifically the approximately $1\frac{1}{4}$ million square miles granted to the Hudson's Bay Company, and territory already claimed by the crown or legally obtained for settlement, the proclamation reserved for the Indians large portions of what are now Southern Ontario and Quebec, the Western Prairies, and probably British Columbia (as one scholar has observed, 'the line of demarcation between the lands reserved by the proclamation and Hudson's Bay Company land is impossible to define with precision because the Hudson's Bay Company land is vaguely described as including the vast territories the waters of which empty into Hudson Bay' (LaForest 1969, 111).

As is seen below, the proclamation failed to settle many issues, including the nature of the economic, social, and political rights that Indians could expect to exercise on the lands reserved for them, and the precise boundaries of such lands. However, by recognizing the land rights of Indians and by requiring governments in Canada to negotiate in good faith with them for the surrender of their land, the proclamation created legal precedents and rules of conduct that – though often abused – could be appealed to by future generations of Indians. (Note, for example, references to the Proclamation in Mercredi and Turpel 1994, 30–1, and 33.)

Following the proclamation, Indians conducted land transactions only with representatives of the crown. We can see a major example in pre-Confederation transactions of Upper Canada – the Robinson Treaties of 1850. In 1846, after the discovery of minerals along the north shores of Lakes Huron and Superior, the local Indian people, familiar with the procedures set down by the Royal Proclamation of 1763, petitioned the governor general of Canada, asking that no mining development take place until suitable arrangements had been made with them, the true owners of the land (Zlotkin 1985, 273). In September 1850, W.B. Robinson met with the chiefs and 'Principal men' of the Ojibwa at Sault Ste Marie to negotiate what have since been called the Robinson–Huron and Robinson–Superior Treaties. These agreements provided compensation for lands ceded to the crown and granted continued 'full and free' hunting and fishing rights to the Indians on such land except on 'such portions of the said territory as may from time to time be sold or leased to individuals or companies' (Zlotkin 1985, 273).

After Confederation the national government, which had been

assigned responsibility for 'Indians and land reserved for the Indians,' continued making treaties. Between 1871 and 1921, it negotiated eleven numbered treaties with the Indian peoples in the northern and western parts of Canada. Though differing in details, these documents contain the same core provisions as the Robinson treaties. In exchange for surrendering 'all their right and title' to the specified lands, the Indian people were guaranteed annuities in perpetuity and special 'reserves' for their own use. Treaties 1 to 7 (1871–7), designed to open the west to agricultural settlement, also promised the provision of tools, livestock, and seed grain to those Indian people who took up farming. Treaties 3 to 11 also guaranteed hunting and fishing rights on surrendered land, 'subject to such regulations as may from time to time be made by her [Majesty's] Government of her Dominion of Canada, and saving and excepting such tracts as may from time to time be required or taken up for settlement, mining, lumbering, or other purposes' (Zlotkin 1985, 274).

The creation of Indian reserves was a key element of these treaties. A reserve has been defined as 'any tract or tracts set apart by treaty or otherwise for the use and benefit of or granted to a particular band of Indians, of which the legal title is in the Crown, but which is unsurrendered and includes all the trees, wood, timber, soil, stone, minerals, metals or other valuables thereon or therein' (Bartlett 1985, 469).

The establishment of reserves began before Confederation, and their purpose was described well by Treaty Commissioner Alexander Morris: 'I regard this system as of great value. It at once secures to the Indian tribes tracts of land which cannot be interfered with by the rush of immigration, and affords the means of inducing them to establish homes and learn the arts of agriculture' (Bartlett 1985, 468). The reserves, in other words, were meant to protect Indians' property rights and to domesticate them. Morris also added his opinion that the Canadian system of alloting smaller reserves to individual Indian bands in the areas where they were living was far preferable to the American system, which placed whole nations in large reservations, sometimes far from their original location. The latter arrangements, he felt, posed a greater threat to white settlement and therefore would result in more conflict between Indians and white settlers. The Canadian reserve system, he felt, would strengthen the attachment of Indians to the land and would 'diminish the offensive strength of the Indian tribes should they ever become restless' (468).

It is clear that the reserve policy was designed to achieve several objectives: to clear the way for white settlement by negotiating the surrender of land from Indians, to compensate the Indians for the loss of such land

and to protect their long-term property rights on special reserve lands, to domesticate the Indians, and to protect white settlers against Indian retaliation 'should they ever become restless.'

The establishment of reserves by treaty took place primarily in parts of Ontario and in the Prairies. In British Columbia and the Maritimes many reserves were set aside by cabinet order under public lands legislation, while in southern Ontario and Quebec a variety of laws and treaty processes were employed (Bartlett 1985, 469).

The Current Situation

In 1980, 70 per cent of the 300,000 status Indians in Canada lived on reserves. There were 2,242 separate tracts of reserve land totalling 10,021 square miles, which comprises 0.28 percent of the land area of Canada. There are Indian reserves in every jurisdiction except Newfoundland. The amount of reserve land per Indian in Canada is approximately thirty-four acres, varying between eight acres per capita in Quebec and the Atlantic provinces and eighty in Alberta. Forest land covers 44 per cent of the total area of Indian reserves (Bartlett 1985, 476).

Final settlement of treaty-land entitlement has yet to be achieved in the Prairies. In Saskatchewan, for example, the provincial and federal governments have acknowledged at least fifteen Indian claims to further entitlement (of thirty claims made by Indian bands). Before 1930 the Indians of that province were allocated 1.5 million acres. In that year the dominion government transferred the right to natural resources on Prairie crown land to the provinces, with the stipulation that each province would make unoccupied crown land available to Canada so that it could fulfill any outstanding land entitlements that might have been overlooked. It appeared at that time that requests for further entitlement would come only from northern bands, where there was plenty of crown land to distribute (Bartlett 1985, 477–8). However, research since that time has indicated that over one million acres of land is still outstanding for fifteen Indian bands in the province, with over half of the acreage located in the agricultural area. As one scholar has observed, 'Saskatchewan will be hard pressed to find this amount of suitable land in all the Crown holdings occupied or vacant. But this is a legitimate debt which should not be allowed to continue' (478). Similar settlements are being claimed in Manitoba and Alberta.

Much controversy continues to surround the method by which negotiations were carried out with the Indians, the adequacy of the remuneration granted to them in exchange for the surrender of the land, and the value of the land given them for reserves. A crucial difficulty, to which I return below, involves the kind of property rights actually given to the Indians on their reserves. In every province with reserves, the province claims a property interest or entitlement of some kind. Title resides in the crown, usually in right of Canada. This means that First Nations have only a partial set of rights on their reserves; they have user rights, some 'enjoyment rights' (shared with the province), and no disposal rights. Nevertheless, by requiring that those who wish to obtain Indian land must pay compensation and by entering into treaties with Indian bands for the surrender of land and the creation of reserves, both the British and the Canadian governments clearly acknowledged the existence of an Aboriginal title to land.

In the Prairie provinces and in Ontario negotiation of treaties provided for legal settlement of Indian land claims (though many misunderstandings remain, and further settlements are required). This process of land acquisition was not completed, however, in Newfoundland, the Maritimes, Quebec, British Columbia, and the north. The Aboriginal peoples of these regions continue to assert their ownership of their lands and press for recognition of their claims.

At the present time, therefore, the Aboriginal peoples of Canada are pressing for resolution of two types of property grievances – first, for correction of abuses and omissions associated with the establishment of Indian reserves and the signing of treaties (specific claims), and second, for recognition of Aboriginal property rights on lands where Aboriginal rights were never extinguished by treaty or superseded by law (comprehensive claims).

Included in the second category are the claims of the Metis people, whose rights the Constitution Act of 1982 explicitly recognizes but who have largely been excluded from the process of property negotiation, since the government of Canada has taken the view that they have no land claims (Morse 1985, 634).

In 1995 there were about six hundred specific claims on Ottawa's official waiting list, registered by Aboriginal peoples who charge that treaties signed by their ancestors were violated in some way. The federal government receives about sixty new claims a year and settles about thirty (Toulin 1995). Some specific claims call for monetary compensation, and some for land, and many settlements have involved both. The amounts are usually less than $10 million per claim, but some are substantially higher. In 1994 taxpayers paid $78.7 million in cash settlements. The land demands, as noted above for Saskatchewan, are considerable. They include parts or all of some major urban areas, such as Toronto.

Comprehensive claims number about fifty, of which ten were being negotiated in 1995. They are wide ranging and tend to involve vast blocks of land and cash. There has, however, been some success in resolving these. This includes two settlements in northern Quebec in the late 1970s and several since then. Among the major recent agreements are the Inuvialuit claim in the western Arctic and the Tungavik claim in the eastern Arctic. The Inuvialuit claim involved a cash grant of $170 million and title to 91,000 square kilometres of land for the twenty-five hundred Inuvialuit who make up about 10 per cent of the Inuit population of northern Canada (Greenwood 1993, 18). The Tungavik Federation of Nunavut claim saw two million square kilometres of territory ceded to the Inuit of the region. The agreement also included mineral rights and a cash settlement of $1.17 billion, spread over fourteen years. The Inuit of both the western and eastern Arctic also created a new political jurisdiction with a form of self-government (Toulin 1995). Meanwhile in Quebec the Cree people are proposing a Cree nation that would involve a substantial part of that province. In British Columbia, native communities have advanced twenty-one claims involving 75 per cent of that province's land. Claims in regions such as Labrador and the central Arctic have taken on a new urgency with the discovery of large deposits of base metals in the Voisey Bay region of Labrador and diamonds in the central Arctic (Toulin 1995; Damsell 1996).

Following the Oka standoff in 1990 the federal government established an independent land claims commission, the ICC, to settle disputes. The commissioners are mainly from Aboriginal communities and have only advisory powers. Ottawa in fact rejected the first two settlements that they recommended. This has prompted the commission to call for a new claims policy 'wherein Canada is not the judge of claims against itself' (Toulin 1995).

Aboriginal and Non-Aboriginal Views of Property and of Historical Rights

The conflicts that have produced such a large number of property grievances and claims by the Indians, Metis, and Inuit of Canada have many origins and therefore will not be resolved easily or soon. Behind many of them, however, there is one overriding problem, and that is the different understanding that Aboriginal and non-Aboriginal Canadians have concerning the nature of Aboriginal property rights. It is this issue therefore that deserves special attention. This section attempts to clarify the nature of these differences and how they have led to the recent spate of court actions and negotiations. The concluding section suggests how some of the conflicting views of property rights might possibly be resolved.

The Aboriginal peoples of Canada have long been regarded as having some kinds of property rights in Canadian land. They themselves, as has been noted, maintain that they have prior and primary rights to the vast sections of Canada that they were the first to occupy. Their claims are essentially two-fold. First, they were in sovereign occupation of Canada at the time of contact with Europeans, and second, their sovereignty, and hence their legitimacy and continued existence, have not been extinguished by the subsequent occupation of Canada by immigrants (Asch 1984, 30).

Regarding the first claim, no one disputes the prior arrival of Aboriginal people on what is now Canadian territory. What many non-Aboriginals have contested, both explicitly and implicitly, is their 'sovereign occupation' of the land. These words, as is seen below, have come to mean an orderly, politically structured, and socially well-organized occupation of a territory – something that Aboriginal peoples claim was true of their occupation and that non-Aboriginals have tended to deny. Regarding the second claim, there are also conflicting views. Aboriginal peoples maintain that while they were willing to share their land with the newcomers, their concept of property was such that it did not occur to them that their land treaties with the newcomers gave the latter exclusive rights to the land. As Duke Redbird, a Metis spokesman, states, 'The concept of "title to land" was alien to the native consciousness except as a natural birthright. The emphasis in native culture was on use of land, not formal possession' (quoted in Elliott 1985, 50). In its *Statement on Aboriginal Title*, presented to the Standing Committee on Indian Affairs and Northern Development on 29 March 1973, the National Indian Brotherhood (the predecessor of the Assembly of First Nations) argued that colonial governments imposed their own property concepts on indigenous peoples and severely limited Aboriginal rights in the process (Elliott 1985, 51).

This view has a profound bearing on the understanding of how treaties affected Aboriginal rights. The new settlers assumed that the documents extinguished Aboriginal title. Aboriginal people consistently deny this. As Mary Ellen Turpel and Ovide Mercredi (1993) have recently written, 'First Nations see the treaties as calling for a sharing of land in exchange for promises made to First Nations about their continued land rights and the recognition of their customs and their autonomy ... First Nations people had no concept of individual ownership of land, so the idea that land could be ceded by a treaty was a shocking and alien concept' (61–3).

We turn now to an examination of how these basic and very different concepts and interpretations of rights have been treated by Canadian legislatures and courts in their attempts to allocate property rights to Aboriginal people. I deal with three questions below (see Elliott 1985, 51–121). First, a question of *legal status*, to what extent is Aboriginal title recognized in Canadian law? Second, a question of *scope and content*, how extensive are Aboriginal property rights, and to what do they pertain? Third, a question of *autonomy*, to what extent are Aboriginal rights free from interference by others? What, if anything, can restrict or extinguish them? What redress is possible if resources are expropriated or damaged by others?

Legal Status

In Canada's English–French property system, claims to property must be established through legal means. The English legal system recognizes three direct sources of law: royal prerogative, common law, and statutes and constitutions passed by legislatures. My concern here is to show how, and to what extent, these three sources of law have both supported and thwarted Aboriginal property rights in Canada.

First, the royal prerogative was expressed by King George III in his Royal Proclamation of 1763. It is, as we saw above, an important source of Aboriginal rights in Canada. It affirmed the rights of Indians to large tracts of land in Canada, albeit to be held in the name of the crown and not be sold except to the crown. The proclamation seems to confirm a pre-existing Aboriginal title. Today in Canada the part of the document that deals with Indian people has the force of a statute, and it has not been repealed by any Canadian statute (Elliott 1985, 56).

Second, the common law, as developed through the decisions of Canadian courts of law, has supported several notions of Aboriginal title. The first is that such title is rooted in a legal act – the Royal Proclamation of 1763. The second, potentially in conflict with the first, is that Aboriginal title also derives from the fact of Aboriginal occupation and use of land – a concept that has roots both in British common law and in traditional Aboriginal views.

One of the first major tests of the legal status of Aboriginal title under common law was *St. Catharine's Milling and Lumber Company v. The Queen* (1889). In this case the Ontario government sought to assert its property rights to Indian land by challenging the dominion government's right to grant a timber licence. Ruling in favour of the province, the Judicial Committee of the Imperial Privy Council maintained that Indian rights were derived solely, at law, from the Royal Proclamation of 1763.

Up to January 1973 the Canadian common-law position on Aboriginal title differed little from the position stated in the *St. Catharine's* case, eighty-four years earlier. Canadian courts attributed legal status to Aboriginal title solely on the basis of the 1763 proclamation. While this gave some legal support to Indian claims, and has indeed been used extensively by First Nations and other Aboriginals to press their claims, it was subject to the geographical and other uncertainties of the proclamation. The proclamation makes no explicit reference to pre-existing rights; it does not apply to the vast lands granted to the Hudson's Bay Company; and it does not clearly apply to the westernmost provinces.

In 1973, in *Calder v. Attorney General of British Columbia*, the Nisga'a people of northwestern British Columbia sought a declaration that they had Aboriginal title to their land based on occupancy from time immemorial and that this title had not been terminated. Three members of the Supreme Court of Canada agreed that they had a title derived from original occupancy and use. Three others agreed with this contention but concluded that the rights were subsequently and effectively extinguished by the BC government. The seventh member ruled against the Nisga'a on a legal technicality, so the case failed to provide a legal precedent for recognition of Aboriginal property rights based on occupancy and use. Nevertheless, as legal scholars noted, none of the judges rejected the proposition that title based on occupancy and use could have legal status at common law. As Elliott (1985) notes, 'The real significance of *Calder* lies in its strong suggestion that Aboriginal title is not necessarily limited to the confines of the Royal Proclamation of 1763, but may be based on the concept of prior occupation of lands' (75).

Following the *Calder case*, Canadian courts have dealt with Aboriginal land rights on numerous occasions, but they have failed to give clear legal recognition to occupancy-based title. A case that has not been appealed, and which gives credence to such rights, is *Baker Lake*, in which Justice Mahoney of the Federal Court of Canada ruled that the Inuit of the Baker Lake area of the Northwest Territories had an occupancy-based title to their land. However, this decision has not been accepted as a clear precedent for further rulings, partly because it relied heavily on *Calder*, which itself did not create such a precedent (see Elliott 1985, 84).

In 1991 *Delgamuukw et al. v. the Queen* in British Columbia aroused a storm of protest from Aboriginal people and their supporters across the country. The Gitksan-Wet'suwet'en had made a claim for ownership of and jurisdiction over 57,000 square kilometres of land drained by the Skeena River and its tributaries. This territory is rich in timber, minerals, and other resources and includes the towns of Hazelton and Smithers. The Indians based their claims on the Royal Proclamation of 1763 and on occupation and use from time immemorial. In addition, they felt that their case was strengthened by the *Sparrow* case of 1989, in which the Supreme Court had confirmed Aboriginal fishing rights in the lower Fraser River (Schreiner 1991, 20).

Chief Justice Allan McEachern of the BC Supreme Court ruled, however, that any rights which the Indians may have had were extinguished when Britain established sovereignty in the colony and permitted settlement. His decision was in keeping with opinions expressed by several judges in *Calder* and in subsequent cases. Nevertheless, the ruling created considerable consternation because of the reasoning it employed and because it seemed to reverse more recent decisions such as those in *Sparrow*.

Because Justice McEachern decided that any rights which the Indians had held had been extinguished by previous government actions, it was not necessary for him to rule on what kinds of rights existed prior to their extinguishment by governments. However, following previous court decisions, he dismissed the contention that Native rights in British Columbia were supported by the Royal Proclamation of 1763. As well, while not rejecting claims to property rights based on occupation and use, he contended that Indian occupation of the territory had not been pervasive or 'civilized' enough to establish such a right. It was his comments in this regard that particularly provoked controversy. Justice McEachern observed, for example, that 'the evidence suggests that the Indians of the territory were, by historical standards, a primitive people without any form of writing, horses, or wheeled wagons,' and he accepted the suggestion of government witnesses (testifying against the claims) that 'the Gitksan and Wet'suwewet'en civilizations, if they qualify for that description, fall within a much lower, even primitive order' (Monet and Skanu'u 1992, 188). He explicitly rejected the testimony of anthropologists regarding the ordered life of the Indians and their longstanding control over the area. 'Some of this evidence had a decided complexion of unreality about it,' he claimed. 'Aboriginal life, in my view, was far from stable and it stretches credulity to believe that remote ancestors considered themselves bound to specific lands' (188). In conclusion, he ruled that he must decide this case 'only according to what [the plaintiffs] call "the white man's law"' (187).

Justice McEachern's ruling was greeted as a victory by private companies hoping to make greater use of BC natural resources. 'Native Ruling Frees Resource Projects,' was the headline in Canada's leading business paper, the *Financial Post* (Schreiner 1991; also Joyce 1993). However, it was extremely disappointing and even shocking to many observers (see, for example, Monet and Skanu'u 1992). Particularly disturbing was Justice McEachern's acceptance of a viewpoint that has frustrated Aboriginal property claims for a long time. As noted above, Canadian courts are willing to accept a common-law defence of property based on use and occupation. What they have not been willing to accept is that Canadian Aboriginals occupied their land in an acceptable way. The elements required to establish Aboriginal title 'cognizable at common law' were spelled out by Justice Mahoney in *Baker Lake* as follows (Elliott 1985, 93): '1) That they and their ancestors were members of an organized society. 2) That the organized society occupied the specific territory over which they asserted the Aboriginal title. 3) That the occupation was to the exclusion of other organized societies. 4) That the occupation was an established fact at the time sovereignty was asserted by England.'

The absence of written records and the nomadic life of most Aboriginals made it difficult, of course, for their descendants to satisfy these strict requirements. The question of what constituted an 'organized society' posed particularly difficult problems. The failure of most Aboriginal groups to build permanent settlements and to erect fences around clearly specified plots of land seemed to preclude organized social and political life – basic components of 'civilization,' in the eyes of some officials and judges.

The following statement by the Indian agent at Kamloops, BC, in 1885 captures very well the sentiment that prevailed among Canadians of European origin well into the twentieth century: 'Some of the old Indians still maintain that the lands over which they formerly roamed and hunted are theirs by right. I have to meet this claim by stating that as they have not fulfilled the divine command "to subdue the earth" their pretensions to ownership in this respect are untenable' (quoted in Usher and Bankes 1986, 12).

Before Judge McEachern's decision, Canadian courts had sought to be more culturally sensitive to Aboriginal practices, and many had accepted the conclusions of anthropologists and the claims of Aboriginal leaders that the Aboriginal peoples had developed organized political and social structures, which had served them well (see Friesen 1984; Berger 1992). Though these people adhered to a communal view of property, and did not countenance anyone's having title to property, they established property rules for hunting and fishing that were both efficient and conservationist. John Tanner, who was kidnapped by Shawnee Indians in 1789 at age nine and sold to Ojibwa (who then placed him in the care of a very protective mother), tells the following story about a hunt near the present town of Portage La Prairie in Manitoba: 'We left all our canoes and went up into the country to hunt for beaver among the small streams. The Indians gave Wa-me-gon-a-brew and myself a little creek where were plenty of beaver and on which they said none but ourselves should hunt' (quoted in Levernier and Cohen 1997, 98–9). By such assignment of temporary exclusive property rights, and by communal standards ensuring conservation of resources, Aboriginals by and large created a satisfying and self-sustaining life for themselves both before and after Europeans reached the shores of Canada.

In the *Calder* case of 1973, Justice Judson had said: 'Although I think it is clear that Indian title in British Columbia cannot owe its origin to the Proclamation of 1763, the fact is that when the settlers came, the Indians were there, organized in societies and occupying the land as their forefathers had done for centuries' (quoted in Elliott 1985, 92). In that same decision, Justice Hall noted that the courts should not be inhibited in their assessment of Aboriginal ownership 'by a preoccupation with the traditional indicia of ownership.' He continued, 'Possession is of itself proof of ownership. Prima facie, therefore, the Nishgas are the owners of the lands that have been in their possession from time immemorial' (92).

Peter Usher has summarized the results of research on the Inuit and on other Aboriginal groups, with their possible implications for Canadian common law:

The Inuit, like other Aboriginal peoples in Canada, not only occupied distinct territories according to systematic patterns over long periods, but also had relatively stable systems of political authority, land tenure, and resource harvesting which, if their continued existence over generations is anything to go by, worked. This system of law is known to lawyers as a *lex loci*, and may be conceived as the local equivalent of English common law. In the light of several historic court decisions in the 1970s, it is possible to assert that these groups have a *lex loci* which is, on the evidence, of a class which can be presumed to have survived the assertion of a territorial sovereignty by the Crown. (Usher and Bankes 1986, 16)

Unfortunately Justice McEachern acknowledged neither the new insights that had been gained into the pre-European life of the Aboriginals nor the direction taken by the courts cited by Usher above. He refused therefore to grant property rights of a class that could withstand the assertion of territorial sovereignty by the province of British Columbia.

In 1993 the BC Court of Appeal overturned portions of his ruling, deciding that not all the Aboriginal rights claimed by the Gitksan and Wet'suwet'en had been extinguished. However, this was only a partial victory for the Natives.

In view of Justice McEachern's ruling that only the 'white man's law' can be followed in adjudicating Aboriginal land claims, and in the light of some previous decisions that implicitly took a similar position, it appears that possession and occupation will continue to form a weak basis for recognition of Aboriginal property rights in Canada. Canadian common law has therefore failed so far to accommodate itself to the customs and practices of Aboriginal cultures. Despite the severe restrictions noted earlier, the 1763 proclamation still provides the most reliable legal basis for Aboriginal title in Canada.

Third, in addition to royal prerogative and common law, there is another source of law in the Canadian system: statutes and constitutions. To date, Parliament and the provincial legislatures have passed no general laws recognizing or affirming Aboriginal title. However, there are a number of federal and provincial statutes that are consistent with such title. These include the Manitoba Act of 1870, the Dominion Lands Act from 1872 to 1908, and a number of provincial enactments (see Elliott 1985, 84; Cumming and Mickenberg 1972, for a detailed list and discussion).

The most recent and significant legislative enactment that is potentially supportive is the Constitution Act of 1982. Section 35 recognizes and affirms existing Aboriginal and treaty rights of Canada's Aboriginal peoples and states that the phrase 'aboriginal peoples of Canada' includes Indian, Inuit, and Metis. In addition, section 52 provides that 'the Constitution of Canada is the supreme law of Canada, and any law that is inconsistent with the provisions of the Constitution is, to the extent of the inconsistency, of no force or effect.' It is possible, therefore, that the affirmation of 'existing' Aboriginal and treaty rights (keeping in mind the ambiguity of the word 'existing') will enable Aboriginal peoples to solidify rights they have already achieved or at least prevent federal and provincial legislatures from eroding them further. One scholar suggests that among the rights comprehended by section 35 may be 'title to land and hunting and fishing rights' (Lyon 1985, 419).

Other Aboriginal rights, such as language and culture, may find increased protection through the new Charter of Rights and Freedoms. First Nations leaders have, however, reacted negatively to the Charter as a whole. They have done so, first of all, because they had no input into its preparation and adoption. Second, they feel that it places too much emphasis on individual rights and neglects collective rights. National Chief Ovide Mercredi phrased his criticism in positive terms: 'We believe in maximizing individual autonomy without sacrificing a sense of community responsibility' (Mercredi and Turpel 1993, 102).

Most Aboriginal leaders strongly supported the Charlottetown Constitutional Accord, which was voted down in a national referendum in 1992. In the words of a First Nations' advocate, the accord contained 'the most comprehensive set of reform proposals on Aboriginal issues in the history of Canada' (Turpel in Mercredi and Turpel 1993, 208). It would have recognized the inherent right of self-government, agreed to treaty implementation, and accepted Aboriginal peoples as equal partners in Confederation. However, many of the provisions were agreed to hurriedly in the last weeks leading up to the vote, creating confusion and suspicion among many voters, including Aboriginal people. Only about 8 per cent of the First Nations' population voted, and of these about 60 per cent rejected the Accord (Mercredi and Turpel 1993, 209). It was clearly a severe blow to those leaders who saw a unique opportunity to give constitutional support to their economic and political aspirations.

Scope and Content

Aboriginal property rights are a matter not only of legal title, as discussed above, but a question of scope and content. Where property title has been achieved, as on reserves and on lands gained through negotiated settlements, what does 'title' actually mean? What kinds of rights does it confer?

As noted above, in English common law the largest recognized property interest is the fee simple absolute. Though qualified by the crown's ultimate property rights, as expressed in the doctrine of eminent domain, it gives the owner unrestricted use, enjoyment, and disposal rights. In *St. Catharine's Milling* (1889), which is one of the major cases in Canada defining Indian title, Lord Watson held that Indian property rights were less than the rights conferred by fee simple absolute for three reasons: fee simple interest is fully alienable (can be sold to anyone), while Indian title can be alienated only to the crown; fee simple cannot be unilaterally revoked by the crown, but Indian title can; and fee simple is freely inheritable, while Indian title can be inherited only by Indians.

In keeping with these restrictions, the courts have granted only use and enjoyment rights to Aboriginal people, with even these rights interpreted restrictively. In the *St. Catharines* case, Lord Watson ascribed 'usufructury' rights to Canadian Native peoples. Cumming and Mickenberg (1972) note that 'usufruct' is a term of Roman law, little known in the common law. It conferred both use and enjoyment rights on the holder. Courts subsequently have equated it to use alone and even around that have placed restrictions (40; see also Elliott 1985, 88).

Autonomy

The narrow and limited property rights granted to Native peoples by Canadian courts have been restricted further by legislated curbs on Native autonomy. Because the Indian interest in land was ruled to be much less than a fee simple, it could not be regarded as 'private land.' Instead, it was considered crown land, in a way far exceeding the crown's normal property interest, as expressed in eminent domain. It was thus subject to the provisions of the Constitution Act, 1867, that distributed crown land to the provinces. Provincial rights therefore superseded Native rights, and in areas where rights had not been established by treaty (as in British Columbia – hence Justice McEachern's decision), provincial rights extinguished Native rights. As well, laws passed by both the federal Parliament and provincial legislatures defined and limited particular uses of Native land.

Federal and provincial powers over Indians are extremely complicated. As LaForest (1969) observes, 'Provinces cannot legislate respecting Indians qua Indians or lands reserved for Indians qua lands reserved for Indians. At the same time an Indian reserve remains part of the province and consequently persons on the reserve are subject to the general laws of the province' (176–7).

Using what seem occasionally to be overlapping rights, Parliament and legislatures have passed many laws reducing the autonomous exercise of the already limited rights of Aboriginal peoples. In his survey of Inuit rights, Usher has observed that the absolute minimum rights granted to

Aboriginal peoples by the crown in every major proclamation, treaty, and statement regarding Aboriginal peoples are the rights to hunt, trap, fish, and gather in areas of traditional use and occupancy.

It might therefore be expected that this minimum would be defensible against encroachment and capable of remedy and redress when violated. In practice, however, the courts have interpreted Aboriginal interests and rights restrictively ... They have held ... that Aboriginal rights to hunt, trap, fish and gather may in some circumstances be modified or abridged by federal and provincial fisheries and wildlife legislation. By the same token, Aboriginal people have not been able to obtain legal redress for the destruction or degradation of traditional resources by third parties who have obtained competing resource or land rights from the crown. Similarly, compensation for damage to these resources or for the expropriation of Aboriginal land or resource rights is difficult if not impossible to obtain. Finally, despite their dependence upon fish and wildlife resources, Aboriginal peoples have no special power to regulate or manage these resources or their allocation, harvest or use under provincial or federal resource management programs. (Usher and Bankes 1986, 5)

This is a rather lengthy litany of restrictions, but it reflects accurately the way in which governments have imposed such limitations.

Two issues related to the autonomous use of resources deserve further comment: compensation for expropriation or harm, and the management of resources. To understand the Canadian position regarding compensation for the extinguishment (in effect, expropriation) of Aboriginal land by the crown, it is instructive to note a fairly recent decision in the United States. Because the Fifth Amendment of the U.S. constitution stipulates that private property shall not be taken for public use without just compensation, it was assumed until the *Tee-Hit-Ton* case of 1955 that American Indians were guaranteed compensation for the extinguishment of Aboriginal title. However, in that case the U.S. Supreme Court held that Aboriginal title is not a property right but a right of occupancy and thus not subject to the protection of the Fifth Amendment (Elliott 1985, 116). This ruling was cited by Justice Judson of the Supreme Court of Canada in the *Calder* case of 1973, in which the court had also to decide on compensation for the extinguishment of Aboriginal rights in British Columbia. Justice Judson implied that the same rule should apply in Canada. Though that particular case resulted in a stalemate, Canadian courts have generally concluded that the extinguishment of Aboriginal title does not obligate the crown to provide compensation. I noted above that there is no guarantee of compensation in Canada for the taking of any property by the crown. However, as Elliott (1985) argues, there is a 'common law presumption' that in the taking of private property compensation is required. Even such a presumption does not exist with respect to Aboriginal title (117–18).

Aboriginal peoples have also had a very difficult time receiving compensation for damage to their resources by other parties. Consider the example of the pollution of the English River in northwestern Ontario (cited in Usher and Bankes 1986, 10). For centuries two Indian bands whose reserves are located on the river earned their living from fishing. They made, in fact, a good living from a commercial fishery and a sport fishery. In 1970 it was discovered that the chief fish stocks contained high levels of methyl mercury, presumably because of discharges of elemental mercury by upstream pulp-and-paper mills. The commercial fishery had to be closed, and the sport fishery was severely curtailed. The community was devastated, financially and morally. However, nearly sixteen years passed before the bands obtained compensation from industry and government. It took numerous protests and media publicity to get even this result. As Usher observes, 'The view of the Ontario government appears to have been that the bands had neither grounds nor title to sue by virtue of a proprietary interest in the fishery. This is in spite of hunting and fishing rights guaranteed by Treaty 3, rights which in the view of the Ojibwa existed before the treaty and were merely affirmed by it' (1986, 10).

Such examples reinforce in the minds of Aboriginal peoples the idea that their rights to property are not only limited but extremely insecure. This feeling is exacerbated by their inability to manage the resources supposedly under their control. Through administration of the Indian Act and implementation of laws regarding management of fish and wildlife, federal and provincial bodies have assumed frequent and quite direct control of major Aboriginal resources. It is important to understand not only the legal basis of this intervention but the kind of thinking that informs it. Government resource-management agencies have generally regarded Aboriginal resource practices, and particularly the commitment to common property, as an impediment to sound management (Usher and Bankes 1986, 5). Governments and courts have favoured exploitation of resources by non-Aboriginals operating within the framework of a supposedly superior private-property system. In large areas of northern Canada Aboriginal peoples, as we have seen, have received very limited rights to manage and harvest resources. Private non-Aboriginal companies, in contrast, have obtained rights that are exclusive to the holder, confer profit (enjoyment) rights, and provide security of tenure.

Usher argues persuasively that this supposedly scientific and 'efficient' management of resources by the crown and private corporations rests on a rather controversial view, described above, which holds that private ownership and management are inherently superior to common ownership. The work of Scott (1955), Hardin ([1968] 1993), Marsha Gordon (1981), and others, referred to in chapter 3, seemed to demonstrate that common property leads inevitably to wasteful use of resources and, in the case of many natural resources such as fish and wildlife, to their ultimate extinction. However, these scholars assumed that there was no communal control over use of resources when the resources were owned in common. Gordon, for example, noted that England's manorial system set up elaborate communal rules to prevent abuse of resources (see Usher and Bankes 1986, 22). He observed: 'Stable primitive cultures appear to have discovered the dangers of common property tenure and to have developed measures to protect their resources' (quoted by Usher and Bankes 1986, 22).

What is easily overlooked is that Aboriginal cultures have adopted similar communal rules. Usher concludes incisively: 'The commons without law, restraint or responsibility is an appropriate metaphor not for these societies, but rather for laissez-faire industrial capitalism and the imperial frontier, both of which were the historical contexts for such events as the Arctic whale fishery, the Pacific salmon fishery, and the buffalo and passenger-pigeon hunts. Hardin's herdsmen [who overgrazed their cattle on the common pasture] were putting into practice the economics not of medieval times but of Adam Smith. Their behaviour is what we expect when community and its restraining institutions are absent' (Usher and Bankes 1986, 23).

By and large, Aboriginal groups have used resources effectively and conservatively. The English River incident discussed above contains within it a terrible irony. For centuries the two peoples on that river had made a good living from fish, based on common ownership and individual initiative, guided by community standards. Their fishery was ruined not by their practices or their form of ownership, but by private companies upriver that ignored the negative external effects of their operation.

Unfortunately such ironies abound in Canada's treatment of Aboriginal property rights. First, those who were in Canada originally have had the most difficult time obtaining broad and secure rights to the land. Second, while the genius of the common law in most countries has been to accommodate law to the unique characteristics of different cultures, in Canada it has failed up to this point in accommodating the basic political and economic needs of its first citizens. Third, though the communal form of common property practised by Aboriginal peoples has proven effective in using and conserving natural resources, government and business have attributed superior virtues to private property, even when, as recent events have shown, their management has coincided with major crises in several of Canada's basic resources.

What Can Be Done?

The ironies mentioned above summarize a few of the more blatant injustices that have marked Canada's treatment of Aboriginal property rights. The past record does not hold out much promise that these and other injustices will be corrected in the near future. Recent court decisions, the failure thus far to build on the constitutional initiatives of 1982, and the backlash that seems to develop in the non-Aboriginal population whenever Aboriginal peoples assert their rights – as witness the Oka crisis in Quebec and the 1995 outcry in British Columbia – all underscore the fact that Aboriginal peoples constantly find themselves navigating treacherous waters when property rights are the issue.

Nevertheless, a number of recent developments indicate that solutions are not impossible. It is to these initiatives that one has to look when asking what can be done. First, several governments, notably the federal government in the north and the provinces of British Columbia and Saskatchewan, are making serious and increasingly successful efforts to settle outstanding land claims. There is hope that substantial land transfers will have been achieved by the end of this century, as indicated at the beginning of this chapter. The Nisga'a people of British Columbia, for example, concluded an agreement with the province and Ottawa early in 1996, which was hailed as a benchmark for future land claims in that province. It promised them a cash settlement of $190 million and considerable control over seven hundred and seventy-two square miles of the Nass valley on the BC northwest coast. As this book went to press, the Nisga'a people had just ratified the agreement in a referendum.

Second, the constitutional amendments effected in the Constitution Act of 1982 opened doors that cannot be shut, and the chances of undergirding Aboriginal rights through constitutional change are much greater today than they were before 1982. Third, the Aboriginal desire for self-management ('self-government,' to couch it in broader, more political terms) is being met with greater understanding on both federal and provincial levels. A First Nations' experiment in self-government in Manitoba is already past the drawing boards. Those who carefully examine the thoughtful treatment of this subject by First Nations' leaders such as Phil Fontaine will undoubtedly find much that makes eminent sense – and little if anything that warrants alarm.

The 1996 report of the Royal Commission on Aboriginal Peoples (RCAP) made numerous, very specific and concrete proposals that, if implemented, would greatly strengthen Aboriginal property rights. It called on the federal and provincial governments to promote Aboriginal economic development 'by recognizing that lands and resources are a major factor in enabling Aboriginal nations and their communities to become self-reliant' (recommendation 2.5.12). It urged them to draft a national code of principles 'to recognize and affirm the continued exercise of traditional Aboriginal activities on Crown Lands' (2.4.48) and made several recommendations to increase Aboriginal access to natural resources and to increase participation in the fruits of resource use by others. It also recommended that an Aboriginal Lands and Treaties Tribunal replace the Independent Land Claims Commission. The new tribunal would have far greater powers, covering both specific lands claims and the treaty process, and would take into account 'Aboriginal customary and property law' (2.4.35). These are only a few of the numerous innovative proposals – constitutional, legal, political, economic, social, and cultural – put forth by the RCAP, serving to demonstrate that solutions to the issue of Aboriginal property rights are indeed available.

The greatest problem seems to lie with public opinion and with courts that seem to reflect rather than lead that opinion. The treatment of Aboriginal history and values by the courts has been at best condescending and at worst hypocritical and myopic. Is it good enough to judge others by 'white man's' law, when other laws even more ancient than those of the white man are present? Can one even speak of 'just' laws when they are imposed on others without their consent to the system? Since 'white man's' law has proved capable of adapting to different cultural values – as it has done over time in both England and Canada – can it be said that a judgment is consistent with that law's tradition and genius when it categorically rejects the need to take other traditions seriously? The courts have it within their power to grant proprietary property rights to Aboriginal peoples based on common-law precedents. Several court decisions leave one hopeful that rights based on occupancy will soon be granted and that this will remove many of the restrictions currently placed on Aboriginal control of resources. Unfortunately, little of this is likely to happen without further expensive court cases, social confrontations, and growing bitterness among Aboriginal peoples. In this land, which the Indians call Turtle Island, justice is indeed slow in coming. Transforming property rights in areas where Aboriginal peoples have ancient rights remains one of the most urgent and important issues in Canada's political life.

5

Citizen Property Rights

Concern about abuses in the market place is as old as the recorded history of civilized man.

Edward Belobaba 1985, 3

We know in general that even well-functioning competitive markets may fail to allocate resources properly over time.

Robert Solow 1993a, 173

The Protecting of Community Interests

Previous chapters have noted several challenges to Canada's existing property system. Private owners of resources are contesting government ownership, adult partners have radically changed the distribution of property within the family, and the property negotiations of Canada's First Nations people with several levels of government are reshaping the economic and political landscape. The actions in these three areas alone constitute a fundamental adjustment to the arrangements and rules that have governed Canada's property system.

On still another front, many Canadians are challenging the ways in which resources are used by property owners. Critics have in mind two distinct, though related abuses. They object, first, to the negative effects of resource use on social and economic life in Canada. This is what economists refer to as negative 'externalities.' Second, a growing number of individual citizens and organizations fear that current resource use may be extremely harmful to future generations. The charge is that many resource owners ignore the future in the speed and manner in which they are using resources.

The two problems involve issues of the environment and sustainability. They affect the current and future condition of our 'ecosphere' – 'the living space shared by all living creatures (including man) – and the creatures themselves' (Dorfman and Dorfman 1993, 79). Concern centres especially around the purity of air and water, the quantity and vitality of natural landscapes, fauna, and flora, and, particularly, such widespread conditions as the accumulation of greenhouse gases in the atmosphere, acid precipitation, and deforestation. It also centres around access to and use of parks and wilderness areas for recreation and leisure.

Robert Solow, an American Nobel laureate in economics, has noted that while current environmental problems and future sustainability are in some ways separate issues, subject to different solutions, they are also closely related. 'The environment needs protection ... because each of us knows that by burdening the environment, by damaging it, we can profit and have some of the cost, perhaps most of the cost, borne by others. Sustainability is a problem precisely because each of us knows or realizes that we can profit at the expense of the future rather than at the expense of our contemporaries and the environment. We free-ride on each other and we free-ride on the future' (Solow 1993b, 183). When a company pollutes the air it ignores the external effects of its operation on persons in the current population who breathe that air. When it fails to replenish the forest resources that it is using it ignores the external effects of its operation on future generations. More and more citizens are protesting such abuse of resources, both in their own name and in the name of future generations.

Citizen Property

In mounting this challenge, critics are essentially insisting that they should have a greater say in how resources are used in our economy. In other words, they would like to enlarge their property rights at the expense of the current formal owners of resources. This movement towards greater property rights may be understood as a movement towards more citizen property.

I define 'citizen property' as property rights sought or claimed by ordinary citizens, either as individuals or as groups, permitting them to ameliorate current and future negative effects of current resource use. It is made up of rights sought by private citizens for public purposes. In pursuit of their objectives citizens may often appeal to courts, and to governments, for legal and administrative assistance, but citizen property is not in and of itself a new form of government property. It does not substitute state property for private property.

What many citizens want is greater rights to protect themselves and their descendants from the abuse of the earth's scarce resources by both private and state owners of property. There is no presumption here, or in the concerns raised by most futurists or environmentalists, that government institutions as such are inclined to use resources more carefully than are private owners of resources. To quote Robert Solow once more: 'It is far from clear that the political process can be relied on to be more future-oriented than your average corporation. The conventional pay-out period for business is of the same order of magnitude as the time to the next election, and transferring a given individual from the industrial to the government bureaucracy does not transform him into a guardian of the far future's interests. I have no ready solution to this problem. At a minimum, it suggests that one ought to be as suspicious of uncritical centralization as of uncritical free-marketeering' (Solow 1993a, 175). With regard to current negative externalities, such as environmental pollution, both the experience of the heavily polluted former socialist countries and the practices of our own governments, as discussed below in this chapter, indicate that citizens desiring wiser resource use must be prepared to exercise their rights against both private and government corporations.

The enlargement of citizen property therefore does not dilute private property rights in favour of greater state rights; it requires instead a wider distribution of rights, a greater sharing of rights between formal owners of property – both private and state – and the citizenry at large. The result should be a more broadly based system of private rights. The concept of citizen property being promoted here is very similar therefore to T.H. Marshall's (1964) 'social citizenship' and 'citizen rights.'

Implicit in this analysis is a certain understanding of human motivation. Those individuals in our society who argue for redistribution of property rights so that they can reduce resource abuse both now and in the future are concerned about their own welfare as well as with the good of society. This view of the individual as a responsible citizen who cares about the public good transcends the narrowly focused individualism promoted by today's free-marketeers. It is also critical of those reform traditions that tie the legitimacy of the individual to the state. The view promoted here is well articulated by Daly and Cobb, who distinguish between homo economicus as pure, selfish individual (the 'model' person assumed in most economics texts) and homo economicus as person-in-community. They argue that the latter deserves much more attention in social and economic analysis (Daly and Cobb 1989, 7). A similar argument is made by John Ralston Saul (1995) in *The Unconscious Civilization*: 'Real individualism,' he maintains, 'is the obligation to act as a citizen' (165). Such citizens are assumed to have basic rights to determine how society uses its resources, and as citizens they will choose frequently to exercise them.

Individuals may choose to exercise citizen property rights in various ways. They may, for example, purchase voting shares in private corporations with the express purpose of improving the corporate use of resources. Those lacking either the means or the inclination to follow this route may join groups of like-minded citizens, appealing to the courts and to governments to recognize and enforce the common law's respect for 'people's' right to property. Governments may on occasion prove more receptive to such initiatives than private corporations, not because – as noted above – they are staffed by more public-minded persons or committed to a broader public agenda, but because the citizenry in a political democracy has greater opportunity to 'do' something about unacceptable government decisions. Private corporations may be under greater pressure from shareholders and competitors to act efficiently, but government bodies may be more susceptible to pressure from citizens to act responsibly.

The chief purpose of this chapter is to examine the role of citizen property in getting resource owners, whether private or public, to use resources more responsibly – to adopt production techniques and objectives consitent with a healthy physical and social environment and a sustainable future. The next section asks why markets often act irresponsibly from this dual perspective. The section after that examines the technical dimensions of coping with environmental problems and guaranteeing sustainability in Canada; there follows an analysis of the political dimensions of this issue. The final section examines possible solutions to these problems, returning to the question of effective citizen property rights.

Market Failure in the Use of Resources

The market system, based on the free (i.e., uncontrolled) exchange of goods and services and the private ownership of resources, is acknowledged by most economists to be the best system ever devised for allocating resources among commodity uses. Even Daly and Cobb (1989) in their critique of the system give it this pride of place. Following a line of reasoning developed particularly by Hayek (1944), they emphasize the remarkable ability of the market to collect, communicate, and use masses of scattered, piecemeal information on resource availability and prices to allocate resources efficiently. 'Individual consumers know their preferences better than anyone else and act directly to satisfy them in the marketplace. Individual producers know their own capacities and options better than anyone else and they too act on this information in the market. This essential feature of *decentralized* decisionmaking is what permits all this knowledge to be used' (Daly and Cobb 1989, 45).

As Adam Smith first argued more than two hundred years ago, the market, through a seemingly invisible hand, spontaneously creates order out of the chaos of millions of daily independent economic decisions. Basic requirements for this system to work are that individual producers have control over resources (private ownership), they are free to use those resources where they will produce the greatest profit, and competition prevents them from exploiting the consumer.

Unfortunately, markets can fail in a number of ways. First, one of the basic requirements – vigorous competition among a large number of independent producers – may be absent. The presence of undue market power among relatively few producers permits price-exploitation of consumers and frustrates the legitimate ambitions of other potential producers. Second, even when the basic requirements are met it may 'fail' on several counts. A competitive market, for example, is 'amoral' with regard to distribution of income. Participants are rewarded according to entrepreneurial skills, luck, and inheritance (start-up resources), but not according to basic needs. A market system inevitably therefore poses questions of fairness. Further, and more central to the current inquiry, a market system does not, by itself, possess mechanisms for preventing significant abuses in use of resources – for both current and future generations.

Producers in a market system may harm the current population in several ways. They may, for example, produce goods and services that are shoddy or directly harmful to users, taking advantage of consumers' ignorance. The tobacco industry is only one glaring example of an industry that has imposed inestimable health and financial costs on millions of people, and short of radical government intervention it will continue to do so.

As Belobaba observes, 'The basic concern – about protecting consumers from marketplace abuse – has been a concern of governments for centuries' (Belobaba 1985, 3). 'Consumer protection,' which has resulted in hundreds of special laws in most industrialized countries, refers particularly to protection against the direct harmful effects of specific goods such as tobacco, faulty automobile brakes, and dangerous drugs. Citizens have had to petition governments for a long time to limit the property rights of producers in order to gain protection from such products. In most cases it appears that the producers themselves, whether private or state organizations, are unlikely to identify and solve such problems on their own initiative.

The concern of this study has more to do with the indirect effects, or by-products, of production. Economists refer to these as 'externalities.' Most discussions of this problem confine their concern narrowly to the indirect physical consequences of production, such as the water pollution accompanying pulp and paper output or the air pollution resulting from metal smelting. These are of course serious problems and receive further attention in this chapter. However, current populations are harmed indirectly by the market system in significant but less tangible ways as well. Daly and Cobb (1989) draw attention, for example, to the erosion of 'moral capital' and community in a market system. The system encourages individualistic self-interest (the pursuit-of-profit motive), but at the same time it depends for its operation on such values as honesty, thrift, and mutual care. Such values, Daly and Cobb argue, 'will not long withstand the reduction to the level of personal tastes that is explicit in the positivistic, individualistic philosophy of value on which modern economic theory is based.' In the long run, they fear, 'the market system does not accumulate moral capital; it depletes it' (50–1). In *The Social Limits to Growth*, Fred Hirsch (1976) concludes that depletion of moral capital in a free market system may be more costly than depletion of physical capital.

A sense of community is a related victim of the market economy. By focusing on the pursuit of individual gain, and by encouraging producers to locate production anywhere in the world, wherever costs are lowest, it diminishes feelings of interdependence and cooperation among people. Robert Reich observes that in the past conservative philosophers such as Edmund Burke considered that 'a nation constituted a contract, a form of partnership not only between those who are living but between those who are living and those who are to be born ... The partnership was a moral one; citizens had obligations to one another' (Robert Reich 1992, 16). Edward Schwarz (1982) shows how such views permeated American political thought until fairly recently – and the irony is that a commitment to community is diminishing at the same time as 'it now appears certain that a strong local community is essential to psychological well-being, personal growth, social order and a sense of political efficacy' (264). George Grant (1970) observed the same tragic irony in Canada in *Lament for a Nation*, a concern revived most recently by writers such as John Ralston Saul (1995).

The clash between market values and community, between a narrowly perceived system of private property and social well-being, often surfaces in very concrete ways. For example, a grocery supermarket decides to close down one of its stores in order to construct a larger one in another area. The store to be closed is not necessarily losing money, but the company feels that the new one will make greater profits. The supermarket has no difficulty defending this decision in terms of free-market, private-property values. It is the owner of its resources and can use them where they will earn the most money. What is easily forgotten, however, is that a grocery store is often a significant social institution as well as a private business, and its removal harms that community.

An interesting example of this occurred in Winnipeg two decades ago when Safeway decided to relocate one of its stores in the Corydon Avenue area. Local residents were alarmed. They pointed out, in letters to the newspapers and in petitions to their political representatives, that one of the reasons they had moved into the area was the proximity of the Safeway store. The store was surrounded by a large number of apartment blocks, housing numerous senior citizens who could not walk far. Grocery shopping for them after closure would be more expensive and inconvenient. The store representatives argued, of course, that they owned the business and could do with it as they liked. The residents replied that Safeway had benefited considerably from their presence in the past, and since the store was not losing money it should not abandon them now.

Economic theory suggests a simple solution: if a store in the area was still a viable proposition, a new store such as the old Safeway would soon appear. However, for several reasons this was unlikely to happen, and did not happen. First, Safeway would not be inclined to sell its building to a potential rival, because its new store was only a mile away from the old. And a new owner, faced with the cost of a new building, and having to compete with a new Safeway store nearby, could hardly hope to match the profitability of the original store. Second, all private firms go where profit margins are highest, and potential rivals would go through the same thinking process as Safeway did, opting for larger stores in larger markets.

In view of all this, was a different solution possible? No one responded seriously to the main point made by the residents: that a large grocery store is simultaneously a private business and a social institution. Ignored was the fact that the success of a private business depends at least partly on its being a social institution and that its closing therefore has serious social implications, which the owners should consider in making their decision. A different solution might have been possible if residents had been recognized as having some property rights in an institution to which they had contributed a great deal and which had prompted at least one of their major life decisions – their choice of residence. The citizen demands were indeed a demand for such rights, which our current adherence to very narrowly defined private-property rights has little chance of meeting.

The Safeway example underlines a weakness in much of our thinking about the indirect negative consequences of business decisions. Most of the environmental literature deals with the indirect, physical consequences of business expansion. Economists measure how a new hydro transmission line, for example, will damage communities and resources through which the line will pass or how expansion of a smelting operation will increase air pollution. They pay relatively little attention to the social consequences of closing or downsizing a business. In recent years a virtual cult of downsizing has gripped the business community, resulting in massive layoffs of workers. This happens even in businesses that are in no danger of bankruptcy. The search is for increased profits, and in that quest workers are deemed readily expendable. It is assumed that private owners have an unrestricted right to make such human-resource decisions.

Ignored in the analyses of economists and the calculations of business owners is the crucial social and community role that most businesses play. They provide not only a job but a livelihood to people, a sense of purpose, and a focus of community stability. In the course of building up their enterprises, many businesses foster an image of community, appealing to workers as members of a family and to consumers as 'valued' long-term customers. However, in the pursuit of larger profits it is considered perfectly legitimate for these same businesses to ignore all community rhetoric, all claims to workers' and consumers' allegiance. Both workers and consumers are essential stakeholders in most private businesses. An adequate system of property should find some way of recognizing this. As is seen in the next chapter, a number of market economies have been extremely innovative in this area, especially with regard to workers' rights. Unfortunately, Canada is not one of these economies.

Why do markets fail to protect even the physical environment from serious abuse? Raising this question takes us to the heart of growing concern about the health of the physical environment for both current and future generations. It also prompts a more critical examination of our market system. Garrett Hardin, whose classic 1968 essay, 'The Tragedy of the Commons,' helped to bring environmental issues to the forefront of economic debate, wrote in his paper that such issues force one to 'exorcise the spirit of Adam Smith.' He regretted that Smith had contributed to a 'dominant tendency of thought that has ever since interfered with positive action based on rational analysis, namely, the tendency to assume that decisions reached individually will in fact be the best decisions for an entire society' (Hardin [1968] 1993, 8). In other words, even though a market system allocates resources efficiently, it does not produce the best social results. The spontaneous order it produces is not necessarily the most beneficial one for society.

The problem of the market, as Stephen Brooks states succinctly, is that its individual decision-makers have no incentive to consider the collective implications of their individual choices (Brooks 1993, 213). Choices in the market are based on prices, but prices do not include all the costs borne by society in the course of production. There is a divergence between private and social costs. Some of the costs incurred in production may be ignored by producers because they can be sloughed off on other members of society, including those still to come. As noted above, economists refer to those costs that are not included in the pricing of a product as 'externalities.' To the extent that such costs are ignored, the products will be underpriced; they will be offered at lower prices and in larger quantities than is optimal for society, either now or in the future.[1]

The market as such has no mechanism built into it that will force producers to deal with the negative external results of their actions. This fact has significant implications for the virtues frequently attributed to the market system. As Daly and Cobb (1989) write, 'All conclusions in economic theory about the social efficiency of pure competition and the free market are explicitly premised on the absence of externalities. The undeniable importance of externalities in today's world is therefore a serious challenge to the relevance of these conclusions' (55).

Coping with Market Failure: The Technical Imperatives

So what can be done in a market system to minimize the impact of current production on the current and future physical environment? Take current environmental damage first. One cannot eliminate the harmful effects of production entirely; for many industries, including those producing essential goods and services, this would prove incredibly expensive and would therefore reduce output and employment to intolerably low levels. The basic objective should be to eliminate the core of the problem, the divergence between private and social costs. This in turn requires two technical procedures: an estimate of the difference between private and social costs – that is, an estimate of the external costs of production – and a method of imposing these costs on the production process so that they are incorporated into the price charged to consumers. In other words, put an appropriate price on pollution. The market by itself, for reasons mentioned above, is unlikely to do either of these things. The ultimate solution therefore is not only technical but political. What is needed is strong community pressure on businesses, governments, and courts to make sure that the technical processes are carried out. This political requirement I examine in the next section, paying special attention to Canadian experience. First, in this section, I look at the technical problems of estimating the true costs of pollution, assigning the costs fairly, and ensuring that all affected stakeholders (including future generations) are properly represented in policy-making.

The first technical challenge – estimating the amount of environmental damage caused by a particular producer – usually involves numerous difficulties. In most cases there are both tangible and intangible costs. For example, pollution along the Fraser River directly affects the BC fishery and the livelihood of fishers. The cost of this impact we can estimate directly in terms of the fixed cost of converting some people and equipment from fishing to an alternative occupation, plus the difference between what they earned in fishing and what they earn in the new occupation, plus the cost to consumers who must eat chicken instead of fish (see Ruff 1993, 25). But there are other, less tangible costs, such as loss of recreation opportunities for families and sportsfishers as well as increased health hazards. There is also, of course, the harm caused to the fish themselves, an important element of the ecosphere. (Economists often ignore the damage done to nature; see, for example, Ruff 1993, and, for a more sensitive treatment, Daly and Cobb 1989.)

How does one estimate the price of intangible harm? One might estimate the value that people place on clean water and air by observing how much more they are willing to pay for equivalent property in non-polluted areas. Another method is to ask people how much they would be willing to pay to have the pollution reduced. A study in Manitoba conducted in preparation for construction of a new hydro-transmission line through wilderness areas asked members of a sample population of that province how much they would be willing to pay additionally on their monthly hydro bill in order to save the wilderness. Wilderness areas could be saved by having the new line built along a more expensive route, which would leave the wilderness intact. The interviewers found that the average respondent was willing to pay $133 more per year to achieve this result. Extrapolated to the whole population this would have been more than enough to reroute the line and save the wilderness (Mason 1995, 9). In the end the line was not built because of reduced demand from potential electricity buyers.

Assume that a careful estimate of both tangible and intangible costs has been made. How should these now be imposed – our second technical problem – so as to improve the environment without necessarily destroying the industry that creates the harm? One direct and common method is for the government to require a certain amount of pollution to be eliminated within a given period. Penalties are imposed for non-compliance. The firms involved will face additional costs in reducing pollution, which will undoubtedly increase the price and reduce the quantity demanded of their products. This is, in itself, a desirable result. However, numerous practical difficulties emerge: government regulators must carefully monitor the actual reduction in pollution and impose a penalty that will encourage compliance without crippling the firms. Perhaps even more important, if each firm is given a similar pollution-reduction target, those that were already making efforts to reduce pollution – the relatively 'good' firms – will undoubtedly face greater expense than those relatively 'bad' ones, which were not. In other words, the 'good' businesses will be punished more than the 'bad' ones, an outcome that defies all notions of fairness. This result follows from the observed fact that it becomes increasingly more expensive to reduce pollutants as one approaches 'zero pollution.'

A simpler and more effective solution is to set the price – in effect a tax – for each unit of pollution and force each firm to pay that price. Each polluter is motivated to reduce pollution up to that point where further reductions cost more than the tax. In general the 'good' companies will reach that point with less expense than the 'bad' ones. This method is therefore 'fair' on two counts: those who produce and consume goods that cause pollution pay the costs, and those who currently pollute the most will pay more to reduce pollution than those who pollute least.

Similar results can be obtained, at least in theory, by permitting firms to trade pollution 'permits.' This method, described by Dales (1993) and Tietenberg (1994), has the government, through a regulatory body, deciding the amount of pollution that will be allowed and issuing corresponding permits. Businesses must purchase the permits, perhaps through a public auction, and can subsequently sell them to each other. The result will be that they will limit their pollution to the level at which the price of the permit equals the additional cost of reducing pollution. The difference between this method and the tax method is that in the case of the latter the government sets the 'price' (tax) of pollution and allows the total quantity to adjust, whereas in the case of tradeable permits it sets the total quantity of pollution allowable and lets the price (tax) adjust itself (see Dorfman and Dorfman 1993, 200). Politically the tax method is easier to sell to the general public because it is clearer that firms are paying a price for polluting, while with tradeable permits it appears that they are paying a price in order to pollute. In theory, however, the result should be the same.

In terms of citizen property, it is important to consider who should implement the procedures to reduce pollution – our third technical problem. In many cases a large number of 'stakeholders' – people affected by the environmental damage and by attempts to do something about it – are involved. Take, for example, a pulp-and-paper mill that damages the river into which it discharges its effluents, thereby harming all those who use the river. In addition, it may seriously harm the wilderness in which it harvests its trees – a concern to people far beyond the region. All citizens who feel that their welfare is harmed by the mill should have some say in determining the price to be imposed on it for its pollution. At the same time, the employers and employees of the company are also significant stakeholders, facing potential hardships from anti-pollution initiatives. If the mill preceded fishers on the river, the mill could even make a reasonable case that the fishers are interfering with its use of the river and should be held responsible for some of the additional costs that will be imposed on the mill. Ruff suggests therefore that in addition to requiring an agency to calculate damage to the environment as well as to the offending firm, a referendum or some other method of public polling is required, to permit people affected to influence the price to be imposed on pollution (Ruff 1993, 32; see also Mitchell 1991). This issue receives further attention in the concluding section of this chapter.

Because current production may impose external costs on future generations, as well as on the current population, producers attempt to 'free ride' on the future as well as on the present, and the market system is unable to prevent either. Commentators have suggested that imposing an appropriate price on pollution might lessen current environmental damage considerably. Presumably the problem of future harm – of sustainability – can be handled in a similar way. What is required is that the costs of current resource use for future generations be adequately considered. In the case of renewable resources, such as fisheries, forestry, and agriculture, harvesters should be forced to include in their costs, and therefore in the price to the consumer, long-term replenishment costs. For non-renewable resources, such as petroleum, a high-enough tax might greatly lessen current use, thereby stretching out its availability into future. The tax revenue could provide eventually for development of alternative energy sources (including retrieval of petroleum reserves that are otherwise too costly).

Unfortunately, future generations are invisible stakeholders with no input into price and resource-use strategies. As Solow observes, 'It is fair to say that those people a few generations hence are not adequately represented in today's market. They don't participate in it, and therefore there is no doctrinaire reason for saying "Oh well, ordinary supply and demand, ordinary market behavior, will take care of whatever obligation we have to the future"' (Solow 1993b, 182).

Numerous economists have suggested that the needs of the future are particularly neglected in cases where resources are subject to common ownership. Hardin's 'The Tragedy of the Commons' showed how overgrazing has historically occurred on unrestricted commonlands prior to their enclosure ([1968] 1993). There was no mechanism requiring herdsmen to consider the effects of their herds' grazing on all the other herdsmen. When the land was subsequently enclosed, and herdsmen were assigned individual property rights, they took care of the land with an eye to the future. Overgrazing was now a loss for them and their progeny. Similar solutions have been proposed for other resources often held in common, particularly forests and fisheries (on the latter see H. Scott Gordon 1993). In recent years Iceland and New Zealand have introduced individual property rights into their fisheries by establishing individual transferable quotas (ITQs). These fishing quotas are acquired and remain the property of the owner, to be bought and sold in the market. This system still requires an annual total quota set by some body, which estimates what is appropriate for the sustainability of the resource. Nevertheless, Canadian resource economist Peter Pearse maintains that 'fishers who find themselves with secure, defined shares of the productive capacity of a fish stock soon realize they have a common interest in protecting and enhancing it, and begin to co-operate in management, regulation and enforcement' (quoted in Corcoran 1995).

Many individual owners of resources may be motivated by self-interest, including the interest of their progeny, to consider the future carefully in their use of resources. M.J. Troughton, for example, observes that in Canadian agriculture 'until recently the relatively small scale of farm operating, its somewhat mixed nature and level of local recycling, coupled with the individual stewardship by the farmer, helped to limit soil erosion under normal conditions' (Troughton 1994, 79).

However, for a number of reasons, private ownership is no guarantee of long-term sustainability. First, as Hardin himself stressed, many fundamental elements of the ecosphere, such as air and water, cannot be easily fenced in. 'Therefore,' he concluded, 'the tragedy of the commons ... must be prevented by different means, by coercive laws or taxing devices' (Hardin [1968] 1993, 11). Dorfman and Dorfman (1993) anticipate enormous economies in the joint consumption or use of many resources. For example, they contrast housing and streets. 'It is economical to divide living space into family-size lots and devote each of them to housing one or a few families, but it would be fantastically wasteful to provide each family with its private road to the central business district' (81). They add, 'Most resources in the environment are analagous to streets, not houses' (81).

Solow argues that even the most rational use of resources by individual producers fails to ensure their conservation for future generations. When calculating the present value of future returns, producers rationally discount the future. For example, a $100 return seven years from now is currently valued at $50 if the interest rate is 10 per cent (looked at in the opposite way, a person who invests $50 today at a compound interest rate of 10 per cent will have an investment worth $100 in seven years. Therefore, $100 seven years from now is equivalent to $50 today). Solow then asks, what are the owners of an iron-ore mine likely to do if they expect that their rate of profit will grow by less than the current compound rate of interest? His answer: they will conclude that their resource deposits are a bad way to hold wealth, and they will get out of the resource business as quickly as possible by using the resource up in order to convert ore into money. The result will not be favourable to future generations.

Solow also notes reasons why the discount rate applied by private owners of resources may not be the same as the one society would use. First, individuals will include among the risks for which they discount future returns those that are real to them – such as resource transfers from one firm to another resulting from changing fortunes – but which are not risks from society's point of view. Second, individuals care about their after-tax return, and society about before-tax return. For these reasons and others, individuals are likely to apply a higher discount to future returns than society would and consequently to exploit a resource more rapidly, and more completely, than society as a whole would allow. Solow agrees with those economists who question whether it is appropriate at all, from society's point of view, to discount future returns. 'In social decision-making,' he argues, 'there is no excuse for treating generations unequally' (Solow 1993a, 171). This analysis causes Solow to express broad agreement with the observation of an earlier economist, Harold Hotelling, that many products in our private-market system 'are now too cheap for the good of future generation ... they are being selfishly exploited at too rapid a rate, and ... in consequence of their excessive cheapness they are being produced and consumed wastefully' (162–3).

Given the market's inability to deal adequately with both current and future externalities, it is small wonder that the public has put pressure on government and on the courts to correct the market. The next section provides a brief overview of legal and legislative actions in Canada with respect to both environmental and sustainability concerns.

Coping with Market Failure: The Political Imperatives

Canada's efforts in recent decades to protect its environment and to create conditions for a sustainable future are part of a world-wide response to an ecological crisis. The crisis in turn results from a deeply ingrained, world-wide pattern of development that appears to be destructive of the environment at its very core. This aspect of the crisis is described in the report *State of the World* (Brown 1996): 'Evidence continues to accumulate that it is in the very nature of industrial economic systems to degrade the environment on which they depend and hurt the people they serve' (Roodman 1996, 168). Both private businesses and governments are caught up in destructive development strategies that neither a concerned public nor the courts seem able to correct.

Global trends tell the story all too clearly. The world's population has doubled since 1950, and the global economy has nearly quintupled in size. In just the ten years from 1985 to 1995 the world's economy grew by $4 trillion – more than from the beginning of civilization until 1950 (Brown 1996, 3). The spiralling human demands that are driving this expansion are beginning to outgrow the capacity of the earth's natural systems, because resources are being both used up and degraded. 'Evidence of the damage to the earth's ecological infrastructure takes the form of collapsing fisheries, falling water tables, shrinking forests, eroding soils, dying lakes, crop-withering heat waves, and disappearing species' (Brown 1996, 4).

Unfortunately, public awareness and concern wax and wane in response to periodic ecological disasters and some highly publicized warnings. One of the earliest such admonitions was Rachel Carson's *Silent Spring* (1962). Her effective disclosure of the harmful effects of agricultural chemicals led to the appointment of an American presidential commission, which examined and eventually banned the use of carginogenic DDT. Before Carson, the environmental movement aimed at conserving nature. It did not conceive environmental degradation as a problem endemic to urban-industrial society. Indeed, as Stephen Brooks has observed, the roots of environmentalism in North America go back to the nineteenth century, when organizations such as the Sierra Club (founded 1892) and the Audubon Society (1895) were set up for conservation purposes (Brooks 1993, 218). This early movement, however, did not challenge the fundamental values and practices of industrialism, even though it faced formidable opposition from forestry, mining, and agricultural interests.

The publication of Carson's work, plus other studies, and a series of environmental disasters, brought a new type of environmentalism to the forefront. The disasters included some major oil spills, one in the English Channel in 1967 and another off the coast of Santa Barbara, California, in 1969. These spills were followed by a chemical leak at a Union Carbide plant in Bhopal, India (1984), that killed over ten thousand people; the discovery of a hole in the ozone layer over Antarctica (1985); the partial meltdown of a nuclear reactor at Chernobyl in Ukraine (1986); and the massive oil spill of the *Exxon Valdez* off the coast of Alaska in 1989. The pressure of growing population on the earth's resources was highlighted in the Club of Rome's first report, *The Limits to Growth* (Meadows et al. 1972). Global energy problems were dramatized by the OPEC's oil embargo of 1973, while an increasing number of scientific reports demonstrated widespread deterioration of such vital resources as water, air, and forests.

The Canadian public, governments, and courts have responded to these developments in a number of ways, and with varying degrees of success. On the one hand, some crises, such as overpopulation and resource depletion, were not pressing problems within Canada's own border. On the other hand, Canadians were directly affected by the depleting ozone layer, the impact of acid rain on air and forests, the deterioration in particular of the Great Lakes and of the ocean fisheries, and the environmental effects of a number of major development projects.

Several factors have affected the Canadian response. First, I examine the legal and constitutional constraints on dealing with the environment and the overlapping as well as conflicting interests of business, governments, and environmental groups. Second, I look at the rather uneven environmental policies that have emerged. Third, I analyse these responses in terms of the three major responsibilities of environmental authorities outlined in the previous section.

Constraints on Action

The legal foundation of the common law provided a number of grounds on which individuals and groups could contest and seek redress for actions affecting the environment (cf. Schrecker 1992). Most of these grounds had to do with the common law's protection of property ownership. 'Nuisance' denoted unreasonable and unnecessary interference with the enjoyment of property. 'Riparian rights' protected downstream owners of property adjoining a body of water against interference with the flow and quality of water by upstream users. 'Trespass' referred to unauthorized entry or damage to property. 'Strict liability' made individuals liable for damage done by the escape of dangerous materials from their property.

The Canadian constitution makes no direct reference to the environment. Unlike the constitutions of many states, Canada provides no enshrined guarantee to a clean, healthy environment (see VanderZwaag and Duncan 1992, 4). Instead, the federal and provincial governments are given responsibility for different sectors of the economy and, with that, the power to determine environmental behaviour in those sectors. For example, the federal power over sea-coast and inland fisheries enabled Parliament to pass the Federal Fisheries Act, and its power to control navigation and shipping supported its passing of the Waters Protection Act. In addition, federal responsibility for 'peace, order and good government' permitted it to create the Canadian Environmental Protection Act. International obligations also fall under federal authority, resulting in such legislation as the Migratory Birds Convention Act and the International River Improvements Act and Canada's commitment to environmental goals enshrined in international conventions.

However, the provinces have much more authority over the environment because of their jurisdiction over property and civil rights. In addition, most crown lands outside the northern territories are provincially owned. This mixed jurisdiction over resources has occasionally produced conflict between federal and provincial governments over environmental issues.

Canadian citizens can use the common law, and the laws of Quebec, to protect themselves against environmental abuses. Governments can pass legislation that reinforces and possibly enlarges the intent of the law, or they can use their statutory powers to protect resource users against citizens' complaints. Canadian governments have done both, frequently.

Environmental Policies

The public's growing concern about environmental issues in the 1960s and 1970s prompted all levels of government to pass legislation in those areas. As two scholars note, 'Canadian politicians and bureaucrats have prided themselves on being international leaders in supporting sustainable development and forging new institutions and laws to protect the environment. When the Canadian Environmental Protection Act (CEPA) was first released as a draft bill in December 1986, the then Minister of Environment, Tom McMillan, called it the most comprehensive piece of legislation in the western hemisphere' (VanderZwaag and Duncan 1992, 3). As will be seen, Canada has little reason to boast of superiority in environmental matters. Nonetheless, it has made numerous advances in the last few decades.

On the federal level a major advance occurred in 1970 with the creation of the Department of the Environment, prompted in large part by growing public demand for government action. In one 1970 survey 69 per cent of Canadians indicated that pollution was a 'very serious' problem, while another found that Canadians ranked pollution as the issue most deserving attention by government (M. Paul Brown 1992, 26). The new department took over responsibilities in management of resources previously held by such departments as Energy, Mines and Resources, Fisheries, and Transport. In addition it was to establish pollution-control guidelines, to assess the environmental effects of development projects, and to facilitate federal–provincial cooperation in environmental matters. After a flurry of well-publicized activity, including the passage by Parliament of several pieces of environmental legislation, such as the Canada Water Act and the Clean Air Act, both public and government enthusiasm waned. Environment Canada sank to the status of a junior ministry, under a minister of fisheries and oceans by 1977, and thus drifted to the periphery of federal decision-making (M. Paul Brown 1992, 27).

In the late 1980s a resurgence of public concern about the environment, prompted by the disasters mentioned above and perhaps also by a new cycle of economic expansion, produced a new wave of government action. The Environmental Protection Act, hailed so effusively by Environment Minister Tom McMillan, was a prime example. This act in turn had been prompted by several other developments. One was the visit to Canada in May 1986 of the Brundtland World Commission on Environment and Development, established by the United Nations in 1983. The commission urged Canada and other nations to make exploitation of resources, the direction of investment, and the orientation of technological and institutional changes consistent with future as well as present needs (M. Paul Brown 1992, 32). The commission's impact was increased by its message of 'sustainable development,' stressing the possibility that environmental responsibility and long-term economic development were positively linked. In response to its visit, the Canadian Council of Resource and Environment Ministers (CCREM) established a National Task Force on Environment and Economy, forging the basis for ongoing cooperation between the various levels of government in this area.

By the end of the 1980s a world-wide environmental movement had achieved what seemed to be unstoppable momentum. *Our Common Future*, the report of the World Commission on Environment and Development (1987) led UN member nations to take up the clarion call of sustainable development. International conferences and agreements followed, including the Montreal Protocol of 1988, requiring reduction and eventual elimination of ozone-destroying CFCs; the Toronto Conference on the Changing Atmosphere in 1989; and the 'Earth Summit' on the environment in Brazil in 1992. In Canada, the federal government announced an ambitious 'Green Plan' in 1990, under the new environment minister, Lucien Bouchard. This involved a $3-billion commitment to clean air, water, and land; sustainable use of renewable resources; protection of special spaces and species; preservation of the integrity of the north; and other objectives (see M. Paul Brown 1992, 38). Unfortunately, this plan, along with many other initiatives, was sharply curtailed as both the public and governments became more concerned with employment and public debt in the 1990s.

Assessing Implementation

An extensive review of government environmental programs is beyond the scope of this study. However, I noted at the start of the previous section that environmental authorities should, first, assess the external costs likely to accompany a particular development project; second, distribute those costs fairly; and third, ensure that all interested parties are represented.

How have Canadian governments carried out the first task? All levels of government now undertake environmental assessments. The 'environment' in question is usually understood to be the natural environment, but sometimes it also includes social and cultural effects (this is true, for example, in Ontario). At the local level, zoning by-laws and other land-use regulations amount to a form of assessment. By now, any major urban project – a sports complex, road system, or shopping mall – is certain to be examined for its effects on the surrounding area. On the provincial level, impact studies of major new industrial projects and government infrastructure programs are routine requirements, though they are not required by law in all provinces.

Federally, a formal environmental assessment process has been in place since 1973. However, the government has not always felt compelled to enforce it, unless required by federal courts to do so. The most glaring example of Ottawa's reluctance to follow its own assessment guidelines occurred during construction of the Rafferty and Alameda dams on the Souris River in Saskatchewan. The federal government approved this project without an environmental assessment. The Canadian Wildlife Federation successfully challenged this omission in court. The government next carried out an assessment and approved the project. Once again the Wildlife Federation took it to court, this time for failing to carry out the assessment in accordance with its own guidelines. The Federal Court again ruled against the government.

The proper enforcement of the environmental assessment process produced a serious conflict between Ottawa and the Saskatchewan government. Ottawa eventually tried to halt the project, without success. As Stephen Brooks observes, 'Faced with powerful economic interests and a government committed to a development project, it did not appear that environmental assessment stood much of a chance' (Brooks 1993, 231). A similar scenario was played out in Alberta, with construction of the Oldman River Dam (see VanderZwaag and Duncan 1992, 12–13). These developments, as Brooks has noted, bear out the truth that was put into verse by the economist Kenneth Boulding a few years ago in 'A Ballad of Ecological Awareness' (quoted by Brooks 1993, 231–2):

The cost of building dams is always underestimated
There's erosion of the delta that the river has created,

There's fertile soil below the dam that's likely to be looted,
And the tangled mat of forest that has got to be uprooted.

There are benefits, of course, which may be countable but which,
Have a tendency to fall into the pockets of the rich,
While the costs are apt to fall upon the shoulders of the poor.
So cost-benefit analysis is nearly always sure
To justify the building of a solid concrete fact,
While the Ecological Truth is left behind in the Abstract.

Government assessments of environmental effects often do influence the project planning of both business and government, but, as the examples above indicate, governments are sometimes loath to enforce their own standards if these will jeopardize potential economic gains within their jurisdictions.

Assessing the damage caused by pollution and establishing appropriate standards has been a major challenge for government. Where Ottawa has jurisdiction, as in the Great Lakes or offshore waters, it has attempted to establish standards and to enforce them. In the case of the Great Lakes, major problems have been encountered in getting adequate cooperation from the United States, which is the major polluter. Provinces have created permit systems to regulate air and water pollution, requiring companies likely to pollute the environment to apply for a permit before construction and to abide by regulations thereafter. Unfortunately, as Brooks (1993) observes, 'the flexibility of these guidelines has always been notorious' (233). For example, Sudbury's Inco smelting operation, the single largest source of acid-rain pollution in North America, has been granted lenient extensions of the provincially set targets for reducing its sulphur-dioxide emissions since these targets were first set in the 1970s. Earlier, in 1948, the Ontario legislature dissolved an injunction placed by the Ontario Supreme Court on the discharge of noxious pollutants by the K.V.P paper mill in Espanola (cf. Schrecker 1992, 85).

A second duty of environmental authorities – to impose a price on negative externalities – has also produced a mixed record. Generally, the cost of pollution is imposed not through a tax, or through a system of tradeable permits, as recommended by most economists, but through pollution-reduction targets, enforced by penalties. Unfortunately, the penalties have frequently conveyed the message that failure to reach the targets is not a particularly serious matter. For example, Dow Chemical received a fine of $16,000 in 1985 after pleading guilty to the accidental release of a toxic dry-cleaning fluid, which also contained the deadly chemical dioxin, into the St Clair River. A study released in 1989 found that fines levied by Quebec courts for pollution-related provincial offences between 1984 and 1988 averaged just $667.16 per conviction (cited in Schrecker 1992, 92). This phenomenon, Schrecker suggests, 'may reflect the widespread perception that because environmental offences normally involve the effects of activities whose job-creating and wealth-generating consequences are desirable, they are "morally ambiguous"' (92). Moreover, as Brooks notes, the defence of 'due diligence' – that a company took reasonable care to avoid causing pollution – makes conviction difficult.

Third, ensuring appropriate participation in policy-making is very difficult. Governments have often failed to be aggressive in measuring environmental damage and in imposing appropriate costs on those causing the damage. There is considerable overlap between government objectives and business objectives. From the beginnings of industrialism in Canada, citizens who tried to use the protections of the common law against the negative effects of industrial production found themselves in opposition not only to the businesses creating the effects but to governments under whose jurisdiction those businesses were operating. Both private business and government were more interested in expanded production than in the protection of the environment. With respect to water use, D. Leslie Shaw (1973) writes that the riparian rights protected by common law have proven inadequate in a modern industrialized society where 'the economic doctrines which underlie modern development strategies are usually predicated upon the maximum exploitation of a resource' (251). She notes further that within our legal and legislative system there exist more than sufficient powers to ensure water quality. 'What is lacking is not the capacity but rather the willingness to so regulate natural resource exploitation in accordance with definitive sociopolitical goals' (261). The result, as Reid Kreutzwisser (1991) concludes in his study of water resource management in Canada, is that 'despite life-giving properties and impressive economic value, Canada's water resources have not been especially well appreciated, used or managed' (153). His findings show that 'industrial discharges continue to be the major source of water quality degradation in Canada due to both the volume of discharge and the wide variety of pollutants ... The pulp and paper industry alone contributes over half of all biological oxygen demand loadings to Canadian waters' (159).

With regard to Canada's valuable forest resources, Jules Dufour (1991) repeats the findings of a number of environmental studies that 'the precarious situation of Canada's forests is largely due to the fact that they have been given over entirely to industry for the sole purpose of harvesting. Other users have not been allowed to participate in forest planning and development' (94). As he notes further, government departments such as those responsible for land, forestry, and fish resources 'were set up in the first place not to serve nature, nor even the public, but to serve industry and commerce' (94). Thus, G. Bruce Doern argues that 'environmental policy is energy policy' in Alberta, and William Coleman describes the relationship between the pulp-and-paper industry and the BC government as a 'clientilist' one, in which the industry's preferred policy options prevail (cited in Skogstad and Kopas 1992, 47). The *Economist* in 1993 drew the world's attention to the state of the BC forest industry. It noted that in general 'British Columbia's record on managing logging is not exemplary,' and logging standards 'are far more lax than those employed by the U.S. Forest Service.' It chided the government particularly for granting MacMillan Bloedel, a giant lumber company, additional logging rights in Clayoquot Sound, one of the largest untouched forests in the province. Most reprehensible, in the *Economist*'s view, was the fact that the government made this grant after buying shares in the company (1 May 1993, 41).

The close involvement of the BC government with a private company leads into the second reason why governments often act timidly when assessing and controlling environmental damage. Not only are their objectives similar to business's, and not only do their departments work closely with business, but governments are directly involved in many activities that harm the environment. In fact, as Stephen Brooks (1993) concludes, 'Governments are themselves among the worst offenders when it comes to pollution' (233). This is the result of their involvement in such activities as sewage and garbage disposal and energy production. Nuclear and coal-fired energy plants are among the prime contributors to air pollution.

Governments have proved reluctant to impose stringent restrictions on their own pollution or to provide rigorous environmental assessments of government projects. For example, the Quebec government's huge hydroelectric development in James Bay was initiated without any environmental studies, on the grounds, as Thomas Meredith observes, 'that whatever the environmental cost, the economic benefits would be greater.' Meredith adds sarcastically that 'this was not a view shared entirely by the Cree!' (Meredith 1991, 230).

The flooding of several Aboriginal communities by Manitoba Hydro when it diverted the Churchill River is another case in point. Hydro, and the Manitoba government which owns it, simply assumed that the rights of residents of Manitoba as a whole to electricity superseded the rights of the Aboriginal peoples to continue living on their traditional lands and in their home communities. Similarly, in 1956 the Ontario government created legislation to dissolve court-imposed injunctions against municipal sewage-treatment plants. In fact, the law disallowed all common-law actions against government based on riparian rights. It sacrificed individual property rights in order to permit municipalities to discharge effluent as cheaply as possible (see Brubaker 1995).

While such major decisions would raise difficult political issues at the best of times, they cannot be adequately addressed if one set of rights is simply ignored. These decisions must, at a minimum, be arrived at by widespread consultation and debate about effects and alternatives.

Governments have tended to use their statutory powers to reduce the ability of courts to defend private individuals and groups against the negative effects of government actions. Governments jealously guard their right to defend what they perceive to be the public good, and, as Schrecker notes, they have tended to identify the public interest with industrial and commercial growth (1993, 91). If such growth damages the environment, that is a price that many governments are prepared to pay.

Protecting the Present and Future Environment

Despite considerable advances in the assessment and curtailment of environmental damage by both courts and governments, experience suggests that the concerns of many citizens about Canada's current and future environment will not be adequately addressed until they obtain greater citizen property rights. This in turn will require at least four elements, examined below – better understanding of what constitutes a healthy society, legal reform, possibly some constitutional reform, and, most important, a more democratic approach to environmental decision making.

Before examining these requirements I wish to stress that many of the serious environmental problems described in this chapter defy easy solutions. In numerous cases, harmful environmental effects go hand in hand with necessary productive activity. As Stretton and Orchard (1994) observe, 'We can't have air, land, and sea transport without some risk, so the question is how much' (249). In addition, many effects are extremely difficult to measure. Further, solutions to a number of very serious problems, including air pollution and the destruction of the earth's vital ozone layer, are inherently transnational and require close international cooperation. Since the countries that must work together often have different economic and political policies and goals, partly because they are in different stages of development, agreements reached have limited objectives and are weak in implementation. In the meantime, the world suffers on.

There are nevertheless a number of significant things that countries such as Canada are already doing and on which they can build even further. First, this country has many persons concerned about environmental issues. As one scholar observes, 'The environmental movement's greatest resource is its large, varied, and highly committed membership' (Jeremy Wilson 1992, 110). Wilson has identified at least eighteen hundred groups, without even including small grass-roots organizations such as neighbourhood recycling committees and school clubs. The groups include national ones, such as Greenpeace, which has over 300,000 members; the Canadian Wildlife Federation, which claims 620,000 members, supporters, and affiliates; the Canadian Nature Federation (36,000 members); and Friends of the Earth (25,000). There are also provincial and regional organizations, such as the Western Canadian Wilderness Committee (over 25,000 members) and Pollution Probe (20,000). Eliminating overlapping memberships, Wilson estimates that between one and two million Canadians belong to at least one group (110–11).

Defining a Healthy Society

These groups obviously enjoy considerable support, some of it coming from government and industry. However, to increase their effectiveness, as well as that of government agencies, a number of changes in Canadian society are necessary. There must be some rethinking of what constitutes a healthy society. This may also require a rediscovery of the importance of community and government, not least among scholars in the social sciences. Fortunately, much rethinking has already occurred, as exemplified in economics by the emergence of social-choice theory. One of its leaders, Amartya Sen, begins by attributing to most human beings a much broader range of concerns than is usually the case in economics. He notes that even Adam Smith attached instrinsic value to such human virtues as justice, generosity, and public spirit. He grants that self-interest is especially strong in economic life, but even there human beings wish to contain such interests within collective rules and principles of morality (Sen 1986).

Sen also suggests that the health or success of a specific society must be gauged differently than it often is. He takes issue, for example, with John Rawls (1971), whose *A Theory of Justice* focuses on the broad provision of 'primary goods,' such as income, wealth, and liberty, to enable people to pursue their respective objectives freely. Sen proposes the addition of such conditions as public health and a healthy environment. He notes, for example, that 'A person who is not particularly poor in income, but who has to spend much of that income on kidney dialysis, can be taken to be suffering from poverty' (Sen 1990, 52). The United States, which on the basis of narrow economic indices is considered one of the most successful nations in the world, has social arrangements for public health that 'are more deficient than those of many other countries that are much poorer' (52). In 1993, for example, the United States was the fifth-richest country in the world in terms of per-capita gross national product but tied for fourteenth in terms of average life expectancy at birth and for twenty-first in terms of infant mortality (World Bank 1994, Tables 1 and 27). Both general environmental conditions and a relatively weak health-care system help to account for this dismal record.

What is wrong with the vision of economists and many others is the focus on the 'narrow economy,' whose health is measured in GDP growth figures, which largely ignore the social health of a society, including the depletion and deterioration of the resource base. As Daly and Cobb (1989) remind us, 'The industrial economy is only a part of what Wendell Barry has called the "Great Economy" – the economy that sustains the total web of life and everything that depends on the land' (18). Such a vision is beginning to catch on, but it undoubtedly needs constant reinforcement.

Legal Reform

In order for a broader understanding of a healthy society to materialize, the decision-making structure (i.e., the property structure) of society will need to change. Negatively, this must involve greater checks on the use of resources by both state and private resource owners. Positively, it requires careful implementation of private-property rights in some common resources, greater appreciation of government's regulatory role in the economy, and enlargement of citizens' property rights. The remainder of this chapter deals with these positive requirements.

As noted above, the fishery and the forestry may be prime examples of 'common' resources whose use, for both current and future populations, might be improved by greater application of private-property rights. However, numerous problems must be recognized, and solved, if there are to be genuine improvements. For example, a fair method of distributing rights must be established, unlike the one applied to the fisheries in New Zealand, where rights were sold to the highest bidders, resulting in an oligopoly of a few large companies (see Ridley and Low 1993, 82). In addition, there must be maximum total annual 'catches' (or cuts, in the forestry industry), since overuse of the resource is not completely solved by a private system. Both government and citizen involvement may be necessary for this purpose. In New Zealand, for example, the government has often issued too many fishing permits, under pressure from the large private fishing companies, resulting in overfishing. Fortunately, environmentalists and small fishers have a voice in the public process that determines total catch levels and have fought successfully to lower quota totals (cited in Brown 1996, 180).

Both the potential and the pitfalls of private use of resources must be recognized. I noted above, for example, that private ownership in agriculture led in the past to fairly careful stewardship of resources. A Canadian expert has observed, however, that the development of 'industrial agriculture' has led to increased mechanization on larger and larger field units under the control of private corporations. The land is still owned privately, but it is now used with much less regard for its long-term viability. 'The key,' the writer maintains, 'is the nature of decision making with respect to agricultural production. In the past, even in commercial systems, decisions as to the ultimate goal of production were still partly in the hands of producers (farmers) ... Farmers have a long-term attachment to land whose well-being they must balance with market demands. Industrial agriculture shifts decision making from the individual to the corporate, non-farm location. The decision as to what to produce and the economics of production can ignore the impact of the decision' (Troughton 1991, 80–1).

In January 1996, the Manitoba government announced new regulations for hog producing that would encourage doubling of production and formation of much larger, integrated companies. It did so despite opposition from the majority of hog producers in the province, and despite evidence such as that cited above, which indicates that larger ownership units tend to ignore environmental concerns. As in the case of the New Zealand fisheries, governments are often swayed by business interests, and by a common business–government interest in greater output, to ignore the broader concerns of the community.

It is through government, however, not through the marketplace, that citizens' concerns about the environment are addressed most effectively. In their study of the myriad tasks assigned to governments, Stretton and Orchard (1994) begin by observing that the load placed on governments is almost overwhelming. 'Western governments are supposed to contrive stable prices and full employment. They are supposed to restrain inequalities of wealth and opportunity and see that everyone can achieve a basic standard of living. They currently wrestle with various effects of an ageing population, and of women's changing rights, opportunities and stresses. Their environmental management is improving but still has far to go.' Nevertheless, 'All these problems call for better rather than less government. None of them is soluble by unaided market forces' (1).

In a recent work on the same subject, Peter Self reminds us: 'The state's role ... is structurally and morally prior to that of the market. The market system is a cultural artifact, dependent upon political rules and capable of being changed by those rules.' He laments the fact, therefore, that 'a shift to more aggressive and short-sighted forms of self-interest is being brought about by the retreat of democratic governments from responsible economic and social policies' (Self 1993, 254 and xiii). And in a similar vein, a Canadian social critic contends: 'It is naive or disingenuous for those leading the fight against government to suggest that society will be reinvigorated by smaller government. Responsibility will simply have been transferred to an equally if not more sluggish bureaucracy in the private sector. What's more, by demonizing the public civil servant they are obscuring the matter of the citizen's legitimacy and of the public good which only that legitimacy can produce. People become so obsessed by hating government that they forget it is meant to be their government and is the only powerful public force they have purchase on' (Saul 1995, 75–6).

Constitutional Reform

Though the evidence suggests that these critics are correct – that a healthy environment and other 'public goods' require government intervention in the market – a few conditions must exist to ensure that governments do take appropriate action. This seems to be especially critical in environmental policy. One necessary condition is the presence of constitutional provisions preventing governments from defying legitimate public concerns. Another is the presence of a vigorous body of citizens, endowed with property rights, able to take appropriate action of its own as well as to put pressure on both government and private business to 'do the right thing.'

The frequent failure of both federal and provincial governments in Canada to enforce their own environmental standards, and their willingness to thwart the environmental concerns of others through offsetting legislation and court challenges, has prompted a number of legal and environmental experts to recommend constitutional protection of the environment. As early as 1972, the Canadian Environmental Law Association (CELA) was calling for an 'environmental bill of rights.' Initially this was meant to encourage new legislation embodying stronger support of the environment. Indeed, Ontario, Alberta, and British Columbia have cast legislation in such language.

However, the failure of these legislatures to provide adequate environmental protection, despite the language of their laws, prompted CELA in 1978 to propose an amendment to the constitution. It did so in the course of hearings on Bill C-60, the forerunner to the Constitution Act, 1982 (cf. Stevenson 1983, 401–2). The amendment recommended by CELA would have affirmed 'the right of the individual to environmental quality and environmentally sound planning' and also 'the right of an individual to access government information' (402). Though Bill C-60 was never enacted, Parliament's constitutional committee totally ignored CELA's representations. This may explain why CELA did not make similar recommendations to the hearings which produced the Constitution Act.

In view of past government actions, constitutional protection of the environment seems absolutely essential in the long run. In Stevenson's words, it is necessary 'to build an environmental counterbalance to set against the traditional legal rights, in particular the right to use one's property as one desires' (1983, 397). Ted Schrecker writes: 'Business has generally been very well served by existing patterns of consultation and negotiation with government. ... One of the principal arguments for environmental rights is that they might serve to counterbalance the political influence, and the exclusivity of the decision-making process, that business enjoys by virtue of its economic resources' (Schrecker 1992, 102).

In the short run, some constitutional protection emerges through creative actions of the courts. David VanderZwaag and Linda Duncan (1992, 16–17) provide examples of how some Canadian courts have been open to environmental actions on the basis of the Canadian Charter of Rights, which was added to the constitution in 1982. Though the Charter does not explicitly refer to a healthy environment, its protection of such individual rights as life, liberty, and security of the person have already provided at least a small opening for individuals to contest government actions relating to the environment and public health. For example, Energy Probe, an environmental organization, acted against the Canadian government in the Ontario Court of Appeal in 1989. Nevertheless, the application of the charter in the environmental area will probably remain quite restricted, for reasons discussed by VanderZwaag and Duncan (1992). Only a constitutional amendment along the lines recommended by CELA promises the kind of support for which environmental groups are calling.

The key, as two Canadian lawyers argued in 1981, is to give a substantive right to environmental quality 'the same prima-facie weight as a property right. This would give it substantial clout both against the actions of the State and against private property rights' (Swaigen and Woods 1981). As well, Swaigen and Woods maintained, a substantive right to environmental quality 'must be a function solely of the citizen's rights as a citizen.' In other words, an individual or group should be able to bring an action against environmental abuse without regard to any specific injury to itself. What is required is the recognition of citizen property – the rights of citizens to have a fundamental say in how resources are being used. Unfortunately, as Peter Self observes, 'citizenship as a positive and active function has little place in the writing of modern political economy' (Self 1993, 256–7).

A More Democratic Process

Exercise of greater citizen rights should go hand in hand with encouragement of greater communal or collective activity in the economy. We have seen the emergence of many environmental groups in Canada. What is needed now is not necessarily more of them, but granting to them of more effective decision-making rights. This requires, in addition to greater legal and constitutional support, better access to environmental information and more direct involvement in the making of decisions. The latter needs further explanation.

The process of environmental decision-making would improve with more democratic decisions at the levels of production and environmental assessment. An article in the *Atlantic Monthly* (Ridley and Low 1993) contrasted irrational depletion of a rich aquifer near Fowler, Kansas, with rational use of the River Turia by some fifteen thousand farmers near Valencia in Spain. Here were two irrigation systems – 'one,' in the writer's words, 'sustainable, equitable, and long-lived, the other a doomed free-for-all.' Neither resource was privately owned. The problem was how to get users to exercise self-restraint. It would have been almost impossible in both cases to assign private-property rights to users; the one resource was hidden below ground, the other was free flowing. In Valencia the farmers got together and developed a method of cooperatively rationing the resource. In Kansas, where farmers proved much too individualistic for their own good, they did not. It is this inclusive approach to resource use that clearly needs strengthening in Canada.

Greater cooperation between citizens and affected parties also needs to be encouraged. Much environmental damage cannot be estimated accurately by the yardsticks recommended by economists. In many cases there are social and cultural as well as economic costs, and the only way to determine these is to obtain input from all those who will be affected by a particular action. Thomas Meredith (1991) stresses that 'evaluations must be representative of, or responsive to, the constituency on whose behalf the impact assessment is being made.' Many groups, he notes, including the Native people of Canada, have too often been ignored by both private business and governments. 'It has always been difficult for developers to understand ... the value that is placed on traditional lifestyles by northern Natives' (234). As an example he cites the case of the NATO training flights over Aboriginal hunting grounds in Labrador.

Fortunately, in the last decade in particular, a more interactive 'policy community' has developed in Canada, within government and between government and citizen groups (see particularly Filyk and Cote 1992, 60ff.). Mitchell (1991) compares several provincial development initiatives in terms of this perspective (273–85). For the Wreck Cove hydroelectric project near the Cape Breton Highlands National Park in Nova Scotia, completed in 1977, a careful environmental assessment took place, involving many groups, but 'only after economic and other aspects had predetermined the range of possible choice' (Mitchell 1991, 274). This obviously does not constitute an effective exercise of citizen property rights. A recent article (CFH 1995) reveals how Manitoba Hydro worked with the the Split Lake Cree First Nation in northern Manitoba to develop a major transmission line by means of numerous consultations with the community, involving social, cultural, as well as economic matters.

Neither private property nor state property therefore is enough to protect the environment or to produce sustainable economic development. Market failure is widespread under capitalism, with external diseconomies and conflict between personal and community priorities being particularly relevant for the environment. Technical solutions fail to deal with matters that are at root political problems. The record of state-owned enterprises also leaves much to be desired, as they often operate along the same principles as privately owned businesses. State regulation of the environmental impact of business also has a very uneven history. Thus there would seem to be no better way of ensuring a healthy environment in Canada, both now and in the future, than through growing acceptance of citizens making decisions. Without recognition of citizens' property rights, private developments such as Safeway's in Winnipeg and government projects such as Wreck Cove in Nova Scotia will continue to inflict substantial social and economic harm on Canadian citizens. The *State of the World* report for 1996 stresses that future prevention of injustices 'will require not just strong laws and the threat of punishment from a strong judicial system, but also a drive to integrate basic civil liberties as explicitly as possible into sustainable development policies' (Brown 1996, 147).

PART THREE
NEW PROPERTY

6

New Property Rights in the Workplace

Most people would be horrified if the town they lived in were controlled in the same way as the corporation they work for. Residents' rights and residents' control have won acceptance, while so far, workers' rights and workers' control have not.

Stephen E. Barton 1983, 923

The contemporary workplace, which values obedience and subordination, is in marked contradiction to our emerging social values, which celebrate individual expression, freedom, and initiative.

Donald V. Nightingale 1977, 32

In April 1990, the Pennsylvania legislature, with a Republican-dominated Senate and a Democratic-dominated House, passed a law protecting local industry against some of the abuses that frequently accompany hostile take-overs from outside. One of the law's provisions guaranteed severance pay for workers dislocated by a take-over and the continuance of existing labour contracts once a hostile takeover bid had begun. Another provision encouraged directors of corporations weighing take-over bids to consider not only the shareholders' interests but also those of employees, customers, suppliers, and the company's surrounding community – the 'stakeholders,' as they were called.

This law evoked a storm of protest in the United States, particularly from members of the business community. *Business Week* said that the last provision in particular 'undermined a key concept of capitalism: a board's fiduciary duty to shareholders'; *Forbes* magazine called it 'socialism Pennsylvania style'; and the venerable *New York Times* weighed in with the shrill assessment that this was 'the sorriest example of state intervention' (quoted in Hill 1995, 18). This reminds one of the rather hysterical reaction to Lee Iaccoca's nomination of a union leader to Chrysler's board, noted above.

Far from being engaged in a sorry or unusual spectacle, Pennsylvania's legislature was doing what governments have always done: redefining property rights in response to demands of their constituents. In the past, as *Business Week* correctly observed, governments granted unique legal support to the ownership claims of shareholders. This legal tradition, however, emerged only in the last century and a half and, being itself an accommodation to the changing requirements of a particular type of industrial society, could hardly be considered a definitive solution to the problem of what constitutes appropriate property arrangements. As one American critic noted, the Pennsylvania law simply, and quite within the purview of governments, 'took away some influence from the stockholders – the absentee owners who often live hundreds, if not thousands of miles from the community – and gave that influence to those who lived in the community in which the corporation was based' (Hill 1995, 18).

Among those who lived in the community were, of course, the workers. The law drew attention to the failure of current property laws to meet a broad spectrum of community needs (in line with concerns developed in the previous chapter), particularly to grant adequate property rights to employees of modern corporations. The expression 'employee property rights' refers especially to the rights of workers to participate in corporate decision-making. In its efforts to strengthen the influence of employees in Pennsylvania corporations, the controversial law brought to the attention of a larger public an aspect of present-day property systems that remains extremely problematic. This despite a massive amount of academic analysis and, especially in western Europe, considerable political experimentation.

In the United States, as well as in Canada, unfortunately, rather widespread recognition of serious anomalies and weaknesses in the current mix of worker–management–shareholder decision-making rights has so far produced few examples of fundamental change in individual companies and even fewer reforms in property law. The situation is troubling in several respects. First, it flies in the face of earlier justifications of property, which linked property to work. After a century and a half of industrial capitalism, most workers find themselves virtually without property rights in their place of work. Second, the forms of subordination practised in modern corporations run counter to more democratic practices in most other spheres of life, including political life, as revealed by the quotations used to introduce this chapter.

The weakness of the current system is manifested in deep-seated conflict between workers and managers appointed by stockholders. Further, psychologists have long identified a serious lack of meaning, or sense of purpose, in the workplace. The hierarchical form of modern business undoubtedly contributes to this problem. In most businesses the average worker has little influence over company policy; consequently, workers have a difficult time satisfying such basic human needs as status, recognition, and self-actualization.

In the next section I examine why and how workers in Canada arrived at such a subordinate, virtually 'propertyless' situation. There follows a discussion of the four types of arguments for enhancing workers' decision-making rights that are being advanced in many quarters. The chapter concludes with a description of reforms that have taken place elsewhere as well as in Canada, rounded off with an assessment of their impact.

The Emergence of Workers without Property in Canada

We saw in chapter 1 how seventeenth-century English philosophers, foremost among them John Locke, expressed the idea that each person has a right of property in one's own person. From this followed the notion that each person is the proprietor of his or her own labour. Locke transformed this principle of labour as property into one of the most popular arguments in defence of property rights. In his own words: 'every man has a "property" in his own "person." This nobody has any right to but himself. The "labour" of his body and the "work" of his hands, we may say, are properly his. Whatsoever, then, he removes out of the state that nature hath provided and left it in, he hath mixed his labour with it, and joined it to something that is his own, and thereby makes it his property' (John Locke, quoted by Russell 1985, 4).

Strangely enough, a doctrine that emphasized the unity of labour and property was eventually applied to justify its separation. Instead of stressing that workers who have property in their own person retain some basic property rights even when their work is carried out under the direction of others, Locke and his followers argued that when labour is performed in another man's service, a master–servant relationship is established in which the master has sole rights to property. Again, in the words of Locke, 'the grass my horse has bit, the turfs my servant has cut ... become my property without the assignation or consent of anybody' (Russell 1985, 5). This argument is carried forward even into the era of the shareholder corporation, in which the shareholders have the property rights without directly engaging in any of the corporations' work, while employees who are undertaking the work have virtually no property rights. In reflecting on this development Karl Marx observed: 'It ... seemed orginally that proprietary rights were founded in the worker's own labour. But now property appears as the right to appropriate alien labour, and the impossibility of labour appropriating its own product for itself. The complete divorce between property ... and labour thus appears as the consequence of the law that originally identified them' (Karl Marx, in Russell 1985, 6).

Before the advent of industrial capitalism most workers were essentially self-employed. On their small plots of land and in the practice of such diverse crafts as shoemaking and cotton spinning they set most of their own working conditions and directly enjoyed the fruits of their labour. This does not mean that they were well off or unoppressed. Many families eked out a bare existence on their small farms, oppressed by royal taxes and the numerous demands of the local landlord. Those who spun cotton in their own cottages were under considerable pressure to meet the deadlines and expectations of the middlemen who collected the spun cotton for further processing by weavers. However, despite their frequently poor conditions, the majority of workers owned the rudimentary tools with which they worked and had considerable influence over the hours they worked, the form and quality of their product, and other basic elements of a typical work environment.

When, in the course of the nineteenth century, more and more workers found it necessary to leave their small farms and crafts to work as farm labourers on larger commercial farms or as industrial workers in large factories with machinery they did not own, they struggled to maintain the decision-making rights they had previously enjoyed. Recent scholarship has illuminated this struggle in Canada. In a careful study of late nineteenth-century workers' response to industrial capitalism in the Toronto area, Gregory Kealey (1980) shows that workers reacted to their situation in the new factories by fighting hard to retain the decision-making rights they had enjoyed as craftsmen. When individual shoemakers, for example, found that they could not compete in price with shoes made in factories with larger machines, they went to work in factories themselves but quickly formed associations to protect their old rights. Many joined the

Knights of St Crispin, which was organized in Toronto in 1869, and demanded the right to 'control our labour and to be consulted in determining the price paid for it' (Kealey 1980, 45; for similar developments in Hamilton and several other cities see Palmer 1979; 1983, 63–91). To control their labour meant to determine their hours and methods of work, in addition to their remuneration.

Coopers (barrel makers), to cite one more example, fared similarly and made similar demands. They had been virtually autonomous workmen. When driven by economic circumstances to join the new factories, they too asserted their right to maintain their craft traditions. The union they formed did not engage initially in the type of collective bargaining characteristic of unions today. Union members met together, arrived at the price of their labour, informed management of their decision, and struck if their offer was rejected (Kealey 1980, 56). In addition, they assumed control of working hours and restricted production when work was short. They also struggled to control the methods of production and enforced personnel decisions in the shop. As Kealey observes, 'The English shop tradition allowed any two coopers in a shop to request a "roll-up" at any time during working hours to discuss problems with the price list, with shop conditions, or with the quality of materials, or any other grievance. When a roll-up was called, the boss was excluded from the discussion until the men decided on a collective position, which was then communicated to the boss by the "collector" (shop steward). No one returned to work until the issue was resolved' (57).

In essence, the coopers, like other previously self-employed craftspeople, tried to adapt the power they had possessed as artisans to the new industrial age. In doing so they not only asserted previous rights but their inherent right to be treated as 'men.' Again and again workers in various skilled crafts insisted that their skills be properly recognized and their decision-making rights respected. The diminution of such recognition and respect was seen as a direct attack on their manliness. For this reason many workers initially rejected modern forms of unionism, in which workers implicitly recognize themselves as mere 'employees' – an underclass without basic rights of decision-making.

In the first decades of industrialism in Canada, workers in numerous industries refused to acknowledge their new propertyless status and continued against insurmountable odds to assert their old traditions. Some, particularly in the metal and printer trades, organized workers' cooperatives, seeking thereby to extend their control over the work process (see Kealey 1980, 78–80; Grant MacDonald 1989). Most of these ventures failed, but they underline the desperate attempt of workers to rescue those elements of their previous work environment that gave them status and significant rights to make decisions.

By the early part of this century most workers had to give up hope of significant decision or property rights in the new industrial society. As one metal worker lamented, 'We are but little better off than our forefathers who were serfs to the feudal barons. We are serfs to the capitalists of the present day' (Kealey 1980, 78). In fact, as evidence presented above suggests, their serf forefathers often possessed more property rights than they did.

There were several apparent reasons for this defeat. First, the new industrial processes seemed to demand a uniformity of behaviour – in terms of working hours and the quality and quantity of output – which was inherently at odds with the flexible decision-making enjoyed by self-employed artisans. You cannot have workers deciding individually when to begin work on an assembly line, nor is it possible to identify the output of a particular worker. Without such identification, however, differentiated quality and price are impossible (Kealey cites examples of workers actually trying to produce their own products within a factory setting and establishing their own prices – all to no avail).

Second, workers tended to underestimate the entrepreneurial role of the new employers in terms of organization and marketing. As Kealey notes, they thought that capitalists brought only capital to the new production processes (Kealey 1980, 78).

Third, the new capitalists responded to the challenges by strategically altering the environment so that workers were even more disempowered than technology itself dictated. In the early part of this century many Canadian employers vigorously adopted the 'scientific management' principles of F.W. Taylor (see F.W. Taylor 1911). The first principle was to dissociate the labour process from the skills of the workers. That is, the ability of workers to have any say at all about conditions was taken from them and placed into the hands of management. Second, the function of planning the work process was separated from work itself. Workers worked, management planned. This had the effect of creating a management monopoly of crucial knowledge. Third, management used this monopoly to control each step of the labour process. In other words, scientific management meant eradication of any significant form of worker participation in determining conditions, planning, and execution (see Kealey 1980, 81–2; Craven 1980).

New Property Rights in the Workplace 149

Very quickly the new subordinate and ineffectual role of labour was being justified and supported by government and even accepted by large segments of the labour force. The liberal-democratic state found itself in a dilemma. One of its tasks was to encourage economic growth through accumulation and efficient production. This required, in its view, the subjugation of labour to efficient work norms and managerial direction. William Lyon Mackenzie King, a labour scholar by trade and sympathetic to labour unions, argued nevertheless that members must 'recognize that as a class they are destined to continue subject always to the conditions of hire, and govern themselves accordingly' (quoted in Craven 1980, 66).

Another task of the liberal-democratic state, however, is to provide legitimation. It must win the allegiance of a broad range of citizens, including workers, by paying attention to their needs. The latter group, it recognized, might require 'the redefiniton of property rights to include, first, property in work and, second, property in an array of equitable social relations' (Craven 1980, 160). This, however, the liberal-democratic state of the twentieth century has largely failed to do. Instead, as Craven argues, the state decided not to resolve endemic class conflicts 'but to subordinate them to a single, dominant ordering of the society. In an industrial capitalist society, that ordering is capitalist industrialization' (162).

Most workers ultimately sought what protection they could in American-style unions, thereby implicitly acknowledging their relegation to an underclass with virtually no effective property rights. Even this limited type of protection was not easily achieved. It took decades of agitation by Canadian workers to achieve the right to bargain with management over a narrow range of issues. Not surprisingly, owners and managers have strenuously resisted attempts to include planning and policy making in the purview of collective bargaining.

A recent study of industrial relations in Canada observes that there are still no formal structures in Canada that enable unions or employees to participate in the management of firms or industries as a matter of right. 'Unions must win rights to participate at each and every bargaining table at which they sit. Workers, as individuals, play little part in making the decisions that affect their daily lives' (Drache and Glasbeek 1992, 48). Other labour scholars concur that neither federal nor provincial legislation has given workers the right to a say in matters of economic management or personnel policy. 'In the rare instances where workers' representatives sit on the boards of directors of private enterprises it is because they own shares, and hence it is more as shareholders than as workers that they can claim to have a say in the running of the company. Neither federal nor provincial legislation considers the enterprise to be anything but an association of shareholders in pursuit of profits' (Laflamme, Belanger, and Audet 1987, 221–2).

To conclude this brief historical overview: within the typical Canadian business enterprise today there is little real sharing of property rights. Workers have won legal support to pit themselves as a virtually property-less employee class against a class of property-owning employers. A certain balance of power appears to have been achieved. The employers' rights to hire and fire are countered by the unions' rights to withhold services. One can argue that the rights are not evenly matched, that those of the employer are generally more potent than those of the workers. This is especially true in economic downturns, when jobs are hard to get.

However, the relative weakness of labour in the collective-bargaining process is not our main concern here. What is more significant is labour's inability at present to have any effective say in company decisions involving such important matters as investment strategy, plant location, layoffs, and transfers. Though such decisions have a profound impact on workers' lives, workers are generally excluded from participating in them because they are based on property rights that belong almost exclusively to shareholders, exercised through their managerial representatives. The actions described above of Pennsylvania's legislature demonstrate that governments are quite capable of altering property rights in favour of workers and other non-shareholder stakeholders, but virtually no other jurisdictions in North America have seen fit to do so (the extensive property reforms in several western European countries are discussed below in this chapter). The hostile reaction of business and the media to the Pennyslvania innovations reflects the orthodox position of industrial capitalism. What is absent from such reaction, unfortunately, is any awareness that the current orthodoxy denies rights granted to workers in pre-industrial society or that many of those rights might be restored without threatening our system of private property.

For most of this century, attempts to enlarge the property rights of workers have been frustrated by several developments. One was the attack on private property set in motion by Karl Marx in the previous century. The basic premise of the new communism spawned by Marx was that worker property in a modern industrial economy could be obtained only through forceful transfer of property from private capitalists to workers. With this premise, Marx and his followers adopted the unitary view of property held by capitalists. Property could not be shared; it was held exclusively either by capitalists or by workers. Therefore Marx set out to destroy the property rights of capitalists. Capitalists in turn, also assuming that property could be held only by either labour or capitalists, but not by both, vigorously defended their rights against workers.

The triumph of capitalism over Soviet-type communism has seemingly strengthened the capitalist case and further frustrated attempts to enlarge workers' rights. A system of propertyless employees and propertied employers appears to have been not only a historical necessity but a much greater economic success than systems favouring workers' rights. This conclusion, however, is open to challenge on several grounds. First, the defeated socialist states (with the exception of Yugoslavia) never granted extensive property rights to their workers. As Orwell illustrated so brilliantly in *Animal Farm* (1945), communist bosses with exclusive property rights simply replaced capitalist bosses. Lenin himself was enamoured of Taylor's scientific-management approach. The socialist system ultimately favoured by Joseph Stalin failed not only to empower workers with extensive property rights but left them without the defence of effective labour unions. It cannot be argued, therefore, that Soviet-type socialist countries demonstrate the failure of an advanced industrial economy with significant property rights for workers. The case *against* worker rights has not been proven.

There is a growing case, however, for enhanced workers' rights. The main arguments I discuss in the next section. I follow this with a brief description of several Western capitalist countries that have changed their system of property in order to further the rights of workers.

Reasons for Enlarging Workers' Property Rights

A variety of reasons are advanced by proponents in many countries for the enlargement of worker rights in the workplace. These I analyse under four headings: legal-philosophical, ethical-psychological, political, and economic.

Legal-Philosophical Reasons

I have shown at several points in this study that property rights based on participation in productive activity, sometimes referred to as 'acquisition through labour,' find support in a rich legal and philosophical tradition. Laws based on this tradition have been used by spouses to obtain property rights and are currently being used by Canada's Aboriginal peoples to support their land claims. Unfortunately in both these cases, as well as in the one being discussed here, the older reasoning has had to be rescued from several centuries of neglect and even outright rejection.

When proprietory farming gave way to a system of labour for hire and when craftsmen exchanged their self-employed status for wage labour in larger shops, lawyers as well as philosophers tended to assume that such persons thereby sold their claims to the fruits of their labour. After all, among the rights of property ownership is the right to sell one's property. Wage labourers, it was argued, gave up broader property rights respecting the fruits of their labour in exchange for a price paid to them in the form of a wage. Their detachment from control over the fruits of their labour was signified not only by their wage contract with an employer but by the loss of any definable product resulting from their particular labours. Assembly-line production of standardized products made it impossible for individuals to place a personal stamp on their output. It seemed therefore that workers' loss of an autonomous, property-owning status was a natural and legally defensible accommodation to a new system of contractual relationships between workers and employers, freely entered into by both sides and reinforced by irresistible technical forces.

Despite the power of such arguments and their general acceptance in Western market economies, they are based on some dubious reasoning. They ignore, for example, a basic premise of the original doctrine of 'property in labour,' as well as the political character of property decisions and the actual circumstances in which workers gave up their property rights.

As noted above, a fundamental premise of the original doctrine as stated by Locke was that 'every man has a "property" in his own person. This nobody has any right to but himself.' This hypothesis clearly attributes an inalienable property right to each person, which may be altered but not obliterated by the circumstances in which that person chooses to exercise her or his labour. By renting out this labour through a wage contract one does not become a slave bereft of those rights that previously resided in one's person. Even were one to grant that the rights are potentially alienable, a primary principle of private property, following Calabresi and Melamed, is that 'no one can take the entitlement to private property from the holder unless the holder sells it willingly' (cited in Weinrib 1988, 120). As we have seen, workers in Canada defended their property rights on the basis of these doctrines. They did not willingly shut down their own shops in order to become wage labourers in larger shops, and they fought strenuously to maintain their autonomy after entering into wage contracts with the new employers. To argue therefore that the ensuing destruction of property-in-labour was somehow 'natural' or flowed logically from previous legal and philosophical thought is to ignore the highly contentious conditions in which it occurred. It also ignores the means vigorously adopted by employers to reduce the position of workers far beyond what the new technical conditions required, as well as the political support that was required, and given, to legitimize the new property arrangements. As one economist has observed, the market view of freedom is seriously tainted because 'it subsists on the economic coercion of the workers – that is, labor contracts are really orders in the guise of agreements' (Lustig 1986, 135).

It may be that the unitary conception of property prevalent at the time contributed to the eradication of workers' property rights. This made it difficult to distinguish between the different parts of a typical bundle of rights and to consider a division or sharing of rights. For example, it might have been helpful to distinguish more clearly between operating rights and policy-making rights. Most of the former artisans and peasants who became workers in the new industrial system had enjoyed both kinds of rights. However, to insist, as some did, that they should retain basic rights over such operational decisions as the mix and quality of products, individual pricing, and individual working hours was all too easily rebutted on technical and efficiency grounds (though the Japanese and the Swedes in particular have shown that workers' participation in some operational decisions adds measurably to company performance). A stronger case for shared decision-making over policy matters, such as general layoffs, plant relocation, and major investment projects, might have been made instead. However, given the business and political mentality of the time, it is doubtful that compromises of this kind would have produced a very different result. As we see below, such a case has been made successfully in the last few decades by workers in several western European countries but has made virtually no headway in North America.

In North America, as elsewhere, the concept of property-in-labour is surreptitiously gaining importance in one particular area: intellectual property. Workers on an industrial assembly line do not produce anything that is uniquely theirs. Many new products and services, however, are the result of innovative thinking by a single person or a distinct group of persons. The 'labour' that these persons contribute is intellectual creativity.

Intellectual labour has several unique characteristics. One is that it exists largely in the mind. It is therefore literally the possession of a particular person or group of persons, and in a country with considerable labour mobility it is often, though not always, highly mobile. When such labour is exercised within a business corporation or research institution, its possessor usually enters into a wage contract with the employer. However, this arrangement does not necessarily transfer all property rights from the labourer to the employer. A sharing of rights is frequently negotiated. Because intellectual labour in an institutional setting usually depends on the employer's facilities (lab and office space, capital equipment, and so on), the employer is obviously entitled to much of the fruit of that labour. This is recognized in the ownership that the employer assumes over products and ideas that are implemented in the workplace.

In many instances, however, the labourer is able to reserve some of the results of that labour for herself or himself, in addition to the negotiated wage. Otherwise the talents of that labourer might go elsewhere, possibly to benefit a competitor or to support a lucrative practice. Thus a newspaper reporter produces a private book based on research done for the newspaper, a university professor privately publishes a text book, novel, or musical composition produced partly on university time, or an actor or researcher receives royalties in addition to a salary. What these examples show is that it is quite possible for some labourers in the modern workplace to enter into wage agreements with an employer without relinquishing all control over such property rights as an autonomous creation and all profit from the products they produce. As well, such intellectual activity is not confined to so-called intellectuals. Many workers in all kinds of industries are capable of envisaging new products and techniques, and more companies are providing financial incentives to encourage them. The implied sharing of property rights was unfortunately stymied for too long by deliberate attempts to reduce the range of initiatives, and therefore access to property rights, open to 'ordinary' workers. This access remains highly constrained.

A second characteristic of intellectual property is that once it enters the public domain, in the form of a news article, book, computer software, movie, or musical score – to cite just a few examples – others can easily reproduce it. From the consumer's point of view, this is usually a good thing. However, the possibility of 'free riding' could sharply reduce the incentive to create new products and services, which would be detrimental to society as a whole. This threat has prompted governments to provide innovators with some unique property protection. Copyright laws, for example, protect the fruits of the creative efforts of artists, writers, and composers, while patents, trademarks, and industrial design laws protect intellectual property in industry. The law is failing, however, to keep up with copying technology and computer networking, making this one of the areas where improved property rules are urgently required (for Canadian discussions see Keon 1986; Weinrib 1988).

To conclude this discussion of the legal-philosophical arguments for property-in-labour I would add that they do, despite their generally poor acceptance in the recent past, provide a basis for the recovery of greater workers' rights. It was largely the economic power of business owners, buttressed by political decisions, that subverted their application to workers in the last two centuries. Governments still have it in their power – as Pennyslvania and several western European countries have demonstrated – to use a venerable legal tradition to grant property rights to workers on the basis of their participation in the production process. Workers, in the language used by the framers of the Pennsylvania law, are basic stakeholders in one of society's most basic communities: the workplace.

Ethical-Psychological Reasons

We have observed that workers in Toronto and elsewhere strongly resisted the deprivation of their decision-making power when economic circumstances forced them into factories. The loss of such rights, they argued, amounted to the loss of their 'manliness.' Many years later psychologists and business management consultants are beginning to understand what they meant.

A school of psychologists and sociologists has perceived a basic conflict between the way in which workers are currently involved in the work process and their psychological needs (for example, Greenberg 1975; 1981; Walker 1972; note also the quotation from Nightingale 1997 in the introduction above). Instead of 'manliness' they talk about human maturation, which process, they contend, involves among other things a movement from passivity to activity, from dependence to independence, from subordinate positions to equality, and from non-awareness to self-control (see Anton 1980, 15). However, most modern work organizations are characterized by job fragmentation and workers' subordination to a hierarchical chain of controls, which retard development of the worker's personality as a mature individual.

In Canada these ideas have surfaced in a management philosophy called 'participatory management' (PM). It is described as 'a philosophy under which managers actually share their decision-making responsibilities with their subordinates. In many instances, managers still make the final decisions, but only after achieving a consensus with the group'

(Lederer 1978, 52). This definition, however, still leaves workers in a subordinate position. The philosophy goes back to earlier work by Abraham Maslow, who identified a hierarchy of human needs, moving from the most basic such as food, shelter, and rest to love and acceptance (see Maslow 1970). At a high level are the needs for status, ego satisfaction, and personal achievement. The PM school recognizes that business organizations can play an important role in helping people to fulfill these higher needs. Though these types of concerns have failed thus far to generate a far-reaching restructuring of decision making in Canadian business organizations – management gurus come and go – they have undoubtedly, as is shown below, helped to involve more workers in certain types of decisions.

Part of the concern of these psychologists and management consultants is an ethical one. It is simply a good thing to enable more people to achieve maturity in their lives. As Walker comments in his world-wide study of worker participation, such participation is expected to reduce workers' alienation, enhance the development of the worker's personality, and increase job satisfaction (Walker 1972, 1177). Part of the concern is also, and understandably, to provide greater motivation to workers so that they will work more effectively for their companies. It is therefore related to the economic reasons discussed more fully below. As one PM advocate observes, 'People who come to work with a sense of commitment or fervor will do better work than those who feel ignored and manipulated' (Lederer 1978, 58).

A study of a U.S. west coast paper-products firm that involves employees extensively in decision making concluded that workers experienced increased satisfaction and personal growth, with greater opportunities for self-management (Elden 1981). Several other studies have shown similar results (for a summary see Elden 1981, 53–4). However, human nature does not change easily, and other studies (for example, Greenberg 1981; Witte 1980) have found that worker participation does not necessarily translate into a broader kind of political consciousness involving, for example, stronger commitment to cooperation or community concerns.

Political Reasons

In one of the introductory quotations to this chapter Stephen Barton suggests that most people in towns would be shocked if they had as little power to influence the decisions of their town council as workers have on basic corporate decisions. This takes us into one of the most widely articulated arguments for the enlargement of workers' rights in the workplace. It seems fundamentally incongruent to a wide range of social critics that liberal democracies such as Canada have not insisted on the same type of democratic practices in the economic sphere as it has in politics (see, among many examples, Carnoy and Shearer 1980; Dahl 1985; Schuller 1985; Bowles and Gintis 1986). 'It has been assumed,' one scholar observes, 'that political power and economic power are two distinct social phenomena' (Lichtenstein 1984, 21).

Some suggest that liberal democracy is in fact fundamentally opposed to the exercise of democracy in the economy at large and in the workplace in particular. Peter Lichtenstein, for example, argues that 'liberalism condones an autocratic, hierarchical society in which authority rests at the top' (1984, 172). He identifies two wings of liberalism – the libertarian, which would subject the working class to the private power exercised by large corporations, and the neo-Keynesian, which would subject the same people to public power.

Those who promote economic democracy in the form of greater worker participation in corporate decision-making wish essentially, in the words of one scholar, to transfer the ideal of the *polis* to the workplace (Dahl 1985, 94). Why, they ask, should not each person have the same kind of democratic citizen rights in the workplace as in the political sphere? The answer given by those who support the current state of affairs is that citizens require democratic political rights in order to protect themselves against the coercive powers of the state. However, such protection is not required in the workplace because, so the argument runs, that place is not characterized by coercion but by voluntary private transactions. Though organizational hierarchy exists in most businesses, those at the bottom have freely entered into employment contracts with those at the top. The business firm, it is alleged, 'has no power of fiat, no authority, no disciplinary action any different in the slightest degree from ordinary market contracting between any two people' (Alchian and Demsetz 1972, 777). For a good summary of this position see Dahl 1985, 113ff.; Bowles, Gintis, and Gustafsson 1993, 5–6.

This argument requires careful analysis. It is true, of course, that the laws of government can be enforced by physical coercion, and, in the absence of democratic checks and balances, such coercion would undoubtedly lead to many more abuses of citizens than are experienced now. Is it equally true, however, that similar coercion is lacking in the workplace, that the latter is essentially a free market within which people engage in voluntary individual exchanges? Dahl argues:

158   New Property

Decisions made by the government of a firm and by the government of the state are in some crucial respects more similar than this classical liberal interpretation allows for. Like the government of the state, the government of a firm makes decisions that apply uniformly to all workers or a category of workers: decisions governing the place of work, time of work, product of work, minimally acceptable rate of work, equipment to be used at work, number of workers, number (and identity) of workers laid off in slack times – or whether the plant is to be shut down and there will be no work at all. These decisions are enforced by sanctions, including the ultimate sanction of firing. (Dahl 1985, 114–15)

Bowles, Gintis, and Gustafson also maintain that in the capitalist-employment relationship the employer exercises power over the worker. They use the following conception of power: 'Agent A has power over agent B if, by imposing or threatening to impose sanctions on B, A is capable of affecting B's actions in ways that further A's interests, while B lacks this capacity with respect to A.' They believe that 'even under conditions of competitive equilibrium, the threat of dismissal will be used to induce the worker to act in ways favourable to the firm's interests. This power exists by virtue of the employer's location on the short-side of a non-clearing market' (Bowles, Gintis, and Gustafsson 1993, 14). The employer is considered on the short side of the market because there is no shortage of workers waiting to be hired, while conversely workers are on the long side because of an excess supply in the labour market.

Does this, however, understate the difference between the two spheres? One might object that unlike the citizens of a state, workers in a firm are not compelled to obey managerial decisions. They are free to leave and cannot be punished for leaving. This, however, exaggerates the difference. As Dahl points out, citizenship in a democratic state is in one respect more voluntary than employment in a firm. If, for example, the decision of a local municipality is disagreeable to a citizen, that citizen's ultimate recourse is to move freely to another municipality. In contrast, employees who leave a firm have no automatic citizenship rights (i.e., employment rights) in another firm.

Dahl concludes with an observation and a question that go to the heart of this issue. 'Like a state, then, a firm can also be viewed as a political system in which relations of power exist between governments and the governed. If so, is it not appropriate to insist that the relationship between governors and governed should satsify the criteria of the democratic process – as we properly insist in the domain of the state?' (Dahl 1985, 115).

There are many who would probably concede that it would be desirable to extend democratic rights to workers in the workplace if only it were feasible. The qualification is an important one, however, and relates to the economic arguments that are discussed next. Can democratic rights (which are equivalent to property rights as defined in this study) be extended to employees in a firm without reducing its efficiency and financial viability? This is the question to which we turn next.

Economic Reasons

In *Democracy and the Work Place*, H.P. Wilson (1974) quotes the vice-president of a large Canadian corporation as saying: 'I consider the employees as one element in the production process, no more and no less important than any other element' (15). One would like to know more about the meaning of the word 'important' for this executive. Presumably it means that there is nothing especially unique about the role of labour in the production process. Contrast that with the following observation: 'Labour is unique not in being solely efficacious but in being solely *responsible* [emphasis in the original]. All the factors are causally efficacious or "productive," but only labour is *responsible* ... Only human beings can be responsible for anything, and thus only the people involved in production can be responsible for the positive and negative results of production' (Ellerman 1984, 868–9).

Because human beings can act wilfully either to improve or to reduce the productivity of a business enterprise, worker motivation must rank high among the priorities of any responsible business executive. The question that has concerned workers, employers, and social critics alike for over a century is whether workers' participation in company management can motivate them to be more productive. The experiences of workers in a particular form of worker management – the producer cooperative – seemed for a long time to provide a resounding 'No!'

As everyone familiar with Canadian, American, and British labour history knows, there were waves of short-lived producer cooperatives in these countries in the late nineteenth century. Their quick demise helped to convince trade-union leaders that in a capitalist economy unionism and collective bargaining were more realistic ways of achieving gains for workers. As Dahl (1985) observes: 'Most academic observers, including labor economists and social historians, concluded that the labor-managed firm was a rejected and forlorn utopian idea irrelevant to a modern economy' (130–1). More recently, however, there has been a revival of interest in the potentially positive effects of workers' participation in management,

160 New Property

TABLE 6.1 Degrees of employee decision making

1 Employees need not be informed about managerial decisions, except as necessary to conduct their work.
2 Employees have the right to be informed after decisions are made.
3 Employees must be informed before a decision and given a chance to respond.
4 Employees are consulted informally before a decision.
5 Employees must be consulted formally before a decision.
6 Employees participate informally with management in making decisions, with management retaining the right of veto over some decisions.
7 Management and employees jointly make decisions – in some cases employees have parity with shareholder and management interests, and in others, shareholder and management dominate.
8 Employees have the final say in all decision making.

sparked both by comparative empirical studies of economic performance in countries with varying degrees of labour participation and by new theoretical work.

To introduce this topic I first outline briefly the forms in which workers can participate in management. To establish this it is necessary to rank the level or degree of participation as well as the importance or scope of the issues over which workers have decision-making powers. A useful ordering has been developed by a Canadian labour economist (Nightingale 1977). He first lists eight degrees of participation, in ascending order, as shown in Table 6.1.

Nightingale classifies the scope or importance of the issues dealt with by employees. He distinguishes between 'shop-floor' issues (which involve employees' benefits, working conditions and some operational decisions) and policy issues. He then ranks them (in approximately ascending order), as shown in Table 6.2.

Workers participate meaningfully in company decision making when all workers, either directly or through their elected representatives, have at least five degrees of participation (Table 6.1), and are involved in most of the shop-floor issues and in at least some of the policy issues (Table 6.2). Nightingale suggests that 'industrial democracy' exists only when the degree of participation is seven or eight (Table 6.1), and policy issues (fifteen and beyond in Table 6.2) are subject to employee decisions (34).

How far along these scales employees actually operate depends on arrangements within their particular enterprise. For this purpose it is useful to distinguish four institutional forms of the producing enterprise (Fusfeld 1983, 772–3). One is the pure capitalist firm without a union or

TABLE 6.2 Scope of issues dealt with by employees

Shop-floor issues
1 Determination of holidays.
2 Hours of work.
3 Physical working conditions.
4 Safety regulations and procedures.
5 Work methods.
6 Work standards and pace.
7 Assignment and transfer of employees to tasks.
8 Recruitment, selection and training of new employees.
9 Salary grades.
10 Job classification of employees.
11 Appointments of supervisors.
12 Dismissal of employees.
13 Promotion of executives.
14 Determination of employee wages and fringe benefits.

Policy issues
15 Layoffs, job security.
16 Choice of products, pricing and markets.
17 Capital investment.
18 Disposition of profits.
19 Raising capital.
20 Re-organizations, mergers and acquisitions.

Source: Nightingale 1977, 32–4.

employee association, in which authority is exercised exclusively by the owners. Nightingale suggests that in such firms workers will typically (though not always) be restricted to two degrees of participation (Table 6.1) and to level three in scope of issues (Table 6.2). The second form is the capitalist firm with a system of collective bargaining, based on a union or an employee association. In such conditions the degree of participation may increase to six and the level of issues to ten. To move beyond that requires a third form of organization, which differs from the firm with collective bargaining in two respects. First, some of the shop-floor issues previously excluded, such as dismissal of employees and the exercise of supervisory functions, shift to workers – as in works councils, which are common in western Europe, or 'quality circles,' which were initially associated with Japan and Sweden but have been adopted in North America and elsewhere. Second, either through ownership or through election of workers to company boards, employees begin to 'co-determine' company policies. This reform has occurred particularly in western Europe.

162   New Property

A fourth institutional form is the labour-managed firm – the producer cooperative. In this form, workers have all eight degrees of participation and determine all working conditions and company policies.[1]

To return now to our main concern: how does employee participation beyond the level of the first institutional form – the capitalist firm without collective bargaining – affect economic performance? Economists have tackled this question both theoretically and empirically.

When building their theoretical models, economists like to test the most extreme or 'purest' cases, and this approach applies also to this field. Much of the best theoretical work on the economic effects of worker management deals with models in which workers own the enterprise. Until the recent collapse of Yugoslavia, its worker self-management system received a lot of attention from theorists and empiricists alike. Scholars used to joke that if Yugoslavia did not exist, for the sake of their work they would have to invent it.

Early work (see Ward 1958 and Vanek 1970) focused on the unique objectives that a worker-owned firm would have in contrast to a typical capitalist firm. Instead of maximizing profit, it would try to maximize the per-capita income of its members. Drawing on this assumption, Benjamin Ward, among others, concluded that such enterprises would probably save less, invest less, and hire fewer workers than those with a profit objective. Other theorists disagreed, asserting that in order to increase their average long-term income, workers would be just as likely as capitalist managers to save and invest. With respect to employment, if individual firms minimized the size of their labour force other firms would be established to take advantage of market opportunities. In total, then, employment should be as high in a worker-managed economy as in any other (see, for example, Jay 1980 and Schweickart 1980). The results of this research have therefore been inconclusive.

More recent research has examined issues of governance. Bowles, Gintis, and Gustafsson (1993), for example, use agent–principal theory, discussed above in chapter 2, to examine the economic implications of a firm democratically governed by workers. They note that this particular theory has been used almost exclusively to examine problems between shareholders (principals) and their appointed managers (agents). They observe that in a typical capitalist firm there is also a significant principal-agent problem between managers and employees. The shop-floor is a place in which workers and managers may very well be trying to optimize different things. The worker must decide, for example, how hard to work for the employer, how truthfully to transmit information to others, and so on – all problems that also exist between managers and shareholders. Since conflicts can lead to sub-optimal performance of the firm, a presumption exists that reducing conflicts through significant worker participation in decision making could improve performance.

Bowles and Gintis (1986) advance two principal reasons for favouring democratic governance of the firm. The first involves accountability, which is essentially a political reason. 'Because the employment relationship involves the exercise of power, its exercise ought on democratic grounds to be accountable to those most directly affected' (13). The second relates to efficiency. The writers argue that a democratic firm can be more efficient than a non-democratic one because it will use labour inputs more efficiently, for three reasons. First, workers in a democratic firm will treat work as a more rewarding experience and will therefore offer more effort than in the typical capitalist firm. This assumption is reasonable, in their opinion, because workers will have residual claims on the income generated by the firm, not merely fixed wages (27–8). Second, monitoring costs will be lower in such a firm. The writers observe that workers frequently have virtually costless access to information concerning the work activities of fellow workers, and in a democratic firm each has an interest in the efforts made by others. There is therefore virtually costless mutual monitoring (28). Third, because the democratic firm minimizes internal costs, it can offer higher wages. The capitalist firm uses too little wage incentive and too much monitoring (29).

Bowles, Gintis, and Gustafsson (1993) address a troubling question. If democratic firms are more efficient in regulating work, why then do they appear to operate at a competitive disadvantage with typical capitalist firms? In other words, why are there not more worker-run enterprises around? They suggest three reasons (31–2). First, learning to govern a firm effectively takes time and requires a workforce trained in techniques and decision-making. The cost of this approach puts considerable constraints on the firm. Second, a critical mass of similarly organized firms may be necessary to enable many to flourish – the 'economic-environment constraint.' For example, basic features of the capitalist system, such as income inequality, favour capitalist firms (for reasons given below), but these would change in a direction favourable to the democratic company in an economy composed largely of such firms. Third, workers in a democratic firm do not initially have the capital resources, nor the access to outside resources, to capitalize it sufficiently to compete with existing capitalist businesses.

Practical Examples of Workers' Democracy and Their Impact

Because of such problems, it is difficult in theory to envisage worker-owned firms competing effectively in many industries with companies that are less democratically run. In many countries, however, there are outstanding examples of worker-owned enterprises that are performing extremely well, indicating that the factors contributing to greater efficiency, as outlined above, can outweigh the constraints.

The largest and perhaps most successful group of producer cooperatives exists in the Basque region of Spain, in the town of Mondragon. A small factory producing portable paraffin heaters was started there in 1956 by twenty-four workers and ninety-six other local people who provided funds. By the 1980s it had grown into a consortium of one hundred and eleven producer cooperatives distributed across the Basque region and comprising nearly twenty thousand employee-owners. Total sales in 1990 reached $2.9 billion. Products now range from furniture to machine tools, from plastic forms to agricultural chemicals. There are also several agricultural cooperatives, seventeen construction cooperatives providing housing, and a consumer cooperative with two hundred and twenty-five outlets and over 130,000 consumer-members (Tseo and Ramos 1995, 29; see also H. Thomas and Logan 1982; Whyte and Whyte 1988; and Paul Phillips 1992). A study showed that in 1972 the Mondragon industrial firms boasted 40 per cent higher production efficiency than small and medium conventionally capitalist Spanish firms, and 7.5 per cent more than large ones (Tseo and Ramos 1995, 29).

One recent visitor from Canada to this remarkable experiment in worker ownership observes that what is perhaps most significant about it is that it 'has maintained a record of employment growth while paying wages equal to, or better than, private employers in the region. Furthermore, there has been no recourse to lay-offs and unemployment to adjust to the economic downturn in the early 1980s nor to the restructuring demanded by increased exposure to competition of the new global economy and European integration' (Paul Phillips 1992, 38–9).

Such experiments are more widespread around the world than is commonly realized. In Brazil, for example, there are currently about fifteen thousand producer cooperatives, which produce 75 per cent of Brazilian wheat, 40 per cent of sugar, 32 per cent of alcohol, and a large percentage of many other products. These cooperatives own six hundred factories and three hundred rural processing plants (Tseo and Ramos 1995, 30).

In the United States, the Pacific northwest plywood industry is dominated by highly successful worker-owned companies. Studies have shown that workers in these firms tend to produce a larger volume of higher-quality output from lower-quality inputs than is generated in conventionally owned plywood companies, and overall firm performance has improved after an employee take-over from conventional management (Fusfeld 1983, 775).

In Canada it has been estimated that in 1987 there were nearly four hundred worker cooperatives, most developed in the 1980s, with about $300 million of sales and fifteen thousand members. About two-thirds of these are located in Quebec and are particularly strong in the forest industry and in wood-related products such as pulp and paper (Quarter and Melnyk 1989, 12). In various parts of Canada workers own and manage well-known and successful companies, such as the Sun newspaper chain and Algoma Steel. The latter is a good example of a company that was near bankruptcy in the early 1990s, before it was rescued by an employee buy-out, in which employees, through wage reductions and direct purchases, obtained 60 per cent of the company's stock. While performance has not been even, Algoma became the most profitable steel company in North America in 1994, and in 1995 it set new records with sales increases of 11 per cent, to $1.2 billion, and earnings up 13 per cent, to $238 billion. An eighteen-member joint steering committee, representing the union (United Steelworkers of America), management, and outside shareholders, sets strategy and manages the business consensually (Nankivell 1996; Lowe 1995). Similar success has been enjoyed by the Pine Falls Paper Company in Manitoba after it was purchased by employees from Abitibi, when the latter had given up on its viability, and the Spruce Falls Mill in Kapuskasing, Ontario, which was bought by employees and the community in 1992.

My analysis to this point has dealt primarily with a radical form of worker participation – the producer cooperative – and its effects on efficiency. Other theorists have examined the possible effects of less radical forms of worker control on economic performance, and these theories too have been tested. The International Labour Organization (ILO), for example, has argued that granting labour some co-decision-making power in corporations, beyond that usually obtained by collective bargaining, can improve workers' morale considerably and increase productivity as well. In keeping with the ethical-psychological arguments described above, the expectation is that workers' alienation will be reduced, product quality will increase, workers will come up with more innovative ideas, and there will be fewer work stoppages. All this change should have a positive effect on company performance (see ILO 1974; Anton 1980, 16).

In a similar vein, a U.S. commission maintained, after an extensive survey of corporations, that new forms of worker participation are required to increase productivity (U.S. Department of Commerce and Labor 1994, 38). It found that 'a majority of American workers want to have opportunities to participate in decisions affecting their job, the organization of their work and their economic future' (39). A recent study on corporate governance published by the Brookings Institution (Blair 1995) identifies still other reasons for worker participation. It deals with the type of problems the Pennsylvania legislature tried to address: the undue pressure placed on corporate executives today by outside shareholders, including pension funds, mutual funds, and the other funds that manage large blocks of shares, to produce the highest returns in the shortest possible time.

A whole new vocabulary has come into existence to describe the resulting practices: downsizing, outsourcing, global strategies, and so on. In the words of one reviewer, 'The long run no longer exists and the previous investments in plant, talent, and the services, conveniences, shops, roads, bridges, schools, homes, and the like of abandoned cities have become financially invisible if they do not show up on corporate balance sheets' (Sharpe 1996). Margaret M. Blair (1995), the author of the Brookings study, argues that the placement of workers on corporate boards could help to stem this massive substitution of short-term gain for long-term stability. Outside shareholders do not consider the community effects of a short-run strategy; locally based workers do. This is precisely what the Pennsylvania law envisaged. One of the ironies of such a strategy is that it will undoubtedly pit the interests of current against retired workers. It is the pension funds of the latter that form a major part of the funds looking for maximum short-run returns. Nevertheless, it is an interesting hypothesis which, as the Pennsylvania legislation indicates, is already being tested.

We can now examine the empirical evidence regarding the economic impact of workers' participation in management short of complete ownership. What we find is that in many countries, including Canada and the United States, a number of firms have granted considerable decision-making rights to employees, with generally beneficial effects on performance.

In Canada many businesses have well-staffed personnel or human-resources departments, whose staff members embrace the notion that there is a link between a firm's success and the commitment of its employees (Laflamme, Belanger, and Audet 1987, 220). Partly through their encouragement and through worker-union initiatives, practices have developed in some corporations that go beyond the rights normally attained through collective bargaining. For one, a fairly widespread attempt is being made to decentralize decision-making within the firm, especially through quality circles. This approach usually involves weekly meetings of supervisors and workers during working hours to discuss such matters as shifts, allocation of tasks, and specific problems relating to the quality of the product or service (226).

The scope of collective agreements has also grown in recent years, particularly with respect to health and safety. Most companies now have joint committees to formulate and implement policies in these areas. A study of six major enterprises in Canada also found that participation frequently increases when special problems occur, going beyond requirements of the law and existing collective agreements. For example, with respect to collective dismissals because of technological changes, the federal Labour Code stipulates that employers must give notice of motion and reopen negotiations with workers, with a view to modifying the collective agreement. In practice, the companies surveyed had gone beyond this by establishing participatory machinery, in the form of ad hoc committees, to find alternatives to layoffs or collective dismissals. Special programs were then set up. For example, in two enterprises where major changes had been introduced, an early retirement plan was prepared, along with a work-sharing scheme (Laflamme, Belanger, and Audet 1987, 225).

In general, however, there is no strong or general commitment by Canadian governments or firms, or for that matter by labour unions, to increased participation by workers in matters traditionally considered the prerogatives of managers. Corporate shareholders and managers quite correctly see a transfer of managerial rights to workers as a change in existing property rights, and they vigorously resist it. Unions wish to enlarge their rights through collective bargaining but resist more radical forms of property sharing, such as works councils or workers' representatives on company boards, for fear that these bypass union structures and co-opt workers into a more cooperative relationship with managers.

In the early 1980s a parliamentary subcommittee on finance, trade, and economics briefly considered a bill that would promote profit sharing in businesses and require corporations with over one hundred employees to elect two employees to their boards of directors. Its basic purpose was 'to improve employer/employee relations and enhance the productivity of business enterprises' (Standing Committee on Finance, Trade and Economic Affairs 1982, 7).

I presented an invited brief to the committee supporting its proposals on the basis of western European experience. Afterward, I had an illuminating encounter with a labour leader who also gave a brief. When asked to indicate whether he would speak in favour of or against the bill, this leader lowered his voice and replied:

I personally think we must create better relations between workers and employers in this country, and having workers on boards of directors should contribute to this. It is also appropriate that governments use their powers of coercion to implement such reforms, because if either unions or management suggest them it will be interpreted as a sign of weakness by the other side. In fact, even though I will support them in confidence before the committee I will openly oppose the proposed changes when I leave the committee room. Nevertheless, governments are there to act as impartial umpires and they must have the courage to impose necessary solutions on partisan bodies.

As it turned out, Parliament did not see fit to pass the bill on second reading.

The report of the earlier Royal Commission on Corporate Concentration (1978, 301) observed that share ownership was not a prerequisite for election to company boards in Canada, so there was nothing to prevent unions and management from arriving at an understanding to elect workers as directors. This has not, however, become an established practice in Canada.

Employees in Canada could potentially achieve more control over corporate decision making through purchase of shares. In fact, a push in the United States to promote employees' shareholding and profit-sharing has had some influence on Canada. By the late 1980s nearly nine million American employees were enrolled in 8,700 Employee Stock Ownership Plans (ESOPs) (Quarter and Melnyk 1989, 6). Companies receive tax benefits through the sale of shares to employees. The impact on employees' decision-making has been quite small. In most ESOPs, they hold only a minority of the corporation's stock, and even when they hold a majority they may not be eligible to elect members to the boards of trustees that administer the funds (6–7). A study by the U.S. General Accounting

Office found that employees' ownership of shares has no effect on corporate performance unless it is combined with a plan to increase employees' participation in decision-making (Quarter and Melnyk 1989, 3). There are thousands of profit-sharing plans in Canada, many of them similar to ESOPS, but virtually all of them are restricted to managerial employees and, like their U.S. counterparts, have no discernible impact on employees' decision-making.

Several countries in western Europe have moved much further than either Canada or the United States in this matter. One of the first to initiate reforms was Sweden, which in 1948 had workers appointed to the country's main planning board and since then has promoted worker representatives on company boards. In the opinion of some, however (see Fusfeld 1983, 777) the movement towards co-determination in (West) Germany is the most important worker-participation scheme, because of its comprehensive nature and in particular its application to large firms. The German example may therefore illustrate how employees' decision making can go much beyond the bounds of collective bargaining in companies that are not owned.

German *Mitbestimmung* (co-determination) occurs at two levels: within the production plant, through establishment of works councils; and at the leadership level, through employee membership on the supervisory board (which corresponds roughly to a Canadian board of directors). All workers in the plant belong to the works council. (Unions exist in most corporations, but they do not operate within individual plants. Instead, they engage in negotiations with employer groups over wages and so on, at the industry level.) The Works Constitution Act of 1972 divides decisions made by the works council into four types: social matters, staff decisions, plant changes, and vocational training (Roy Vogt 1981, 382). In the first two types most decisions are co-determined by workers and managers. This means in practice that each has veto power over the other. In matters of hiring and firing, however (related to type-two decisions), workers do not have outright veto power. Nevertheless, dismissals without a hearing of the works council are void, and the council has the right of objection for certain reasons, in which case the decision must be submitted for arbitration by a labour court. In case of the last two types of decisions, which include transfers and shutdowns of plant, worker rights are less extensive and fall short of true co-decision. The economic decision is left to the employer, but the works council can force establishment of a 'social plan' to ameliorate the effects of such a decision.

More far-reaching powers have been granted to workers through membership on the supervisory boards. These bodies establish long-range policy (including major investment decisions) and appoint or dismiss members of the executive committee, including managers. The supervisory board then has responsibilities that we normally associate with ownership. The Co-Determination Act (4 May 1976) established three forms of workers' participation on supervisory boards. In the first type, in corporations with up to two thousand employees (outside coal and steel), one-third of the seats go to workers' representatives. In the second type, in corporations with more than two thousand employees (again, outside coal and steel), the board consists of an equal number of workers' and shareholders' representatives. For example, on a board with twenty members, there will be ten workers' representatives – six elected from all employees by the employees, three chosen by the union, and one selected by all workers from the ranks of management personnel. The chair, who is usually a shareholders' representative, has an additional vote in case of a tie. Therefore the representatives of the shareholders hold the balance of power. The third type of board exists in the coal-mining and iron and steel–producing industries and was the earliest example of this type of co-determination, having been set up in 1951. The board in these industries consists of an equal number of shareholders' and workers' representatives plus a 'neutral' chair agreed on by both sides. Therefore there is greater worker–shareholder parity on these boards.

The Co-determination Act of 1976 generated a great deal of controversy. Workers wanted the coal and steel model to apply to all industry, while shareholders wanted workers' representation to be reduced substantially. The employers' groups argued in addition that implementation of co-determination across all industries violated their private-property rights as guaranteed in the constitution. After the act was passed, the Confederation of Employers officially challenged it in the courts. The Constitutional Court ruled in 1979 that the act was indeed valid, adding that the state has power to arrange property rights in the way it wishes in order to further the common good (Roy Vogt 1981, 384–5).

Labour in Germany, as well as in other countries such as Austria, the Netherlands, Norway, and Sweden, which have adopted similar reforms, has obtained considerable powers of co-decision-making. Through their participation in works councils workers have considerable say in shop-floor issues, while their membership on boards gives them substantial influence on relocation or shutdown of the enterprise, on appointment of managers, and on major investment projects.

All this has been accomplished without apparently damaging the economy in any way, or leading it towards state ownership. There is in fact considerable empirical evidence that this type of participation significantly improves workers' morale and companies' performance. Several studies of Germany and other countries confirm the expectation that meaningful participation can reduce industrial strife and increase efficiency (see, for example, Gyllenhammar 1977 for Sweden; Schregle 1978 for Germany; and Vaughan 1976 and Whitehorn 1978 for more general comparisons). Some scholars have concluded that the German form of participation has been especially vital in helping (West) Germany through several difficult periods in its post-1945 recovery (Connaghan 1976, 79). In particular, it reduced potential industrial conflict during twenty years of substantial rationalization in the coal and steel industry.

A recent study by two American scholars attempts to measure the effectiveness of different degrees of worker participation in an innovative, comprehensive way (Buchele and Christiansen 1995). They develop an index of workers' rights, based on representational strength and income security. They can correlate this index for several countries with annual increases in labour productivity for those countries for the years 1972–88. They discovered 'a strongly positive relationship between the rate of growth of labor productivity and our index of workers' rights' (34). Over half the variation in productivity growth among countries was 'explained' by variations in workers' rights. For example, the workers' rights index for the United States was 0.36, and annual growth in labour productivity was 0.9 per cent. Canada's index of workers' rights was 1.16, and its productivity growth was 1.7 per cent per annum. Japan had a workers' rights index of 1.63, with productivity growth of 3.4 per cent per year, and Germany's workers' rights index was the highest, at 3.11, and its annual productivity growth was 3.0 per cent (Table 1, 33). These results did not change substantially when increases in capital stock for each country were taken into account. The authors conclude that 'the countries with the weakest workers' rights experienced productivity growth rates below what would be predicted by their growth in capital per worker. And the countries with the strongest workers' rights had productivity growth rates above what would be predicted by their growth in capital per worker' (36).

This part of the study has shown that the arrangement of decision-making rights within the workplace constitutes a major aspect of Canada's property system. There are many good reasons for enlarging the property rights of employees. This hypothesis I advance not as a panacea for the social and economic problems of our society, but as an attempt to restore to the working population the rights that mature citizens ought to have. Far from injuring the country, reforms in this area, available evidence suggests, could contribute substantially to its economic and social improvement.

Workers in western Europe have received increased property rights in the workplace, through works councils and membership on boards of directors – through their participation in an enterprise, not through share purchase. They have therefore put into force a means for obtaining property rights that is deeply imbedded in the European legal and cultural tradition, which is also Canada's tradition. There is no reason why similar steps cannot be taken in Canada. Changes will not happen, however, without courageous action by governments, since there are enough vested interests that will defend the status quo, even if it can be shown that the status quo is injurious to the economy and to the individual well-being of many Canadian citizens.

7

New Property in Jobs and Social Investments

The cover story on Paul Martin ('The bean counter,' Dec. 13) made me see red. You talk about 'transfers to persons' as though we were being given something by the government that we did not earn. I bought and paid for my old age pension when we lived on hamburger and never knew if the money would last until the next payday. The government took the money and promised it was buying a vested life old age pension at 65. No one said, when we were paying what we could not afford: 'We may tax it all back if your income goes over a certain arbitrary level.' I am rapidly reaching pensionable age. If any government messes with my old age pension, I will promptly hire the best lawyer I can and sue for breach of trust.

Letter to the Editor from F.D. Cooper, Victoria, *Maclean's*, 1 Jan. 1994, 4

The convictions expressed in this letter to a Canadian magazine take us back to chapter 3, where the term 'new property' first occurred. The American legal scholar Charles Reich coined the term some thirty years ago to describe the new kinds of 'things' on which people rely for their sustenance (Charles Reich 1965a, b). As Reich observed, people used to depend largely on physical things such as land and fixed assets associated with land to provide themselves with a decent standard of living. The owners of these things managed to protect their interest in them by having them legally designated as 'property.' Nowadays, only a small minority of the population owns land from which income is derived, and only a small minority owns the new capital resources of industry. Instead, most people work for others, and they depend on things other than land and physical capital to provide life's necessities.

The most important 'thing' on which people depend today for their living is, of course, a job. However, they also count on a wide array of other 'things,' most notably investments that generate income and security, referred to here as 'social investments.' Canadians make all kinds of social investments, both privately and through their governments. They place their earnings in private savings institutions, purchase stocks, bonds, and other financial instruments that produce long-term income, and make regular contributions to private pension plans to guarantee an adequate flow of income after job income terminates. They have also chosen to protect themselves through investments in government programs. Their tax payments ensure such social benefits as health and education, at the same time as special contributions to (un)employment insurance and pensions provide protection against loss of income during job loss and in retirement.

The average Canadian depends on a job and on social investments for adequate lifetime income just as surely as earlier generations, and a minority of Canadians today, depended on land and capital. However, the law has not seen fit to accord to these new life-supporting things the property protection extended to land and capital. It was a ruling by the U.S. Supreme Court (*Fleming vs. Nestor*, 1960) that Social Security benefits do not constitute an 'accrued property right' that prompted Charles Reich, and numerous others since, to develop the theory of the 'new property.' Their objective has been to secure for the new things on which most people depend the same type of property protection that the old things, now held by a minority, have had. From this perspective, a pension purchased through government, as per the letter writer above, should be as fully protected from theft or abuse as any piece of land or other physical asset owned by a Canadian. 'It is a purpose of the ancient institution of property,' several U.S. Supreme Court justices remind us, 'to protect those claims upon which people rely in their daily lives' (cited by Baker 1986, 745). Such action serves, as Baker argues, the basic 'welfare' function of property.

What Reich calls 'new property' is an essential element of what Marshall (1964) has termed 'social citizenship.' Distinct from 'political' or 'civil' citizenship, it entails a set of rights, 'ranging from the right to a modicum of economic welfare and security to the right to share to the full in the social heritage and to live the life of a civilized being according to the standards prevailing in the society' (71). Marshall, however, focuses on rights to education and social services. I broaden the concept here to include property rights in employment.

The inability of employers to hire all available labour, their power to dismiss employees, and governments' ability unilaterally to alter or discontinue major social benefits support the claim that 'old conceptions of property limited to the protection of interests in land and physical objects will no longer serve as adequate protection for the individual' (Levine 1973, 1085). The problem I examine in this chapter is how to provide better protection, possibly in the form of new property rights, to the new things that people find absolutely essential for their lives – first, jobs; second, the 'social safety net'; and third, health care and education. Then I look at recent events in Canada and their implications for these property rights.

New Property in Jobs

I observe below in this chapter that in 1994 the average Canadian tax filer (of whom there were slightly fewer than fifteen million) received $26.85 in social benefits (largely transfer payments from government) for every $100 of employment income earned (Statistics Canada, 1996). What I emphasize below is the contribution of social benefits – a vital part of the new property – to the average Canadian's annual income. People depend heavily on income earned through employment. The income figures above indicate that the average Canadian taxpayer receives almost 80 per cent of current income through employment. The holding of a job, therefore, is by far the biggest single 'asset' through which most people support themselves. 'We have become a society of wage earners, with the result that the employment relationship is one of the most important institutional mechanisms in society' (MacNeil 1983, 368).

In chapter 6 we examined property rights within the workplace of those who have jobs. Differences in initial income, access to capital, talent, and luck allowed some people to achieve control over such productive resources as land and capital, while the majority have not. A fair and socially effective property system, I suggested, should give all participants in society, especially those in the workplace, some property rights over these vital resources. A broader distribution of property rights does not require a revolution destroying the property rights of current owners in order to transfer them to others. Instead, the propertyless could enlarge their control over use of resources through greater participation in the decision-making process.

Our concern now is with the right to have or hold a job. Since most people cannot do without employment, it would surely seem imperative that society adjust its property rules so as to enhance the job-getting and job-holding abilities of its members. For this reason 'an increasing number of commentators are calling for recognition of the "universal and equal property right in employment"' (MacNeil 1983, 368).

But what do property rights in jobs mean? The first necessity is to get a job. Unfortunately, just as some people are more able for various reasons to obtain land and capital than others, so some have easier access to jobs than others. How does one provide access to all? It is perhaps useful to contrast the approach taken by some socialist economies in the past with that of a typical market economy. In the former, individuals were restricted in their freedom to create their own jobs but were virtually guaranteed work in the state sector. In market economies, in contrast, persons are free to create their own jobs but are not guaranteed a right to work for others. In other words, individuals have an unrestricted right to create a job, but no guarantee of finding one.

The virtue of socialism was to grant universal property rights in jobs. People need jobs and got them. However, the state mechanisms used to direct workers to jobs contributed to the erosion of human freedoms that was already occurring for other reasons. Further, it proved impossible to find productive jobs for everyone, or to encourage high levels of productivity among slothful workers and managers who interpreted the right to work as an opportunity not to work. (In a right-to-a-job society the right to dismiss indolent workers or managers is, in practice, seriously restricted. The state has the burden of finding another job for every person dismissed.) The virtue of the market system in this respect is the contribution that labour mobility in a 'free' job market makes to individual freedom and efficiency. Its defect is that because many people have neither the financial nor 'natural' resources to create their own jobs, and because it would be economically disadvantageous for employers and for society to hire large numbers of unproductive workers, it usually does not assure nearly everyone who needs a job that they will have one.

Short of guaranteeing work, however, there is much that society can do to increase access to jobs and to ameliorate the financial problems created by an inability to find one. First, society has a responsibility to correct market 'failure' through non-market mechanisms. The efficiency requirements of market-oriented businesses may often produce results in terms of product quality, quality of the environment, or quantity and quality of jobs that are objectionable to consumers, workers, and capitalists alike. Yet, in the absence of intervention from agencies representing the interests of society as a whole, decisions may be taken that are destructive to almost everyone. In the words of an American legal scholar, who espouses the contribution of property rights to liberty, 'A significant portion of most people's lives is devoted to productive activity. Many people consider this activity to be an important aspect of who they are. A meaningful notion of freedom requires that people's activity and the collective world created by this freedom not be entirely independent of their preferences. Given the large stake of both capitalists and workers in the nature of their social world, concern for individual freedom requires that the structure itself be subject to conscious, human control. This implies the need for collective control of the structure' (Baker 1986, 790). In other words, basic human needs, such as access to jobs, should not be left entirely to the dictates of the market. Society should intervene on behalf of those to whom access may be most limited.

Second, society not only needs to increase access to jobs but has the ability to do so. It can do so in many ways: through its support of education and health, job training, and direct creation of jobs in social services and social infrastructure. Many in modern business say that governments do not create real jobs. In fact, in Canada and elsewhere they have managed to create a large number of good, long-term jobs, most of which contribute immeasurably to our quality of life, as noted above (chapter 2). Governments have a role to play in providing jobs to people who might not otherwise get them, and such positions have often been the gateway to the mainstream economy for immigrants and minorities. Even if one accepts the business view that 'real' jobs are created only in response to consumer demand, there is no reason to assume that large numbers of government jobs fail to meet this test. There is ample evidence that a majority of Canadians choose to purchase such goods as hospitals, highways, and schools, and such services as medicare and education, through their tax payments to government, instead of buying them from private sources.

Society also eases the inability to find a job by providing many citizens with both private and state-financed social benefits. This, of course, is especially vital to those who cannot qualify for almost any job because of physical or mental disabilities. Before examining this more, however, which would take us into a discussion of the 'new property' in social investment, a further comment on protection of jobs is necessary.

If it would be both unwise and impossible to guarantee everyone a job, what about the right to continue in a job once it has been obtained? What does it mean to create a property right in jobs with respect to their continuation? Property laws protect citizens against theft of their assets. Should citizens be protected against the 'theft' of their jobs?

Once again, the realities of human nature and modern economies suggest that an absolute guarantee of a particular job could be harmful and may, in any case, be impossible. A threat of dismissal may still be a necessary incentive for some persons to perform adequately. Even universities, which almost guarantee lifetime tenure to instructors, withhold such protection for a probationary period, during which time the employee's performance is evaluated under the discipline of possible dismissal. It is also beyond doubt, as one Canadian scholar observes, that 'in times of rapid change, neither the government nor the economy will succeed in providing continuous employment for all.' Therefore, he concludes, 'Guaranteeing security in the job itself is an unrealistic goal' (MacNeil 1983, 375).

What can be done is to accord jobs some of the protection provided by property laws, particularly that of 'due process.' In the words of a legal scholar, 'Our concept of property must be expanded to encompass the employment relationship, to protect against wrongful discharge. 'A more exact definition might be 'the protection of the worker's interest in his employment from discharge without just cause' (Levine 1973, 1085). University tenure fits this requirement almost exactly; it does not guarantee continuation of a job, but it makes dismissal without due process or the showing of just cause almost impossible (these protections can generally be lifted in cases of 'financial exigency'). To grant a property right in a job means therefore that positions cannot be taken away without such legal safeguards as adequate notice, reasons for dismissal, a fair hearing and chance of appeal, and possibly compensation.

The search for greater employment security has already produced some of the above job protections. A few have come about through employee–employer contracts, and others through legal challenges in court or through statutory changes. Four devices in particular may be identified: contract law; collective-bargaining limits on unilateral management prerogatives; legislative standards creating a floor of rights and defining circumstances under which employment can be terminated; and procedural standards of natural justice and fairness that emphasize the manner in which employment can be terminated (MacNeil 1983, 369). Each of these deserves a fuller explanation.

Contract law. For a long time contract law left the employer with an unfettered right to terminate an employment contract. However, over time the courts have come to recognize, 'through the fictional device of an implied term in the contract of employment' (MacNeil 1983, 369), that workers may be entitled to reasonable notice before termination other than for cause. Courts have emphasized the difficulty of finding alternative employment as one of the factors that entitles workers to reasonable notice. Nevertheless, if proper notice is given, there is the continuing assumption in contract law that the employee has no right to continue in the job. There is at the same time, however, 'growing jurisprudence which is attempting to define situations where employees should be compensated for the abrupt termination of an employment relationship' (MacNeil 1983, 371).

Collective bargaining. A more direct attack on management's unilateral powers with respect to job dismissal has taken place through the collective-bargaining process. Many collective agreements now contain 'just cause' provisions, which prohibit management from terminating employment in an arbitrary or capricious manner. In addition to the substantive protection given to employees, there is procedural protection in the form of grievance procedures and decisions by mutually acceptable arbitrators. The value of these protections is shown in a study of six hundred and forty-five disciplinary discharges considered by arbitrators in Ontario between 1970 and 1974. The arbitrators found that in 53.5 per cent of the cases there was not sufficient cause for discharge (cited in MacNeil 1983, 372).

Statutory protection. Legislatures have passed laws designed to afford unorganized workers protection that is similar to that achieved through collective bargaining. Nova Scotia was the first province to grant statutory protection against unreasonable discharge. Subsequently the Canada Labour Code and the codes of several other provinces have been amended to include similar provisions. Other statutes, including provincial human rights legislation, protect employees against various types of discrimination. Severance-pay provisions are being increasingly protected and enforced, in recognition of the need to aid employees in adjusting to the loss of jobs. As MacNeil observes, 'Severance pay can be viewed as compensation for the expropriation of rights which the employee had acquired in the course of the job' (MacNeil 1983, 375).

In the public-service sector the position of civil servants has changed dramatically in the last few decades. For a long time, they were subject to dismissal at the pleasure of the crown, with no advance notice or reasons given. Gradually greater job security was achieved, and in the federal jurisdiction the Public Services Employment Act and the Public Staff Relations Act of 1970 granted tenure for an indeterminate period unless some other period of employment was specified. Just cause for termination is carefully spelled out, and appeal procedures are put in place.

Natural justice and fairness. The courts have also imposed on employers the requirement to exercise their functions fairly, in accordance with the dictates of 'natural justice.' Thus in one of several cases cited by MacNeil, a probationary police constable, who was dismissed and not informed of the reasons or given an opportunity to be heard, was held to be improperly dismissed (MacNeil 1983, 379). The probationary status of the employee had not clearly put him under the protection of existing laws, so the courts applied concepts of natural justice or fairness to give him such protection.

Incomes related to jobs have been given extra security through provision of (un)employment insurance – a form of social benefit discussed below.

Through such multilayered devices, a considerable number of Canadian workers have received some of the protection they might enjoy if their interest in their job had the status of a property right. Unusual circumstances in the United States pressed legal scholars there into urging property status for jobs. Several U.S. Supreme Court decisions respecting the employment rights of public employees had ruled that due process protected such employees only if one of the protected interests of life, liberty, or property, as set out in the Fifth or Fourteenth Amendments, was endangered. Therefore, in order to obtain the protection of due process, it seemed necessary to have a person's job recognized as a new form of property.

In Canada due process has been achieved for many workers by the means described above, without recognition of a property right in employment. However, many workers still lack these protections, be it because they are part of a sizeable and growing part-time or seasonal labour force, or because they live in jurisdictions without adequate statutory protection or work in firms without the safeguards of collective bargaining.

Recent studies show that insecurity in many parts of Canada's labour force has increased substantially in the last few years. Businesses have worked aggressively to achieve increased labour 'flexibility' in order to cope with new global competition. Strategies include radical downsizing of the labour force; contracting out, or 'outsourcing'; and substitution of temporary, part-time jobs for permanent, full-time ones. The inevitable result has been a sharp increase in employment volatility. More than 20 per cent of all Canadian workers now lose or change their jobs each year, a historically high rate of turnover (Stanford 1996, 132). Fully half of the new jobs created in Canada during the 1980s were non-standard – either not full time or involving working for more than a single employer. The share of Canadians working a 'normal' work week (between thirty-five and forty hours per week) declined from 71 per cent in 1976 to 61 per cent in 1993 (Stanford 1996, 133). In 1993 60 per cent of all the new jobs created were non-standard; the majority went to women. Women consistently comprise approximately 70 per cent of all part-time workers (Vosko 1996, 260). The increase in insecurity caused by these changes has been exacerbated by major reductions in (un)employment insurance, which are discussed below.

The security enjoyed by workers in the public sector has also decreased considerably through new strategies of contracting out and downsizing. The Conservative government of Brian Mulroney announced a program of major cutbacks to the federal civil service in 1984 ('pink slips and running shoes'). A reduction of fifteen thousand employees was proposed. In fact, over the next eight years of that government less than five thousand jobs were cut, and 'ironclad job security' was granted to non-term employees (80 per cent of the total). During the 1993 federal election the Liberals vowed that the public service would not be cut. Shortly after forming the new government they introduced massive cuts, first in the Department of National Defence and then in most other departments. The public service was reduced by about sixty thousand – a feat accomplished by attractive and expensive early-retirement provisions, as well as by unilateral modifications of job-security agreements negotiated with unions (Lee and Hobbs 1996, 374).

These trends only reinforce what has always been true: that for many Canadians the fundamental need to have and hold a job is still insufficiently protected. Given the recent increases in job insecurity, new ways of achieving greater security will ultimately be demanded by workers. The recent efforts of unions such as the Canadian Auto Workers to obtain 'ownership in jobs' through collective bargaining, by which they are challenging management's unilateral right to decide how investments and jobs within the enterprise are to be allocated, would, if successful, constitute recognition of jobs as a new form of property .

Canadians have long recognized that in the absence of job guarantees or even adequate protection, and with the possibility of undue hardship through illness or other misfortunes, it is necessary to make provision for income flows not directly related to jobs. Both private industry and governments have responded to this need by creating a wide array of social benefits. The focus in the remainder of this chapter is on those investments that Canadians have made in social benefits financed largely through the state. The basic question that I pose is: is it necessary to protect the investment of Canadians in these benefits by according them the status of property?

New Property in the 'Social Safety Net'

During this century Canada has gradually evolved into what some have called a 'welfare state,' and others prefer to call a 'protected society' (see Courchene 1980). Like citizens of most other Western countries, Canadians have asked their governments to use their revenue and spending powers to create a social safety net, to meet the special needs of the poor and unfortunate, and to provide for all citizens greater income security and better health and educational services than the market system by itself seems to provide.

Canadian governments have actually been slower than, for example, their western European counterparts in creating such a safety net, and even today Canadian social programs are judged to be less developed than those of most other capitalist societies (Brooks 1993, 188). Canada, for example, first introduced sickness insurance in 1971, almost one hundred years after Germany and sixty years after the United Kingdom and Sweden; pension insurance was begun in 1927, many years after Germany, Britain, France, and Italy, and the introduction of unemployment insurance in 1940 followed that of most European countries (Brooks 1993, 189). Some of the major features of Canada's current social policy emerged between 1965 and 1970, including medicare, the Canada Assistance Plan (CAP), the Guaranteed Income Supplement (GIS), and the Canada Pension Plan (CPP).

There are two pillars to Canada's social safety net: an income-security system and what might be termed a basic-social-resource program, involving primarily health and education. The total package of social programs is financed by the public and paid out by governments in different ways. Support from the public goes to governments through specific contributions in the case of employment insurance (EI, formerly unemployment insurance) and the Canada Pension Plan. Other programs are financed through tax revenues.

Income security and basic social resources are provided to citizens in three main ways: in the form of direct service, as in health and education; through transfer payments, as in Old Age Security (OAS), GIS, EI benefits, and social assistance; and through tax benefits, which include Registered Retirement Savings Plan (RRSP) deductions, marital and age exemptions, and the integrated child benefit introduced in 1993 (which replaced family allowance transfer payments). Direct service and transfer payments show up as government expenditures, referred to generally as 'direct program spending.' Benefits through tax deductions are in effect tax expenditures, or government revenues forgone because of various tax preferences (also called the 'hidden welfare system' – Rice 1987, 212). Tax expenditures are just as much government spending as direct program spending. In the words of Canada's auditor general, 'a dollar of revenue intentionally forgone is just as important as a dollar spent.' There is no financial difference between providing $1,000 to an individual through a public program and forgiving $1,000 of tax that the individual would otherwise owe (Shillington 1996, 107).

In 1992 all levels of government in Canada combined imposed a tax rate equivalent to 36.5 per cent of gross domestic product (GDP). This figure was slightly below the twenty-four-country OECD average (Shillington 1996, 101). Just less than one-third of tax revenues (11 per cent of GDP) went to health and education in 1990 (Perry 1993, 45), and a similar proportion went for social security and welfare. Social-security taxes (mainly the Canada and Quebec Pension plans and unemployment insurance levies) have in the recent past accounted for 14.2 per cent of all taxes in Canada (Perry 1993, 51). Because of the large proportion of total tax revenues used to support health, education, and income security in Canada, observers often assume that they have been major contributors to the growth of Canada's public debt. That growth in turn has prompted drastic efforts in the last few years to reduce the size of government-financed social benefits (on which more below). A study by Statistics Canada in 1991 showed, however, that from 1975 to 1991 only 6 per cent of the federal debt could be attributed to social spending. In contrast, 50 per cent was an outcome of declining revenue resulting from tax expenditures and corporate tax breaks (Mimoto and Cross 1991).

Before we turn to the specific benefits that Canadians receive from these tax contributions, which involves an examination of the types of programs that have been developed and an analysis of recent proposed reforms, we should consider the reasons for the growth in benefits (and in the taxes required to finance them). The expansion of the modern welfare state has been attributed to two forces: the increased political mobilization of the general population, which has forced governments to respond to a wider range of interest groups, and the need of governments to promote social harmony and to legitimize the existing economic system in the eyes of those who benefit least from its operation (Brooks 1993, 186). Critics of government, more prevalent in the United States than in Canada, stress the 'empire-building' tendencies of government itself. Government programs grow because politicians and civil servants alike see the vast amounts of money raised through the unique taxing powers of government as an opportunity to create ever-larger programs over which they exercise power and control.

To the extent that this is true – and who would doubt that state officials are as likely to be self-serving and hungry for power as human beings in general – the government is inclined to take a paternalistic attitude towards its own activities. It sees itself as the owner of the revenues it receives, rather than a trustee, and assumes therefore that it has a unilateral right to create, destroy, and change programs. People such as the letter writer quoted at the beginning of this chapter therefore get the impression that governments think they are using their own resources to 'favour' Canadians with social and economic benefits, favours that can be extended and withdrawn as governments will.

Despite the cynicism towards governments that such attitudes breed, Canadians paradoxically retain a strong faith in the role of government. The social benefits built up through government programs since the Second World War have been created largely in response to popular demand. Canadians by and large prefer to see their health and educational needs taken care of by governments, and even in times of fiscal retrenchment a majority would sooner see these programs maintained than cut back in order to reduce taxes. Canadians also favour government income-maintenance programs and protest strongly when these are threatened. While most Canadians have savings in private financial institutions, they rely heavily on benefits financed through tax contributions to government.

One frequently encounters persons who on nearing retirement have given capital assets to their children, which could have generated a private flow of income, in order to qualify for a government income supplement. For many people there is nothing more treasured than a monthly cheque from government! Canadians also tend to favour government-sponsored home-care programs over private 'for profit' programs and enjoy the benefits of nursing homes financed through taxes. And they accept these benefits without apology, because they see their past tax contributions as a form of social investment from which they are now getting their return. They have, to reiterate the main theme of this chapter, created for themselves a new form of property, and they wish their rights in it to be respected.

In the process of creating new property for themselves, Canadian taxpayers have also built a safety net for those without adequate income and without the means to make a substantial contribution to their own social benefits. In Canada, as in most other countries today, there appears to be an implicit commitment to providing a life-supporting income to everyone, even though so-called guaranteed-income programs have uncertain support. Public debate centres around the legitimacy of certain requests for social support, from apparently able-bodied and potentially employable individuals for example, but there is little hesitation to contribute both privately and through government programs to those considered truly in need. As a noted social-policy analyst and a leading Canadian economist told the House of Commons Finance Committee during its 1995 hearings on a new health and social-transfer system, 'Canadians as Canadians have obligations to each other that go beyond an inter-regional laundering of money. For us, the Canadian community is meaningful if it directly engages important social issues that touch Canadians deeply. For us, Canada is made more meaningful if there are important spheres of shared experience, critical programs such as health care and social welfare the parameters of which we set in common' (Keith Banting and Robin Broadway, Presentation to the Standing Committee on Finance, House of Commons, 9 May 1995, in Maslove 1996, 285).

The result of such perceptions of government's building community has been the slow but vigorous development by various levels of government of social benefits that affect virtually every Canadian. The variety and size of these benefits are impressive.

New Property in Health Care and Education

Canada's national system of health care, known as medicare, has been termed 'our most collective achievement' (Silver 1996, 69). It is based on two pieces of legislation: the Hospital Insurance and Diagnostic Services Act of 1957, insuring hospital services, and the Medical Care Act of 1966, insuring doctors' services. Costs are met from general tax revenue. The legislation imposed five federal–provincial cost-sharing conditions: universal coverage: all Canadian residents covered; accessibility: no hindrance through means tests, extra charges, and so on; portability: all Canadians receiving services anywhere in Canada; comprehensiveness: all 'medically necessary' hospital and physicians' services covered; and public administration: each provincial plan publicly administered on a non-profit basis without the involvement of the private sector.

However, physicians remain private practitioners, and hospitals are generally run by boards of trustees consisting of private citizens. For this reason, as one Canadian health expert insists, it is correct to say that 'we do not have "socialized medicine," but we do have socialized insurance' (Robert Evans 1993, 27).

In 1990, government health-care spending in Canada amounted to about 5.9 per cent of GDP. In the United States the corresponding figure was 4.7 per cent (Perry 1993, 45), but whereas in Canada private spending added relatively little to overall costs for health, in the United States private plus government spending on health amounted to about 13 per cent of GDP – the highest proportion of any country in the world (Robert Evans 1993, 32).

Education is another social-resource benefit to which Canadians commit a sizeable portion of their tax dollars. In 1990 all levels of government spent $34.2 billion on education, or 5.1 per cent of GDP (Perry 1993, 45). These expenditures provide 'free' education for children from kindergarten through high school and have been used to support about 70 to 80 per cent of post-secondary education costs.

For almost two decades, beginning in 1977 with passage of the Federal-Provincial Fiscal Arrangements and Established Programs Act (EPF), Ottawa has supported provincial initiatives in health and education through block-fund transfers. About 32 per cent of the transfer was intended for education, and the remainder for health (Silver 1996, 71). The EPF arrangements have been termed the 'most massive transfer of revenues (and therefore the substance of power) from the federal to the provincial governments in Canadian history' (Malcolm Taylor 1987, 435). Unfortunately, due to the recession of the early 1980s, the federal government began unilaterally to decrease the amount given to the provinces under EPF. This in turn prompted several provinces to permit 'extra billing' by both doctors and hospitals. This change threatened to destroy such basic features of the program as universality and accessibility. Several public inquiries, including the Health Services Review of 1980, revealed strong support throughout Canada for a system of universal health care without extra user charges. As the review's commissioner, Mr Justice Emmet Hall, noted, 'If extra-billing is permitted as a right and practised by physicians in their sole discretion, it will, over the years destroy the program, creating in that downward path the two-tier system incompatible with the societal level which Canadians have attained' (cited in Silver 1996, 74). The result was passage in 1984 of the Canada Health Act, which penalized provinces for extra billing and firmly entrenched the basic principles of medicare noted above. In the last few years, however, new concerns about Canadian public spending and about the long-run efficiency and affordability of Canada's health and education system have prompted basic changes to the amount and type of support that governments plan to offer in the future. These I discuss below.

In addition to basic social resources such as health and education, governments have developed several types of income support. Most of these, including CPP/QPP, EI, GIS, OAS, and social welfare, are received as transfer payments. They are proving crucial to a wide range of Canadians. As noted above, the average Canadian taxpayer in 1994 received $26.85 in transfer payments for every $100 of employment income. This proportion increased by nearly 32 per cent between 1989 and 1994. Government pensions made up $9.58, or 36 per cent of transfer income. Private pensions, which are lumped together with other non-employment transfer payments, made up 24 per cent of the total ($6.35). It is noteworthy that men received almost one-third of their total transfer payments from private pensions; only 15 per cent of transfer payments for women were derived from private pensions. (This information is derived from Statistics Canada 1996.) (Un)employment insurance accounted for another 14.5 per cent of transfer income. This was down considerably from the previous year, partly because of cutbacks that are discussed below (the amount of UI income fell by 14.7 per cent on a constant-dollar basis, to $14.4 billion).

Social-assistance benefits constituted 12 per cent of transfer payments. Social assistance has been financed until recently under the Canada Assistance Plan (CAP), which coordinated federal and provincial funding beginning in 1966. Under this program Ottawa in effect reimbursed the provinces for part of their eligible welfare costs. Unlike assistance given for education and health, virtually no conditions were attached to federal support. Ottawa basically agreed to finance 50 per cent of provincial welfare costs, but starting in 1990 it began to reduce its contributions to three provinces, Ontario, Alberta, and British Columbia, considerably below that. By 1995 it was paying as little as 29 per cent in Ontario (Maslove 1996, 288). In the four years 1990–4 this 'cap on CAP' cost Ontario alone about $5 billion. Problems of funding contributed to a major review of social assistance in 1995 (see below). In a background paper asking 'Why Social Security Reform?' federal minister Lloyd Axworthy noted that in March 1993 some three million Canadians were dependent on social assistance, including 1.2 million children (Pulkingham and Ternowetsky 1996a, 5). Many Canadians also receive benefits in the form of tax expenditures (i.e., through programs of reduced taxes).

These include credits for the Goods and Services Tax (957), child tax benefits (which constituted 5.3 per cent of transfer income in 1994, or $1.43 for every $100 of employment income), and RRSP.

New Social Policies: A Threat to Social Investments?

The above discussion may have, for the sake of brevity, created the impression that Canada's social-benefit programs evolved without too much controversy. Though, as suggested, they have been created largely in response to public demand, and have received broad support, their creation and continuation have been marked by considerable public debate and government indecision. Almost every program has come under intense criticism at one time or another, leading to frequent calls for reform. Indeed, as has been observed, 'the landscape of Canadian social policy is littered with the skeletons of proposals for reform' (Battle and Torjman 1996, 52).

The opposition to particular aspects of the social safety net has originated with different groups of people and for a variety of reasons. Initial attempts to provide government-supported universal health care, for example, were vigorously opposed by most physicians and large segments of the business community. Corporations have frequently placed tremendous pressure on governments to reduce social spending in general, partly out of an underlying antipathy to the growth of the state sector and partly in order to reverse what they consider an unbearable tax burden on themselves and on the rest of the country. The greatest pressure that business brings to bear on government is the threat to reduce investment and production, thus threatening the viability of the economy. For this reason, as one expert on social policy has observed, governments in Canada may have created social policies in response to popular demand, but they have always done so 'within the limits of business confidence ... and in ways that minimize the cost burden shouldered by business ' (Brooks 1993, 187). Canada's social policies have been financed mainly by the citizens who use public education, public health services, and income-security programs, through personal income taxes and social contributions, not by business. Between 1970 and 1990 taxes on personal income increased from 10.1 to 15.2 per cent of GDP, while taxes on corporate income fell from 3.5 per cent to 2.5 per cent (Perry 1993, 49).

Reforms to social programs have also been advocated by a broader range of citizens, and by governments, for other reasons. Many observers feared almost from the beginning, for example, that health costs might ultimately spiral out of control because of the way programs were structured. For example, the fixed-fee-for-service that characterizes physicians' services encouraged growth of demand for such services. In the absence of caps on numbers of doctors and on the total amount of money allocated to their services, there seemed no limit to the drain on the public purse. In fact, as a leading expert on Canada's system insists, 'health care costs in Canada are not "exploding" or "spiraling" ... In real terms ... they have been rising at about the same annual average rate for the last twenty years. And that rate, it should be noted, is considerably *slower* than during the previous twenty, prior to the completion of universal coverage for hospital and medical care' (Robert Evans 1993, 31). However, this has not alleviated all concerns. What has happened, as the above expert acknowledges, is that the economy itself has slowed down, and as a result overall health expenditures have increased from about 7.5 per cent of GDP to about 10 per cent. The real problem, then, is to 'adapt a health care system which has been habituated over decades to steady expansion, so as to fit it within the new, low-growth environment' (32). Hence the continuing calls for reforms in this area.

Other long-term problems in Canada's safety net have also been observed. Canada's ageing population, and its particular demographics, have raised fears that such programs as old-age security and other pensions are unsustainable without increased contributions and/or reductions in coverage. A Department of Finance study published in 1985 indicated, for example, that if the contribution rate for the Canada Pension Plan, which is split evenly between employees and employers, remained unchanged the CPP would be bankrupt by the year 2004 (Brooks 1993, 194). In addition, as Thomas Courchene demonstrated some time ago, there are inequities in the system. Elderly Canadians with significant private income gain most from the current system of benefits. This is because the value of deductions for occupational pension plans and RRSPs increase with income (Courchene 1987; Brooks 1993, 194). The main result, the National Council of Welfare (1990) argues, 'is to enhance the tax advantages of the rich' (52). Similar concerns have been expressed about other programs such as (un)employment insurance and social assistance.

In addition, decentralizing political forces have placed growing pressure on Ottawa to shift more of the funding and sponsorship of social programs to the provinces, where, so the theory goes, local bodies will be able to run them more effectively and efficiently. Finally, particularly since the late 1980s, the business lobby has been able to convince a significant portion of the population that Canada faces a fiscal crisis and that social expenditures must be reduced in order to cope with it.

Because of such concerns, recent federal and provincial governments have used various strategies to 'reform' government programs in general and to reduce state commitments to social benefit programs in particular. With regard to general governmental reform, the federal Conservative government undertook a major review of programs in 1991, which was nothing less than a critical rethinking of the state's role and its operations in society and the economy (Paquet and Shepherd 1996, 43). All government departments were evaluated on the basis of six 'tests,' which included such questions as: does the program area or activity continue to serve a public interest, and is there a legitimate and necessary role for government in it (45)? This review resulted in 1993, under Kim Campbell, in a regrouping and reduction of ministries and programs. One effect was creation of the Department of Human Resources Development Canada (HRDC), the largest of the new portfolios. It encompassed elements and programs from five departments, including Employment and Immigration, National Health and Welfare, and Labour. Part of the purpose was to reduce administrative costs; another was to coordinate social benefits such as unemployment insurance and training programs more effectively. This new super social-benefits department was carried over into the Liberal government that took power in 1993.

At the same time as efforts were under way to streamline government services, substantial changes and reductions occurred in the funding of social benefits. In the late 1980s and early 1990s the federal Conservative government reduced its previous commitment to pension funding by 'de-indexing' benefits to less than the growth of inflation, by reducing unemployment-insurance benefits, and by 'clawing back' family allowances and old-age-security payments from middle-income Canadians. In some cases there were also demonstrable improvements in social services, particularly increases to the child-care expense deduction and substitution of the child-tax benefit for family allowances. Finance Department figures show, for example, that the revised child tax benefit introduced in 1993 cost Ottawa $5.3 billion in that year, which was $800 million more than combined child and dependant tax credits and family allowances in the previous year (*Winnipeg Free Press*, 16 Aug. 1996, B5).

Critics of the changes lamented particularly the piecemeal and subtle ways in which reductions to pensions, for example, were made. 'Social policy by stealth' was a phrase used to characterize this approach (Battle 1990). When the Liberal government assumed power in 1993 it promised not to pursue the politics and policy of stealth. When it decided to launch a major social-security review (SSR), it began with a highly public and visible review process under Minister Lloyd Axworthy at Human Resources Development Canada (HRDC). The SSR launched a major restructuring of social benefits in Canada, with devastating implications for the social investments that Canadians have made in these benefits. Its provisions therefore require careful scrutiny.

The Social Security Review of 1994 and the Federal Budget of 1995

When the Liberal government in 1994 began its review of social policy it pursued almost immediately two different and, to some extent, conflicting objectives. The new minister of HRDC, Lloyd Axworthy, is generally credited with trying to streamline social policy with the hope of making it more effective. The finance minister, Paul Martin, and some of his right-of-centre colleagues, however, provided a strong counterweight in cabinet. Their main objective was to use reductions in social spending to reduce the federal deficit. In the words of one observer: 'Thus began a squaring off between the two most powerful ministers in the Chrétien Cabinet – Martin, who clearly had the support of a number of key colleagues as well as the business and financial community, and Axworthy, who was responsible for the largest single expenditure portfolio ($69 billion), and who had a reputation for being committed to people rather than the reduction of deficits' (Bakvis 1996, 139).

In the autumn of 1993 Martin organized a number of sessions with business leaders and selected economists to promote his deficit-reduction objectives. Axworthy in turn held a few well-publicized seminars with individuals and organizations in the social-welfare field to publicize his position. By early 1994 he had received enough support in cabinet to launch a package of social-policy reforms. In announcing his strategy in the House of Commons on 31 January 1994, he acknowledged that a reform program would have to assist the government's efforts at deficit reduction, but the main focus, he insisted, would be on more effective social policies, not on their reduction.

The reform process was to proceed in three stages. First, the House of Commons Standing Committee on Human Resources Development would hold hearings on social security and the labour market. Concurrently there would be a small task force to assist the minister in proposing reforms. These hearings and deliberations were to result in a 'Government Action Plan' by April 1994. Second, there would be more detailed discussion of the action plan. Third, development, tabling, and debate of legislation would follow, all to be accomplished by late 1994, with implementation in 1995.

The initial work seemed promising. The standing committee launched vigorously into its task and within a few months had travelled the land, gathering submissions from more than two hundred individuals and organizations (Battle and Torjman 1996, 54). By the end of March it had produced an interim report (Standing Committee 1994b). However, the February 1994 federal budget announced reductions of $5.5 billion over three years in (un)employment-insurance benefits. Federal social transfers to the provinces for welfare, social services, and post-secondary education would have to yield minimum savings of almost $2 billion in the two years 1995–7. Many people speculated, correctly as it turned out, that the underlying deficit-reduction plans of Finance would ultimately dominate the process. There were conflicts between the goals spelled out by the task force and those envisaged by the Social Security Review secretariat in HRDC (Bakvis 1996, 141). In addition, the provinces, led by Quebec, were wary of the process and forced cancellation of a federal–provincial meeting scheduled for April. That autumn the imminent Quebec election effectively closed the window on a federal–provincial agreement.

Meanwhile, the review process across the country continued, producing another twelve hundred briefs and an astonishing forty thousand responses to the discussion (green) paper tabled in the House of Commons on 5 October (Standing Committee 1994a). Clearly, Canadians were extremely concerned about the prospects of basic changes to Canada's social-safety net and wanted their concerns to affect government policy. The committee's work ended with its submission to Parliament of its final report on 6 February 1995 (Standing Committee 1995).

In the view of the task force, its work constituted one of the most thorough and comprehensive parliamentary reviews ever undertaken of Canadian social programs (Pulkingham and Ternowetsky 1996, 13). In general, there was widespread acceptance by the public of the need for its work. Many groups shared its view that some programs could be operated more efficiently and that current programs such as unemployment insurance and social assistance should be reformed in order to encourage re-entry of recipients into the workforce. There was at the same time vigorous opposition to major reductions in social services. The committee's recommendations were comprehensive and innovative, ranging from transfer of funds from (un)employment insurance to job retraining and from increased child benefits to direct support for post-secondary students.

What is important here is not the reform proposals as such, many of which never saw the light of day, but the changes to social programs that were actually enacted. The process resulted in such a complex set of proposals that few groups could be persuaded to support them and many opposed recommendations affecting their particular interest. For example, income-contingent repayment for students, which would have provided the federal government with a stronger presence in post-secondary education, was roundly condemned by student representatives. More crucial, however, was opposition from within government. In February 1995, at the very time that Axworthy was releasing the final report of his task force, the minister of finance issued the 1995 federal budget. This document effectively dictated how social reforms would be carried out. 'By the end of January 1995,' one observer notes, 'Axworthy had essentially conceded defeat' (Bakvis 1996, 142).

The 1995 budget announced that the Canada Assistance Plan (CAP) would be combined with Established Program Financing (EPF) for health and education, creating one gigantic block fund, the Canada Health and Social Transfer, or CHST. (Un)employment insurance was to be cut by $2 billion. Of that total saving, $800 million, the so-called UI reinvestment fund, was allocated to a Human Resources Investment Fund (HRIF), which, together with funds from other sources, was to support new employment training. The 1995 budget also announced that Ottawa was considering major changes to benefits for the elderly.

The primary focus was on the new CHST, which replaced federal cost sharing of provincial welfare and social services (under CAP) and transfers to the provinces for health and post-secondary education under EPF. The CHST came into effect on 1 April 1996. It was developed almost entirely within the Department of Finance, without broad consultation either with the public or with other departments, and displayed, in the words of one analyst, 'more evidence of federal expenditure control than of social program considerations' (Maslove 1996, 284).[1]

The main fiscal impact of the CHST has been to reduce transfers to the provinces, compared to what they would have received under the former CAP and EPF programs. Over the two years 1996–98 cash transfers to the provinces were scheduled to decline by about 33 per cent, or about $6 billion. Further smaller declines are planned in the future (Maslove 1996, 285). This change is already posing enormous problems for the provinces, for the municipalities that administer much of the social assistance, and, of course, for the recipients of aid. The cutbacks raise other concerns. For example, the sharp decline in EPF funds calls into question Ottawa's ability to uphold the basic principles of medicare, including comprehensiveness, universality, accessibility, and portability. The reduction in CAP funding is matched by a drop in standards previously imposed by the federal government. Under the old CAP, Ottawa insisted that social assistance be given solely on the basis of need, without requiring the recipients to meet other conditions (this prohibited workfare, for example). A minimum residence period for eligibility was prohibited, and appeals procedures had to be in place. Under CHST, a province needs to observe only one of these conditions – prohibition of a residence requirement.

The reductions in (un)employment-insurance benefits are being achieved through reductions in the level of benefits and in the duration of benefits and an increase in the qualifying period. The hundreds of thousands of seasonal workers across Canada, many of whom are women, will be especially hard hit. The new training programs might prove beneficial, though, as critics point out, at a time of high unemployment in many regions of Canada it is not clear how many jobs will be available for those who are retrained. In benefits for the elderly, the 1995 budget announced that the government was considering a family income test for Old Age Security (OAS). Changes of this type are planned for the year 2001.

Further alterations appear to be in the offing for the Canada Pension Plan. When the scheme was implemented in the mid-1960s, it was designed to replace 25 per cent of the working income of the average worker on retirement. OAS was to replace another 15 per cent. The slow elimination of the OAS through clawbacks, combined with forecast decreases, will gradually reduce the social security purchased by Canadians through their social investments to less than 25 per cent of their average income (Schellenberg 1996, 166). Greater reliance is obviously to be placed on private provisions – a not-altogether-reassuring prospect when one considers that in 1992 only half of people with incomes between $40,000 and $50,000 contributed to an RRSP, despite the considerable tax advantages, and less than half (47 per cent) participated in a registered pension plan. Only one-third of tax filers with incomes between $25,000 and $30,000 contributed to an RRSP, and slightly fewer to a private registered pension plan (166).

It has been estimated that between 1995 and 1999 a total of $15 billion will be taken out of EI, CAP, and the post-secondary-education component of EPF. When we combine this with reductions for health care, we see that about one-quarter of Canada's expenditure on social programs will be lost during those five years alone (Wiseman 1996, 122–3). All this is happening after a brief flurry of public discussion, which indicated wide-

New Property in Jobs and Social Investments   195

spread opposition to major cutbacks, and as a result of plans made largely in secret by government bodies with no experience in social policy. It is also taking place at a time when more than 1.2 million Canadians are unemployed, and several million more depend on some type of social assistance.

It is clear that many Canadians were completely unprepared for this massive change in the basic social fabric of the country. While they supported more effective programs, and some reduction in Canada's overall deficit, they did not want a substantial reduction in the social safety net nor movement away from the Keynesian welfare state towards what Jessop (1994) has called a 'Schumpetarian workfare state.' In fact, many feel that their basic property rights are being violated by recent government actions. Why are the investments of Canadians in social resources and income-security programs less protected from tampering than investments made in capital, land, and other physical assets?

A strong case can be made for extending traditional forms of protection for property to new forms of property, on which the vast majority of Canadians rely 'in their daily lives.' This would entail organizing society and tailoring government policy in ways that create greater access to employment and greater security while in employment. It would also mean that social programs deemed important by Canadians should be recognized as essential property rights and granted a degree of protection no less than that currently accorded to financial and physical forms of private property. It may well be necessary to create new forms of citizen-controlled institutions to protect these property rights from encroachment by private capital and by the state acting on its behalf or, alternatively, to provide constitutional guarantees of access to certain levels of service.

Conclusion:
Restructuring Property Rights

I am not an advocate for frequent changes in laws and constitutions, but laws and institutions must go hand in hand with the progress of the human mind. As that becomes more developed, more enlightened, as new discoveries are made, new truths discovered and manners and opinions change, with the change of circumstances, institutions must also advance to keep pace with the times.

The Jefferson Memorial, Washington, DC,
quoted in Davidson and Davidson 1988, 43

This study has revealed vast differences among people with respect to the merits they assign to different forms of property. Considerable momentum has been created in Canada and in several other Western nations in recent years favouring private property and the shrinking of the state sector. At the same time, many Canadians are concerned about possible erosion of the social benefits they have chosen to purchase through the state. A majority clearly continue to see the state as a bulwark against the insecurities of the marketplace. They are puzzled and angered that the state itself wishes to abdicate that role. There also remains widespread concern about the abuse of the environment by private producers and the support frequently given to such abuse by governments. Neither private nor state control of resources seems to ensure highly satisfactory results. Social discontent is also fostered by the weak response of governments and courts to Aboriginal property claims and by the failure of both private and public businesses to redistribute property rights within the workplace.

The different perceptions of property that lie behind the fears and conflicts just mentioned will obviously not be resolved easily, if ever. They

198 Whose Property?

underline a great need, however, for some new thinking about the nature of property and its current distribution in Canada, and they indicate that the time has come to change laws and institutions in accordance with the resulting findings.

It may be helpful to begin this discussion by noting one attribute of property on which virtually everyone seems to be agreed. My study has shown that whether people favour state property à la Lenin and Stalin, or common property à la scholars such as Macpherson and Grunebaum and Aboriginal peoples, or private property in accordance with the insights of Adam Smith, they all agree on one thing: it is essential for human beings to have property (i.e., to have sufficient control over sufficient resources in order not only to survive but to develop as free and mature persons). As several Canadian scholars have recently reminded us, the absence of property rights drastically diminishes our role as agents.

It is clearly incumbent on every just society therefore to allocate property rights broadly enough so that each citizen has enough rights to ensure both survival and personal development. There is at the same time, however, another requirement: to allocate property so that resources are used most productively, thereby improving the economic and social prospects of society as a whole. A fair distribution of property therefore has both a horizontal and a vertical dimension. There must be a wide dispersion of rights across society, creating a horizontal mosaic of property that at all times affords each citizen sufficient sustenance and opportunity for personal growth. There must also be a strategic distribution, so that those who aspire to use resources more productively, thereby raising the potential of all citizens to improve their lot, have the maximum opportunity to do so. This chapter examines how Canadians might restructure property rights legally, constitutionally, and organizationally, in order to enrich the democratic character of our society and, in the process, to provide greater justice and security for many citizens.

Horizontal and Vertical Dimensions

The historical survey contained in chapter 1 above showed how difficult it has been to achieve these twin objectives. Pre-capitalist societies in Europe created an intricate horizontal mosaic in which nearly everyone, regardless how poor, had guaranteed access to the basic resource – land. This pattern of property granted relative security to large segments of the population. However, because of its restrictions on personal freedom and mobility, and its prohibitions on the sale of land, little economic progress was possible. This arrangement condemned the vast majority of people to short lives of considerable misery, stunting both their immediate chances for personal growth and their future prospects.

The aggressive efforts of some landowners and merchants in late medieval England to use land more commercially gradually loosened the restrictions on labour mobility and land sale. This process was greatly facilitated by usurpation of political power by the landowning and merchant classes. The emerging property system shifted the balance in favour of the vertical dimension identified above, radically altering the horizontal mosaic, in which rights had been widely distributed. Property rights to land were increasingly consolidated in the hands of relatively few people. To the extent, however, that such people used their greater property holdings to increase productivity (and profits) by improving agricultural and commercial techniques, they laid a foundation for the eventual improvement of most people's lives.

The industrial revolution of the late eighteenth and early nineteenth centuries did not change the movement from widely dispersed rights emphasizing security to narrowly held rights favouring economic growth. If anything, it exacerbated the trend. Nevertheless, it produced in its wake a few subtle changes which had considerable long-term consequences. First, the leaders of the new industry challenged both the political and the economic hegemony of the previous leading classes – landowners and merchants. In Britain, for example, industrialists gradually gained control of the House of Commons – a movement culminating with repeal of the Corn Laws in the 1830s. This made Parliament into a more pluralistic centre of power, leading to its opening up to the demands of even more diverse groups less than a century later. In the economic sphere, some of the new industrialists eagerly espoused the individualistic, competitive doctrines of Adam Smith. This position challenged the protective stance that land-based industries, such as that in woollen cloth, had increasingly taken.

In their late-medieval take-over of real property, landowners had sometimes said to those who doubted their intentions that they were taking property into their own hands in order to free society for greater progress. This boast was not without merit (despite the justifiably cynical cry of some peasants that being freed from a lord was not a great bonus when it also meant being freed from the land). However, it was not long before the wealthy new landowners and merchants consolidated their position by imposing protective tariffs on competitive imports and by creating internal regulations, buttressed by royal charters and decrees, which supported monopolies. It became increasingly clear that freedom for the landed and commercial gentry meant little more than their freedom to protect themselves against economic and political challenges from others.

The new industrial class promoted a more individualistic concept of freedom: the freedom of each individual to compete with others and to pursue profit wherever possible. While this claim too often proved hollow – as Adam Smith himself anticipated when warning about the monopolistic proclivities of business people – it did create the basis for the growth of more individual freedoms, highlighted in the mid-nineteenth century by such diverse spokesmen for freedom as John Stuart Mill and Karl Marx and by substantial improvements in parliamentary democracy.

Second, industrial capitalism led to the growth of an urban culture, which created in its wake a more highly organized, literate, and politically conscious society. This process was undoubtedly assisted by a gradual but definite improvement in living standards in the second half of the nineteenth century. The gamble that a more consolidated holding of property rights would result in greater economic prosperity thus seemed finally, by the end of the century, to be paying off.

Industrial democracy has, however, been plagued by some fundamental contradictions. On the one hand, it has supported the development of basic democratic institutions and a culture promoting a wide range of individual human rights. On the other hand, it has restricted democratic practices largely to the political sphere, often actively stymying extension of such rights to the economic sphere. As noted in the introduction, it has done this in several ways: by throwing almost all its support behind private property, with its exclusionary features; by interpreting property largely in unitary terms, thereby stifling attempts to create a better sharing of property rights within business enterprises and within communities affected by business's resource use; by one-sidedly supporting the money purchase of property rights, thereby prejudicing the rights of major groups such as family partners, Aboriginal peoples, and workers who have claims based on occupation and participation; and finally by consistently overestimating the ability of a market economy to satisfy the basic needs of its participants, thereby underestimating the need for protective civic institutions that facilitate and honour a broad range of social investments.

Our system of industrial democracy has, in other words, created a serious imbalance between the horizontal and the vertical dimensions of property. It has given undue weight to the latter, allowing property to be consolidated in the hands of a small minority for the alleged purpose of spurring economic growth. The improvements in standard of living are not without merit, but we should remind ourselves of the many citizens whose lives remain highly insecure and impoverished. It is not a luxury to plan changes that might enlarge the scope of democratic practices in our society.

The market system, with its support of private property and its encouragement of the pursuit of profit, has the virtue of placing property rights strategically in the hands of those who are most likely to use resources most productively. This is an aspect of a just property system that has perhaps been neglected too much by those who are deeply interested in questions of justice. What the market system needs simultaneously, however, also in the name of justice, is democratic institutions which ensure that property rights are distributed horizontally as widely and as equally as possible (with due consideration to efficient allocation of resources). As two commentators observe: 'Nations are built on the motivating forces of both self-interest and civic values. When self-interest and civic values are combined, they reinforce each other so that a nation can enjoy both prosperity and justice. Difficulties arise when society is governed by only one of these two forces because you cannot buy justice in the marketplace, and similarly, you cannot build prosperity on civic pride alone' (Davidson and Davidson 1988, 1). This statement on a just society's twin responsibilities may be faulted only in that it fails to recognize the contribution of the market system to justice. The prosperity made possible by the market surely contributes to justice in so far as it enables more citizens to increase their enjoyment of the world and its resources. Without the encouragement of civic values, however, as the authors stress, the market's contribution to justice is highly questionable at best.

Finding Solutions

The basic problems in Canada's distribution and protection of property rights appear to be as follows. First, the productive resources of this country – land and capital – are controlled by a very small minority of its citizens. Second, old and new economic and social conditions leave many citizens without adequate property rights and protection of rights previously acquired. (This is especially true of single parents coping with the realities of the new family and Canadian social policies, of citizens affected by resource abuse, of Aboriginal peoples facing courts and governments that apply alien property concepts, of people who have property confiscated by the state without due process and adequate compensation, and of workers forced to engage in class warfare with employers because neither side envisages a prospect of sharing property rights in the workplace.) Third, the creation of 'new property,' in the form of jobs and social benefits, has not been recognized sufficiently by governments and therefore has not received the property protection that it requires.

Sharing Property Rights

The solution to the first problem – distributing property rights more broadly through society – requires first of all greater appreciation of the shared nature of property rights. The laws upholding private property rely too much on a unitary view of property. The owners of private businesses, for example, receive carte blanche to open, close, and move their operations, even in cases where it can be demonstrated that such actions will have profound and harmful effects on numerous citizens.

The neglect of a broader community of stakeholders is often apparent as well in the treatment of the environment by both private businesses and government. Existing laws on nuisance and riparian rights, to name examples, are obviously inadequate to protect all those people substantially affected by current resource users. What we require is incorporation in law of a broader concept of 'citizen rights.' Since Parliament and provincial legislatures have thus far failed to produce legislation adequately protecting such rights, the many citizens concerned about these issues will have to pursue other means of protection. One of the most essential means is to unite the numerous environmental groups into a stronger political alliance. In addition to protesting actions considered detrimental to community life, such an alliance could undertake several specific initiatives. A fundamental long-term initiative would be to obtain a constitutional amendment requiring governments to provide greater protection for the environment (see above, 136–8).

Another initiative must be to put increased pressure on the federal government to increase financial support to organizations acting on behalf of citizens' concerns. An immediate task is to protest recent cuts to such government support, while at the same time Ottawa continues to provide tax relief to businesses that incur expenses while lobbying the govern-

Conclusion: Restructuring Property Rights   203

ment on behalf of projects that may harm a community (see Cardozo 1996 for numerous examples of the federal government's reduced support to opponents of its social cutbacks and of the support granted to business lobbies). As my study has shown, most Canadians are profoundly concerned about the protection of what I term 'citizen rights.' One therefore remains hopeful that substantial reforms in this area are possible.

The failure of both governments and private resource owners to appreciate and support the shared nature of property rights is also very apparent in the distribution of property rights in most workplaces. Apart from the fact that a minority of workers in Canada (about 40 per cent) are able to influence a narrow range of conditions in their workplace through collective bargaining, workers have virtually no property rights in their places of employment. Reforms in this area will depend very much on government initiatives.

The two major combatants in the workplace – workers and management – are like two hockey players wearily fighting it out at centre ice. They are both tired, and both in calmer moments may have given some thought to better means of resolving conflict. However, at this moment neither can afford to be seen to give up. They keep clutching each other, hoping quietly that the referee will step in so that they can disengage themselves without losing face. It is time in labour–management relations for the state to step in as referee, to pull the combatants apart, and to put in place new procedures for dealing with conflict. Next to Italy, Canada has in the last few decades lost more work time to industrial strife than any other advanced economy.

Grounds for conflict in the workplace will never disappear. Most corporations will continue to feature ownership by outside shareholders, and the managerial representatives of these owners will continue to have ideas that differ from those of other employees about how work should be organized and how the 'pie' ought to be split up. Interesting but rare experiments in worker ownership will not change this situation. Improvements may emerge gradually through broader-scope collective bargaining. This, as this study has shown, is already happening.

However, there is something that the state can do to reduce significantly the grounds for conflict. As chapter 6 illustrated, it can help to redistribute some of the ownership rights within firms in favour of workers. It can do so without destroying the corporation and without in any way making it more 'socialistic.' The secret, of course, lies in the shared nature of property within the enterprise. Rights are already shared between managers and shareholders, and to a much lesser extent between workers and managers. Economies such as Austria, Germany, Sweden, and others have shown that industrial conflict can be greatly reduced by going even further and placing worker representatives on boards of directors. An attempt was made to legislate such a reform on the federal level in Canada in the early 1980s, but the government's half-hearted commitment to it ensured its failure (see above, 167). One of the most useful things that both provincial and federal governments might do in the near future is to implement such a reform. This move would restore to workers some of the property rights that the private-property system took from them, and it would also constitute belated extension of democratic principles into the workplace.

Broader Participation

Our discussion of possible solutions began by examining some implications of the narrow property-ownership base in Canada, as mentioned in the first point above. In the process of discussing these implications, I have dealt with the major property grievances of some groups, such as citizens and workers, mentioned in the second point. It is time now to consider appropriate responses to the concerns of other groups identified in the second point.

Chapter 3 described how female partners in marriage whose property rights were previously not recognized after the breakdown of the partnership have managed in the last few decades to establish significant rights for themselves. This reform has been accompanied, however, by legal interpretations that emphasize the autonomy or independence of those left on their own after a breakup. Many feminists welcome this change. Others, however, point to significant hardships experienced particularly by women who are left with the care of children and find it difficult, if not impossible, to re-enter the workforce at a level that will give them adequate support. To compound the problem, these single parents usually get little support from former spouses who have gone on to other relationships, and they find it increasingly harder to obtain adequate social-welfare benefits. Preaching 'family values' and urging on such parents greater job-seeking initiative seem like satisfactory solutions only to those who do not face such a situation. The state cannot absolve itself of major responsibilities in this matter. Several provinces are already taking steps to plug the loopholes that permit spouses to shirk financial responsibility for their children and for their ex-spouses. More concerted efforts are required, however. Surely in an era of vastly improved information networks it should not be difficult for governments to track down spouses who are failing to provide support and to enforce orders that make them pay. Political will still seems to be the missing ingredient.

Studies of income distribution in Canada show that approximately 60 per cent of all single parents live below the poverty line. Anyone who has carefully studied these lines and has applied them to his or her own situation knows that they are not extremely generous. People who live below them are not able to afford many of the amenities that we consider necessary for personal growth and enjoyment. The state must commit itself to income programs that help to lift these people above the poverty line. The recent child-tax credits represent a move in the right direction (see above, 190).

The federal government should also seriously reconsider introducing a more effective type of guaranteed annual income. We already have a form of guaranteed income in place. The elderly are supported through various types of pension programs. Other citizens are entitled to enough social benefits for basic sustenance. What is needed is a more effective program, which will both provide greater support for those, such as the disabled and single parents, who are unable to enter the workforce, and also reduce the disincentives that currently discourage people on social welfare from taking jobs. The Macdonald Commission of the mid-1980s recommended just such a reform. Ottawa eagerly adopted the free-trade recommendations of that commission – encouraged by the business community – but it has done nothing with the equally strong recommendation to provide greater income support to the needy through a form of guaranteed income. Without such reforms, large groups of Canadians, particularly single parents, will continue to experience the pain of a socially inadequate distribution of property.

The property grievances of Canada's Aboriginal peoples are slowly being dealt with on both provincial and federal levels. Recent agreements in British Columbia and the settlement of Inuit claims in northern Canada seem to bode well for the future. However, as chapter 4 demonstrated, both the court system and the various levels of government have been much too slow to accommodate law to the property concepts used by Aboriginal peoples when advancing their claims. Both the common law of English-speaking Canada and the civil law of Quebec contain principles of interpretation that, if applied by governments and courts with enough will and cultural tolerance, should produce more favourable results than have so far been experienced by many Aboriginal groups. The public itself will have to display a greater spirit of generosity and cultural sensitivity if progress on the legal and legislative front is to speed up. That, unfortunately, cannot be legislated. In the absence of such a spirit, there is every reason to expect more violent conflicts between Aboriginal peoples and non-Aboriginals.

The property grievances of those whose property is confiscated by the state should be addressed as quickly as possible through a constitutional amendment. Such an enactment should not necessarily go as far as the property amendments contained in the U.S. constitution. As noted above (52), these impose three basic conditions on government 'expropriation': that it follow fair procedures, include fair compensation, and serve a public purpose. The last obligation particularly worries governments in Canada, which fear that it might restrict their ability to use private resources for purposes whose public value is not easily proven in court. There is no reason, however, to delay considering an amendment containing the first two conditions. It seems unfair that citizens are not assured of due process and fair compensation when governments take their property.

'New Property'

The new forms of property mentioned in the third point above – jobs and social benefits – require much more property protection than they receive at present. I acknowledged in the discussion of jobs in chapter 7 that it would be unrealistic for a market economy to guarantee jobs for everyone. I also noted how contract law, collective bargaining, government legislation, and court application of standards of natural justice have already helped to make many jobs more secure than they were in the past. None the less, job security has recently been diminishing, and, unless there is a reversal of the current policies of radical downsizing, people will find it more difficult both to obtain jobs and to hold on to them. This makes it more imperative than ever to support programs such as (un)employment insurance that reduce the costs of losing a job and to implement reforms that can increase job security.

One possible reform has already been noted: requiring corporations to arrange for the election of workers to their governing boards. Where this has happened, workers have been able to get their companies to pay much more attention to their needs in times of downsizing or relocation. No one can prevent a company from moving, selling, or reducing the size of its operation, but a sharing of rights among those most affected by such actions can considerably reduce their insecurity and personal loss.

In addition, provincial legislatures might well consider the type of law adopted in Pennsylvania to protect the interest of various stakeholders when local businesses are bought up by outsiders. There is nothing sacred about the exclusive rights now enjoyed by shareholders, and government actions of this type do not, as the U.S. business press tried to imply, pose a serious threat to private property. What they do show is that with the right vision and some legislative will the people's representatives can act in the interests of a broader community, not just on behalf of one group of investors.

Recent government actions clearly threaten the social benefits that Canadians have chosen to purchase through the state, including health care, education, pensions, and social welfare. Because several provinces as well as Ottawa seem to be responding largely to signals from the business community, not to the many citizens who wish to see such support programs maintained, new ways have to be found to protect services. It may be that only new forms of citizen-controlled institutions could guarantee services against the whims of government. Perhaps nothing short of a constitutional amendment will be adequate to guarantee protection of such property. Such an amendment, of course, could not be accomplished without citizens placing tremendous pressure, electoral and otherwise, on those very bodies that are now acting against their interests.

Conclusion

This study has shown that Canadians wish to see a number of basic property rights protected and enlarged. I have argued that reforms which respond to such wishes will, in most cases, merely represent a very belated attempt to extend to the economic realm democratic practices long accepted in the political sphere. Though many of the property rights recommended in this book evaporated in the course of the growth of a capitalist market economy based on private property, I have attempted to show that their reintroduction would not threaten either the existence or the performance of our basic institutions. Neither do they require introduction of radically new laws. Nevertheless, a serious question hangs over the possibility of their adoption. It arises from the way in which social and economic policy decisions are made in this country. The charge made by some scholars – that our liberal, democratic, and capitalist society is hierarchical and so structured as to protect the interests of the business class at the expense of other interests – deserves to be taken seriously.

A number of studies cited in this work leave no doubt whatsoever that the business community, particularly the leadership of its largest corporations, has a disproportionate influence in shaping the country's public policies. Through lobby groups, business-sponsored 'think tanks,' special access to government ministers, and control of much of the media, it is able to influence the public perception of what governments ought to be doing as well as influence governments into doing those things. Both by training and by natural instinct, however, members of this group are not inclined to think about the public interest. By suggesting that the policies they promote are meant to support primarily their own long-term interests, one is not imputing to them devious motives. They are doing precisely what they insist they are always doing: improving the 'bottom line' of their corporations. What is good for business, however, is not necessarily good for the country.

This is a serious problem in every democratic society. Walter Eucken, one of the great economists of this century, a strong defender of free markets, and an architect of the postwar West German economic recovery, issued this warning: 'Once monopolistic bodies have begun to flourish in a state, they gain considerable political influence, so considerable that the state itself becomes incapable of exercising effective control' (Eucken 1951, 35).

Business enterprise is helped in this endeavour by a pattern of property rights that emphasizes the vertical dimension. I have stressed that a just society cannot neglect this dimension. However, a truly just society, one that attempts to promote democratic rights in all areas where decisions affecting life are made, must put an equal, if not greater, emphasis on the horizontal distribution of rights.

The horizontal dimension of Canada's property mosaic is in great need of repair. A question hangs over this study: will governments and courts, influenced as they are by a small segment of society that promotes its own interests, show greater willingness to support private groups, as well as new laws and constitutional amendments, that advance the interests and the democratic rights of a much larger segment of society?

Notes

Introduction

1 In strictly legal terms, no one owns the corporation. It has an independent existence of its own. Shareholders merely purchase a fractional interest in its assets and are virtually insulated from the risks that it takes. However, this study defines property ownership more broadly in terms of decision-making rights (see chapter 1), and from this perspective shareholders possess some of the major rights normally attributed to ownership.

1: The Evolution of Property Rights

1 There are two competing theories of landholding: allodial and tenurial. Under allodial theory, ownership rights pertain to the thing itself. This theory applies to personal things, or chattels, such as a book or an automobile. However, in the English system of landholding, which was introduced into Canada, the tenurial theory applies. Under this theory, all land is owned by the crown and remains in the crown notwithstanding a crown grant. A person cannot own land but is, strictly speaking, a tenant of the crown. What the person owns is an 'interest' or 'estate' in land. 'An estate may be defined as an abstract entity that is interposed between the tenant and the land itself: the concept of ownership is detached from the land and attaches to this abstraction' (Gillese 1990, 8:1). There are two types of estates: 'freehold,' which is held indefinitely, and 'leasehold,' which has a fixed term. Freehold was an integral part of the feudal system; leasehold was recognized later. Of the three types of freehold estates, 'fee simple' is the nearest thing to full ownership, conferring rights of use, enjoyment, and disposal.

2 Outside Quebec the courts were obliged until 1949 to follow the principles of

English common law, if it was not inconsistent with Canadian legislation, which was always paramount. The final arbiter was the Judicial Committee of the Privy Council in London. Statute laws were, however, innovative in interpreting those principles in response to local needs (Lederman 1958, 34; Shaw 1973, 253).

3 Armstrong and Nelles (1973) theorize that it is in the interest of big business to have government decision-making centralized, to encourage greater rationalization. This goal was accomplished in the United States. 'As a national business and financial community began to emerge in Canada ... its members attempted to do the same thing. They failed' (20).

2: State versus Private Property

1 James Grunebaum (1987, 173 and 177) maintains that a private-property system, even with enough resources, equally distributed, does not secure individual autonomy and freedom. Autonomy and freedom require 'social and not individual control of land and resource use ... Everyone in the community must be able to participate in decisions about how *all* the land and resources are used.'
2 'Economies of scale' are the lower unit costs for large firms; 'market power' consists of the advantages of large size that are unrelated to improvements in production efficiency – for example, greater influence on government policy, easier access to financial markets, and increased ability to counter competition through advertising and other means.
3 The seminal work on this subject remains *The Modern Corporation and Private Property*, by Berle and Means (1932).
4 The crown corporations discussed here are firms with a separate legal entity, as distinct from government agencies, which operate directly under the control of a ministry and only incidentally produce goods for the market.
5 For links to the British program see Tupper and Doern 1982, 6. They also describe the role played by the business community (12).
6 Some have argued that section 7 of the Charter of Rights and Freedoms, which protects the 'right to life, liberty, and security of the person,' implicitly protects the right to property. However, such arguments have failed before the courts, and one Supreme Court justice has clearly stated that this section will not be used to protect those rights that are 'purely economic' (quoted in *Financial Post*, 7 Aug. 1989, 10).
7 'Transactions costs' include costs of negotiating and enforcing contracts.
8 A leading Canadian expert on health care maintains that privatization, 'in the sense of moving back to more payment by users and private insurance,' would

undoubtedly lead to higher overall costs (particularly administrative costs), lower efficiency and greater inequity. 'What it would do is lower the share of costs carried by the healthy and the wealthy' (Robert Evans 1993, 37).

3: Family Law and Family Property

1 The political and economic aspirations of Quebec, which may cause Canada's boundaries to be redrawn, are not treated in this study. More than one book would be necessary for that subject.

5: Citizen Property Rights

1 There are also positive externalities, or external benefits not adequately reflected in the price of a product. For example, if some people wish to be educated and others do not, even those who refuse to attend school may benefit from those who do. A case can be made that the external benefits of education should be credited to those who are being educated and debited to those who are not. This justifies an education tax on everyone, permitting subsidization of those being educated. This tax enables the price of being educated to be reduced and the quantity to be increased, reflecting the true net cost of education and its value to society. In this study my concern is largely with negative externalities.

6: New Property Rights in the Workplace

1 Many cooperatives, such as credit unions, do not belong in this category. Employees in these organizations are subject to managers hired by member-shareholders, and the internal working arrangements parallel those of other capitalist organizations.

7: New Property in Jobs and Social Investments

1 As Maslove (1996, 285) notes, the March 1996 budget made some adjustments, which were a partial response to some of the social-policy concerns raised over the intervening year.

References

Adelman, Jeremy. 1994. *Frontier Development: Land, Labour, and Capital on the Wheatlands of Argentina and Canada, 1890–1914.* Oxford: Clarendon Press.
Aharoni, Yair. 1981. 'Managerial Discretion.' In Raymond Vernon and Yair Aharoni, eds., *State-Owned Enterprise in the Western Economies.* London: Croon Helm.
Alchian, A. 1972. 'Corporate Management and Property Rights.' In Erik Furubotn and Svetosar Pejovich, eds., *The Economics of Property Rights*, Cambridge: Ballinger Publishing. chap. 9.
Alchian, A., and Demsetz, Harold. 1972. 'Production, Information Costs, and Economic Organization.' *American Economic Review* 62 (Dec.), 777–95.
Anastassopoulos, Jean-Pierre. 1985. 'State-Owned Enterprises: Between Autonomy and Dependency.' *Journal of Public Policy* 5 (Oct.), 521–39.
Anderson, Terry L., ed. 1992. *Property Rights and Indian Economics.* Boston: Rowan and Littlefield.
Anton, Frank R. 1980. *Worker Participation: Prescription for Industrial Change.* Calgary: Detselig Enterprises.
Armstrong, Christopher, and Nelles, H.V. 1973. 'Private Property in Peril: Ontario Businessmen and the Federal System, 1899–1911.' In Glenn Porter and Robert D. Cuff, eds., *Enterprise and National Development, Essays in Canadian Business and Economic History*, 20–38. Toronto: Hakkert.
Asch, Michael. 1984. 1984, *Home and Native Land: Aboriginal Rights and the Canadian Constitution.* Toronto: Methuen.
Augustine, Philip W. 1986. 'Protection of the Right to Property under the Canadian Charter of Rights and Freedoms.' *Ottawa Law Review* 18, 55–81.
Avila, Charles, 1983. *Ownership: Early Christian Teaching.* Maryknoll, NY: Orbis Books.
Baker, C. Edwin. 1986. 'Property and Its Relation to Constitutionally Protected Liberty.' *University of Pennsylvania Law Review* 134 (April), 741–816.
Bakvis, Herman. 1996. 'Shrinking the House of HRIF: Program Review and the

Department of Human Resources Development.' In Swimmer, ed. (1996), 133–70.
Bartlett, Richard H. 1985. 'Reserve Lands.' In Morse, ed. (1985), 467–578.
Barton, Stephen E. 1983. 'Property Rights and Human Rights.' *Journal of Economic Issues* 17, no. 4. (Dec.), 915–30.
Barzel, Yoran, 1989. *Economics Analysis of Property Rights* Cambridge: Cambridge University Press.
Battle, Ken. 1990. 'Social Policy by Stealth.' *Policy Options* 11 no. 2, 17–29. Published under the pseudonym 'Grattan Gray.'
Battle, Ken, and Torjman, Sherri. 1996. 'Desperately Seeking Substance: A Commentary on the Social Security Review.' In Pulkingham and Ternowetsky (1996b), 52–65.
Bazelon, David. 1970. 'What Is Property'? In David Mermelstein, ed., *Economics: Mainstream Readings and Radical Critiques*, 53–60. New York: Random House.
Beck, Stanley M. 1985. 'Corporate Power in Canada.' In Bernier and Lajoie, eds. (1985), 182–219.
Becker, Lawrence C. 1977. *Property Rights, Philosophic Foundations*. London: Routledge & Kegan Paul.
Belobaba, Edward P. 1985. 'The Development of Consumer Protection Legislation, 1945 to 1984.' In Bernier and Lajoie, eds. (1985), 1–88.
Berger, Thomas R. 1985. *A Long and Terrible Shadow: White Values, Native Rights in the Americas 1492–1992*. Vancouver: Douglas and MacIntyre.
Berle, Adolf A., Jr., and Means, Gardner C. 1932. *The Modern Corporation and Private Property*. New York: Commerce Clearing House.
Bernier, Ivan, and Lajoie, Andrée. 1985. *Consumer Protection, Environmental Law and Corporate Power*. Research Studies, vol. 50. Toronto: University of Toronto Press and the Royal Commission on the Economic Union and Development Prospects for Canada.
– 1986. *Family Law and Social Welfare Legislation in Canada*. Research Studies, vol. xx. Toronto: University of Toronto Press and Royal Commission on the Economic Union and Development Prospects for Canada.
Bernstein, Claire. 1990. 'Court Ruling Means Marriage is a Business,' *Winnipeg Free Press,* April 8, 16.
Blair, Margaret M. 1995. *Ownership and Control: Rethinking Corporate Governance for the Twenty-first Century*. Washington, DC: Brookings Institution.
Bliss, Michael. 1980. 'Rich by Nature, Poor by Policy: The State and Economic Life in Canada.' In R. Kenneth Carty and W. Peter Ward, eds., *Entering the Eighties: Canada in Crisis*, 78–90. Toronto: Oxford University Press.
Boardman, Robert, ed. 1992. *Canadian Environmental Policy: Ecosystems, Politics, and Process*. Don Mills Ont.: Oxford University Press.

Borins, Sanford F., and Boothman, Barry E.C. 1985. 'Crown Corporations and Economic Efficiency.' In McFetridge, ed. (1985), 75–130.
Bosworth, Derek L. 1986. *Intellectual Property Rights.* Oxford: Pergamon Press.
Bowles, Samuel, and Gintis, Herbert. 1986. *Democracy and Capitalism: Property, Community, and the Contradictions of Modern Social Thought.* New York: Basic Books.
Bowles, Samuel, Gintis, Herbert, and Gustafsson, Bo. 1993. *Markets and Democracy: Participation, Accountability and Efficiency.* Cambridge: Cambridge University Press.
Brooks, Stephen. 1987. *Who's in Charge? The Mixed Ownership Corporation in Canada.* Halifax: Institute for Research on Public Policy.
– 1993. *Public Policy in Canada,* 2nd ed. Toronto: McClelland & Stewart.
Brown, Lester R. 1996. *State of the World 1996.* New York: W.W. Norton & Company and Worldwatch Institute.
Brown, M. Paul. 1992. 'Organizational Design as Policy Instrument: Environment Canada in the Canadian Bureaucracy.' In Boardman, ed. (1992), 24–42.
Brubaker, Elizabeth. 1995. *Property Rights in the Defense of Nature.* Toronto: Environment Probe.
Buchanan, James M. 1975. *The Limits of Liberty: Between Anarchy and Leviathan.* Chicago: University of Chicago Press.
Buchele, Robert, and Christiansen, Jens, 1995. 'Worker Rights Promote Productivity Growth.' *Challenge* (Sept.–Oct.), 32–7.
Canada, Parliament. 1981. *Minutes of Proceedings and Evidence of the Special Joint Committee of the Senate and of the House of Commons on the Constitution of Canada.* Ottawa, Friday 23 Jan. 44: 12.
Canadian Bar Association. 1988. *Aboriginal Rights in Canada: An Agenda for Action.* Ottawa.
Cardozo, Andrew. 1996. 'Lion Taming: Downsizing the Opponents of Downsizing.' In Swimmer, ed. (1996), 303–36.
Carnoy, Martin, and Shearer, Derek. 1980. *Economic Democracy: The Challenge of the 1980s.* White Plains, NY: M.E. Sharpe.
Carson, Rachel. 1962. *Silent Spring.* Boston: Houghton Mifflin.
Cassidy, Gordon. 1994. 'Contracting Out.' School of Policy Studies, Queen's University, Study no. 94-106 for the Government and Competitiveness Project.
Caves, D.W., and Christensen, L.R. 1980. 'The Relative Efficiency of Public and Private Firms in a Competitive Environment: The Case of Canadian Railroads.' *Journal of Political Economy* (Oct.), 938–76.
CFH. 1995. *Bulletin of the Canadian Federation of the Humanities* 17 (winter), 22–6.
Clement, Wallace. 1975. *The Canadian Corporate Elite: An Analysis of Economic Power.* Toronto: McClelland & Stewart, Carleton Library.

Conklin, David W. 1991. *Comparative Economic Systems*. New York: Cambridge University Press.

Connaghan, C.J. 1976. *Partnership or Marriage of Convenience?* Ottawa: Labour Canada.

Corcoran, Terence. 1995. 'Property Rights Only Answer for Fishery.' *Globe and Mail Report on Business*, 16 March.

Courchene, Thomas J. 1980. 'Towards a Protected Society: The Politicization of Economic Life.' *Canadian Journal of Economics* 13 (Nov.).

– 1985. 'Privatization: Palliative or Panacea?' In Tom Kierans and W.T. Stanbury, eds., *Papers on Privatization*. Montreal: Institute for Research on Public Policy.

– 1987. *Social Policy in the 1990s*. Toronto: C.D. Howe Institute.

Coval, S., Smith, J.C., and Coval, Simon. 1986. 'The Foundations of Property and Property Law.' *Cambridge Law Journal* 45 no. 3 (Nov.), 457–75.

Cox, Bruce Allen. 1991. *Native People, Native Lands*. Ottawa: Carleton University Press.

Craik, Elizabeth. 1984. *Marriage and Property Rights*. Aberdeen: Aberdeen University Press.

Craven, Paul. 1980. *An Impartial Umpire: Industrial Relations and the Canadian State, 1900–1911*. Toronto: University of Toronto Press.

Cribbet, J. 1975. *Principles of the Law of Property*, 2nd ed. Mineola, NY: Foundation Press.

– 1986. 'Concepts in Transition: The Search for a New Definition of Property.' *University of Illinois Law Review* 1, 1–42.

Cumming, Peter A. 1973. 'Native Rights and Law in an Age of Protest.' *Alberta Law Review*, 11.

Cumming, Peter A., and Mickenberg, N.H., eds. 1972. *Native Rights in Canada*, 2nd ed. Toronto: Indian Eskimo Association of Canada.

Dahl, Robert A. 1985. *A Preface to Economic Democracy*. Berkeley: University of California Press.

Dahlman, Carl J. 1980. *The Open Field System and Beyond: A Property Rights Analysis of an Economic Institution*. Cambridge: Cambridge University Press.

Dales, J.H. 1993. 'Land, Water, and Ownership.' In Dorfman and Dorfman, eds. (1993), 225–40.

Daly, Herman E., and John B. Cobb, Jr. 1989. *For the Common Good: Redirecting the Economy toward Community, the Environment, and a Sustainable Future*. Boston: Beacon Press.

Damsell, Keith. 1996. 'Whose Land Is It Anyway?' *Financial Post*. 2 March, 7.

Davidson, Greg, and Davidson, Paul. 1988. *Economics for a Civilized Society*. New York: W.W. Norton.

Davies, Maureen. 1985. 'Aspects of Aboriginal Rights in International Law.' In Morse, ed. (1985), 16–47.

Davis, Carole O. 1984. 'A Recommendation for Family Maintenance in the United States: A Comparative Study of Canadian and American Provisions for Support of Dependents.' *Canadian–American Law Journal* 2 (spring), 151–75.
De Alessi, Louis. 1973. 'Private Property and Dispersion of Ownership in Large Corporations.' *Journal of Finance*, 28, 839–51.
– 1980. 'The Economics of Property Rights: A Review of the Evidence.' *Research in Law and Economics* 2, 1–47.
Demsetz, Harold. 1967. 'Toward a Theory of Property Rights.' *American Economic Review* no. 57 (May), 347–59.
Dietz, Gottfried. 1971. *In Defense of Property*. Baltimore: Johns Hopkins University Press.
Donahue, John D. 1989. *The Privatization Decision*. New York: Basic Books.
Dorfman, Robert, and Dorfman, Nancy, eds. 1993. *Economics of the Environment*, 3rd ed. New York. W.W. Norton.
Drache, Daniel, and Glasbeek, Harry. 1992. *The Changing Workplace: Reshaping Canada's Industrial Relations System*. Toronto: James Lorimer & Company.
Dragun, A.K. 1987. 'Property Rights in Economic Theory.' *Journal of Economic Issues* 21, no. 2 (June), 859–68.
Dufour, Jules. 1991. 'Toward Sustainable Development of Canada's Forests.' Mitchell, ed. (1991), 85–109.
Economic Council of Canada. 1985. 'The Scope of Regulation in Canada.' In K.J. Rea and Nelson Wiseman, eds., *Government and Enterprise in Canada*. Toronto: Methuen.
– 1986. *Changing Times*, Twenty-third annual review. Ottawa.
Economist. 1993. 'Selling the State.' 21 Aug., 18–20, 19 June, 112.
Eichler, M. 1983. *Families in Canada Today: Recent Changes and Their Policy Consequences*. Toronto: Gage.
Elden, J. Maxwell. 1981. 'Political Efficacy at Work.' *American Political Science Review* (March). 43–58.
Ellerman, David P. 1984. 'Theory of Legal Structure: Worker Co-operatives.' *Journal of Economic Issues* 18 (Sept.), 861–92.
Elliott, David W. 1985. In Morse, ed. (1985), 48–121.
Eucken, Walter. 1951. *This Unsuccessful Age*. Edinburgh: William Hodge.
Evans, Patricia. 1988. 'Work Incentives and the Single Mother.' *Canadian Public Policy* 14 no. 2 (June), 125–36.
Evans, Robert. 1993. 'Less is More: Contrasting Styles in Health Care.' In Thomas, ed. (1993), 21–41.
Filyk, Gregor, and Cote, Ray. 1992. 'Pressures from Inside: Advisory Groups and the Environmental Policy Community.' In Boardman, ed. (1992), 60–82.
Forsyth, Murray. 1971. *Property and Property Distribution Policy*. London: PEP.

Friedman, Milton. 1962. *Capitalism and Freedom*. Chicago: University of Chicago Press.
Friesen, Gerald. 1984. *The Canadian Prairies: A History*. Toronto: University of Toronto Press.
Fulton, Murray E., ed. 1990. *Co-operative Organizations and Canadian Society: Popular Institutions and Dilemmas of Change*. Toronto: University of Toronto Press.
Furubotn, E., and Pejovich, S. 1972. 'Property Rights and Economic Theory, A Review of Recent Literature.' *Journal of Economic Literature* no. 10, 1137–62.
Fusfeld, Daniel R. 1983. 'Labor-Managed and Participatory Firms: A Review Article.' *Journal of Economic Issues* (Sept.), 769–89.
Gall, Gerald L. 1977. *The Canadian Legal System*, Toronto: Carswell.
Gauthier, David A. 1991. 'The Sustainability of Wildlife.' In Mitchell, ed. (1991), 110–29.
Gillen, D.W., Oum, T.H., and Tretheway, M.W. 1989. 'Privatization of Air Canada.' *Canadian Public Policy* 15 no. 3 (Sept.), 285–99.
Gillese, Eileen E. 1990. *Property Law: Cases, Text, and Materials*, 2nd ed. Toronto: Edward Montgomery Publications.
Ginsberg, Morris. 1965. *On Justice in Society*. London: Heinemann.
Glendon, Mary Ann. 1981. *The New Family and the New Property*. Toronto: Butterworths.
Gordon, H. Scott. 1993. 'The Economic Theory of a Common-Property Resource: The Fishery.' In Dorfman and Dorfman, eds. (1993), 97–108.
Gordon, Marsha. 1981. *Government in Business*. Montreal: C.D. Howe Institute.
Grant, George, 1970. *Lament for a Nation: The Defeat of Canadian Nationalism*. Toronto: McClelland & Stewart.
Green, T.H. 1982. *Lectures on the Principle of Political Obligation*. London.
Greenberg, E.S. 1975. 'The Consequences of Worker Participation: A Clarification of the Theoretical Literature.' *Social Science Quarterly* 56 no. 52 (Sept.), 190–209.
– 1981. 'Industrial Self-Management and Political Attitudes.' *American Political Science Review* (March), 29–42.
Greenwood, John. 1993. 'This Land Is My Land.' *Financial Post* (March), 17–22.
Grunebaum, James O. 1987. *Private Ownership*. London: Routledge & Kegan Paul.
Gyllenhammar, P.G. 1977. 'How Volvo Adapts People to Work.' *Harvard Business Review* (July–Aug.), 102–13.
Hardin, Garrett. [1968] 1993. 'The Tragedy of the Commons.' In Dorfman and Dorfman, eds. (1993). First published in *Science* 162 (Dec. 1968), 1243–8.
Harker, Paul. 1991. 'Energy and Minerals in Canada.' In Mitchell, ed. (1991), 180–202.
Harris, R. Cole, and Warkentin, John. 1991. *Canada before Confederation: A Study in Historical Geography*. Ottawa: Carleton University Press.

Hayek, Friedrich von. 1944. *The Road to Serfdom*. Chicago: University of Chicago Press.

Heidenreich, C.E. 1971. *A History and Geography of the Huron Indians, 1600–1650*. Toronto: McClelland & Stewart.

Held, Virginia. 1980. *Property, Profits, and Economic Justice*. Belmont, Calif.: Wadsworth Publishing.

Hill, Steven. 1995. 'Stakeholders versus Stockholders.' *Humanist* (March–April), 17–21.

Hirsch, Fred. 1976. *The Social Limits to Growth*. Cambridge, Mass.: Harvard University Press.

Hobbes, Thomas. 1983. *De Cive*. First pub. 1647. Oxford: Clarendon Press.

Hoggett, Brenda. 1987. 'Recent Reforms in Family Law: Progress or Backlash?' *Dalhousie Law Journal* 11 no. 1 (Sept.), 5–20.

Hollowell, Peter G. 1982. *Property and Social Relations*. London: Heinemann.

Honoré, A.M. 1961. 'Ownership.' In A.G. Guest, ed., *Oxford Essays in Jurisprudence*, 107–47. Oxford: Oxford University Press.

Hume, David. 1955. *An Abstract of a Treatise of Human Nature* in *Philosophical Essays Concerning Human Understanding*. Indianapolis: Bobbs-Merill.

Iacocca, Lee, and Novak, William. 1984. *Iacocca: An Autobiography*. Toronto: Bantam Books.

Industry Canada. 1995. *Corporate Decision-Making in Canada*. Calgary: University of Calgary Press.

International Labour Organization (ILO). 1974. *Workers' Participation in Decisions within Undertakings*. Labour–Managements Series, No. 48. Geneva: ILO.

Ip, Greg. 1990. 'More Millionaires Than Ever.' *Financial Post*, 17 Dec., 3.

Jay, Peter. 1980. 'The Workers' Cooperative Economy.' In Alasdair Clayre, ed., *The Political Economy of the Third Sector: Cooperation and Participation*. Oxford: Oxford University Press.

Jessop, Bob. 1994. 'Post-Fordism and the State.' In Ash Amin, ed, *Post-Fordism: A Reader*. Oxford: Blackwell.

Johnston, Richard, 1985. *Public Opinion and Public Policy in Canada*. Toronto: University of Toronto Press.

Joyce, Greg. 1993. 'B.C. Court Squashes Land Claim Ruling.' *Financial Post*, 26 June, 10.

Kealey, Gregory S. 1980. *Toronto Workers Respond to Industrial Capitalism, 1867–1892*. Toronto: University of Toronto Press.

Keet, Jean E. 1990–1. 'The Law Reform Process, Matrimonial Property and Farm Women: A Case Study of Saskatchewan, 1980–1986.' *Canadian Journal of Women and the Law* 4, 166–89.

Keon, Jim. 1986. 'Intellectual Property Protection in Canada: The Technology Challenge.' *Canada–United States Law Journal* 11, 27–50.

Kierans, Thomas E. 1984. 'Privatization if Necessary But Not Necessarily Privatization.' Halifax: Institute for Research on Public Policy, Nov.

– 1986. *Re-Mixing the Economy*. Montreal: Institute for Research on Public Policy.

Kitchen, B. 1984. 'Women's Dependence.' *Atkinson Review* 11, no. 2.

Kitchen, Harry. 1994. 'Private Provision of Public Services.' Paper prepared as basis for discussion at a conference on privatization, Economics Department, University of Manitoba, 28 Oct.

Kreutzwisser, Reid D. 1991. 'Water Resource Management: Canadian Perspectives and the Great Lakes Water Issue.' In Mitchell, ed. (1991), 153–79.

Laflamme, Gilles, Bélanger, Laurent, and Audet, Michel. 1987. 'Workers' Participation and Personnel Policies in Canada: Some Hopeful Signs.' *International Labour Review* 126, no. 2 (March–April), 219–28.

LaForest, Gerard V. 1969. *Natural Resources and Public Property under the Canadian Constitution*. Toronto: University of Toronto Press.

Lambrecht, Kirk N. 1991. *The Administration of Dominion Lands, 1870–1930*. Regina: Canadian Plains Research Center.

Laskin, Bora. 1969. *The British Tradition in Canadian Law*. London: Stevens and Sons.

Laux, Jeanne Kirk, and Appel Molot, Maureen. 1988. *State Capitalism: Public Enterprise in Canada*. Ithaca, NY: Cornell University Press.

Lederer, Victor. 1978. 'Decision Making: Should Employees Get In On the Act?' *Administrative Management* (Sept.), 51–62.

Lederman, W. 1958. 'The Common Law System in Canada.' In *Canadian Jurisprudence: The Civil Law and Common Law in Canada*. Toronto: Carswell.

Lee, Ian, and Hobbs, Clem. 1996. 'Pink Slips and Running Shoes: The Liberal Government's Downsizing of the Public Service.' In Swimmer, ed. (1996), 337–78.

Levernier, James, and Cohen, Hennig, eds. 1977. *The Indians and Their Captives*. Westport, Conn.: Greenwood Press.

Levine, Philip J. 1973. 'Towards a Property Right in Employment.' *Buffalo Law Review* (spring), 1081–1110.

Lichtenstein, Peter M. 1984. 'Economic Democracy: The Rawls–Vanek–Sraffa Connection.' *Review of Social Economy* (Oct.), 170–82.

Lowe, Mick. 1995. 'Steel Resolve.' *Financial Post Magazine* (April), 20–6.

Lustig, Jeffrey R. 1986. 'Freedom, Corporations, and the New Whiggery.' In Fred. E. Baumann, ed., *Democratic Capitalism? Essays in Search of a Concept*, 127–58. Charlottesville: University Press of Virginia.

Lyon, Noel. 1985. 'Constitutional Issues in Native Law.' In Morse, ed. (1985), 408–51.
McDavid, James. 1988. 'Privatizing Local Government Services in Canada.' In Michael Walker, ed., *Privatization: Tactics and Techniques*, Vancouver: Fraser Institute. 101–16.
MacDonald, Grant. 1989. 'Organized Labour Encouraged Worker Co-ops in the 19th Century.' *Worker Co-op* (summer), 22–4.
Macdonald, Norman. 1934. 'English Land Tenure on the North American Continent.' In University of Toronto Studies in History and Economics, *Contributions to Canadian Economics*, vol. 7.
McFetridge, D.G. 1985. 'Commercial and Political Efficiency: A Comparison of Government, Mixed, and Private Enterprises.' In McFetridge, ed. (1985), 195–231.
McFetridge, D.G., ed., 1985. *Canadian Industrial Policy in Action*. Research Studies, vol. 4. Toronto: University of Toronto Press and the Royal Commission on the Economic Union and Development Prospects for Canada.
Maclean, John P. 1984. 'Where Provinces Stand on Divorce Settlement Laws.' *Financial Post*, 26 May, 29.
MacNeil, Michael. 1983. 'Property in the Welfare State.' *Dalhousie Law Journal*, 367–82.
Macpherson, C.B. 1962. *The Political Theory of Possessive Individualism*. Oxford: Clarendon Press.
–, ed. 1978. *Property, Mainstream and Critical Positions*. Toronto: University of Toronto Press.
– 1980. 'A Political Theory of Property. In Virginia Held, ed., *Property, Profits, and Economic Justice*. Belmont, Calif.: Wadsworth.
McQueen, Rod. 1993. 'The New World of Corporate Governance.' *Financial Post*, 20 Nov., S14–S15.
– 1995. 'Director's Role Undermined by Stock Options.' *Financial Post*, 8–10 July, 1–2.
– 1996. 'Under the Gun.' Three-part series on corporate governance. *Financial Post*, 4 May, 6–7.
McWhinney, Edward, ed. 1958. *Canadian Jurisprudence, the Civil Law and Common Law in Canada*. Toronto: Carswell.
Malthus, Robert Thomas. 1960. *A Summary View of the Principle of Population*. In *Three Essays on Population*. New York: Mentor Books.
Marshall, T.H. 1964. *Class, Citizenship and Social Development: Essays by T.H. Marshall*. Garden City, NY: Doubleday.
Maslove, Allan M. 1996. 'The Canada Health and Social Transfer: Forcing Issues.' In Swimmer, ed. (1996), 283–301.

Maslow, Abraham. 1970. *Motivation and Personality*, 2nd ed. New York: Harper and Row.
Mason, Greg. 1995. 'Managing Demand Using Contingent Valuation: An Application to Wilderness Valuation.' Presentation to the Department of Economics, University of Manitoba, 17 Nov.
Meadows, Dennis, et al. 1972. *The Limits to Growth*. First report of the Club of Rome. New York: New American Library.
Mercredi, Ovide, and Turpel, Mary Ellen. 1993. *In the Rapids: Navigating the Future of First Nations*. Toronto: Viking.
Meredith, Thomas. 1991. 'Environmental Impact and Assessment.' In Mitchell, ed. (1991), 224–45.
Mimoto, H., and Cross, P.H. 1991. 'The Growth of the Federal Debt.' *Canadian Economic Observer* (June).
Mitchell, Bruce, ed. 1991. *Resource Management and Development*. Toronto: Oxford University Press.
Monet, Don, and Skanu'u (Ardythe Wilson). 1992. *Colonization on Trial: Indigenous Land Rights and the Gitskin and Wet'suwet'en Sovereignty Case*. Gabriola Island, BC: New Society Publishers.
Morse, Bradford, ed. 1985. *Aboriginal Peoples and the Law: Indian, Metis and Inuit Rights in Canada*. Ottawa: Carleton University Press.
Mossman, Mary Jane. 1986. 'Family Law and Social Welfare in Canada.' In Bernier and Lajoie (1986), 43–69.
– 1987. 'Development in Property Law: The 1985–1986 Term.' *Supreme Court Law Review* 9. 419ff.
Mueller-Freienfels, Wolfram. 1985. ' The New Family and the New Property.' *American Journal of Comparative Law 33*, 733–52.
Munzer, Stephen R. 1990. *A Theory of Property*. New York: Cambridge University Press.
Nankivell, Neville. 1996. 'A Good Working Relationship between Management, Union.' *Financial Post*, 29 June, 20.
National Council of Welfare. 1990. *Pension Reform*. Ottawa: Supply and Services.
Nelles, H.V. 1974. *The Politics of Development: Forests, Mines, and Hydro-electric Power in Ontario 1849–1941*. Toronto: Macmillan.
Nepon, M.B. 1983. 'Brief on the Proposed Property Rights Amendment to the Constitution Act, 1982.' Prepared for the Attorney General of Manitoba. 2 March.
Nightingale, Donald V. 1977. 'The Concept of Employee Participation in Canada.' *Industrial Democracy Today* 31–4.
Niosi, Jorge. 1981. *Canadian Capitalism: A Study of Power in the Canadian Business Establishment*. Toronto: James Lorimer.

Norrie, Kenneth, and Owram, Douglas. 1991. *A History of the Canadian Economy.* Toronto: Harcourt, Brace, Jovanovich.
Noyes, C. Reinold. 1936. *The Institution of Property: A Study of the System of Property in Modern Anglo-American Law.* New York: Longmans, Green.
O'Brien, George. 1968. *An Essay on Medieval Economic Thinking.* New York: Burt Franklin.
O'Connor, James. 1973. *The Fiscal Crisis of the State.* New York: St Martin's Press.
Oliverima, Karl. 1974. 'Appropriation in the State of Nature: Locke on the Origin of Property.' *Journal of the History of Ideas,* 211–30.
Ostrom, Elinor. 1990. *Governing the Commons: The Evolution of Institutions for Collective Action.* New York: Cambridge University Press.
Ostry, Sylvia. 1985. 'Government Intervention: Canada and the United States Compared.' In K.J. Rea and Nelson Wiseman, eds., *Government and Enterprise in Canada,* 20–32. Toronto: Methuen.
Ouellet, Fernand. 1980. *Economic and Society History of Quebec, 1760–1850.* Ottawa: Carleton Library.
Palmer, Bryan D. 1979. *A Culture in Conflict: Skilled Workers and Industrial Capitalism in Hamilton, Ontario, 1860–1914.* Montreal: McGill-Queen's University Press.
– 1983. *Working-Class Experience: The Rise and Reconstitution of Canadian Labour, 1800–1980.* Toronto: Butterworth.
Paquet, Gilles, and Shepherd, Robert. 1996. 'The Program Review Process: A Deconstruction.' In Swimmer, ed. (1996), 39–72.
Parkin, Frank. 1986. *Marxism and Class Theory: A Bourgeois Critique.* Social Science Paperback. London: Tavistock Publications.
Payne, Julien D. 1985. 'Family Law in Canada and the Financial Consequences of Marriage Breakdown and Divorce. In Bernier and Lajoie, eds. (1986), 1–42.
Pearse, Peter H. 1988. 'Property Rights and the Development of Natural Resource Policies.' *Canadian Public Policy.* 14 no. 3, 307–20.
Pejovich, Svetozar. 1979. *Fundamentals of Economics: A Property Rights Approach.* Dallas: Fisher Institute.
–, ed. 1983. *Philosophic and Economic Foundations of Capitalism.* Lexington, Mass.: D.C. Heath.
Perry, David. 1993. 'What Price Canadian? Taxation and Debt Compared.' In Thomas, ed. (1993), 42–64.
Phillips, Jeremy. 1986. *Introduction to Intellectual Property Law.* London: Butterworths.
Phillips, Paul. 1991. 'Is Industrial Democracy Feasible? Lessons from Mondragon.' *Canadian Dimension* (March), 38–41.
– 1992. 'Functional Rights: Private, Public and Collective Property.' *Studies in Political Economy* 38 (summer), 61–84.

Pryor, Frederic L. 1973. *Property and Industrial Organization in Communist and Capitalist Nations*. Bloomington: Indiana University Press.

Pulkingham, Jane, and Ternowetsky, Gordon. 1996a. 'The Changing Landscape of Social Policy and the Canadian Welfare State.' In Pulkingham and Ternowetsky, eds. (1996b), 2–29.

– eds. 1996b. *Remaking Canadian Social Policy: Society Security in the Late 1990s*. Halifax: Fernwood.

Quarter, Jack, and Melnyk, George, eds. 1989. *Partners in Enterprise: The Worker Ownership Phenomenon*. Montreal: Black Rose Books.

Rawls, John. 1971. *A Theory of Justice*. Cambridge, Mass.: Harvard University Press.

Rea, K.J., and McLeod, J.T. 1976. *Business and Government in Canada: Selected Readings*, 2nd ed. Toronto: Methuen.

Reeve, Andrew. 1986. *Property*. Atlantic Highlands, NJ: Humanities Press International.

Reich, Charles. 1965a. 'Individual Rights and Social Welfare: The Emerging Legal Issues.' *Yale Law Journal* 74, 1245.

– 1965b. 'The New Property.' *Yale Law Journal* 73, no. 5 (April), 733–87.

Reich, Robert. 1992. *The Work of Nations*. New York: Vantage Books.

Rice, James. 1987. 'Restitching the Safety Net: Altering the National Security System.' In Michael Prince, ed., *How Ottawa Spends, 1987–88*. Toronto: Methuen.

Ridley, Matt, and Low, Bobbi S. 1993. 'Can Selfishness Save the Environment?' *Atlantic Monthly* (Sept.), 76–86.

Roodman, David Malin. 1996. 'Harnessing the Market for the Environment.' In Lester Brown, ed. (1996), 168–87.

Royal Commission on Corporate Concentration (Bryce Commission). 1978. *Report*. Ottawa.

Royal Commission on the Economic Union and Development Prospects for Canada (Macdonald Commission). 1985. *Report*. Vol. II. Ottawa: Minister of Supply and Services.

Ruff, Larry E. 1993. 'The Economic Common Sense of Pollution.' In Dorfman and Dorfman, eds. (1993), 20–36.

Russell, Raymond. 1985. *Sharing Ownership in the Workplace*. Albany: State University of New York Press.

Ryan, Alan. 1984. *Property and Political Theory*. Oxford: Basil Blackwell.

Saul, John Ralston. 1995. *The Unconscious Civilization*. Concord, Ont.: Anansi Press.

Sax, Joseph L. 1983. 'Some Thoughts on the Decline of Private Property.' *Washington Law Review* 58.

Schellenberg, Grant. 1996. 'Diversity in Retirement and the Financial Security of Older Workers.' In Pulkingham and Ternowetsky, eds. (1996), 151–69.

Schmid, A. Allan. 1978. *Property, Power, and Public Choice: an Inquiry into Law and Economics.* New York: Praeger.

Schrecker, Ted. 1992. ' Of Invisible Beasts and the Public Interest: Environmental Cases and the Judicial System.' In Boardman, ed. (1992), 83–108.

Schregle, J. 1978. 'Co-determination in the Federal Republic of Germany: A Comparative View.' *International Labour Review* (Jan.–Feb.), 81–98.

Schreiner, John. 1991. 'Native Ruling Frees Resource Projects.' *Financial Post,* 11 March, 1.

Schuller, Tom. 1985. *Democracy at Work.* Oxford: Oxford University Press.

Schwarz, Edward. 1982. 'Economic Development as If Neighborhoods Mattered.' In John Raines et al., eds., *Community and Capital in Conflict: Plant Closing and Job Loss.* Philadelphia: Temple University Press.

Schweickart, David. 1980. *Capitalism or Worker Control?* New York: Praeger.

Scott, Anthony. 1955. 'The Fishery: The Objectives of Sole Ownership.' *Journal of Political Economy* 63 (April), 116–24.

Self, Peter. 1993. *Government by the Market? The Politics of Public Choice.* Boulder, Col.: Westview Press.

Sen, Amartya. 1986. 'Adam Smith's Prudence.' In Sanjaya Lall and Frances Stewart, eds., *Theory and Reality in Development.* Cited in Stretton and Orchard (1994), 16.

– 1990. 'Individual Freedom as a Social Commitment.' *New York Review of Books,* 14 June, 49–54.

Sharpe, M.E. 1996. 'Ownership and Control,' Review. *Challenge* (Jan.–Feb.), 62–4.

Shaw, D. Leslie. 1973, 'Property, Possession and Ownership: Changing Concepts.' In Philippe Crabbe and Irene Spry, eds. *Natural Resource Development in Canada,* Ottawa: University of Ottawa Press.

Shillington, Richard. 1996. 'The Tax System and Social Policy Reform.' In Pulkingham and Ternowetsky, eds. (1996), 100–11.

Silver, Susan. 1996. 'The Struggle for National Standards: Lessons from the Federal Role in Health Care.' In Pulkingham and Ternowetsky, eds. (1996), 67–80.

Skogstad, Grace, and Kopas, Paul. 1992. 'Environmental Policy in a Federal System: Ottawa and the Provinces.' In Boardman, ed. (1992), 43–59.

Smith, Adam. 1937. *An Inquiry into the Nature and Causes of the Wealth of Nations.* New York: Modern Library.

Snare, Frank. 1972. 'The Concept of Property.' *American Philosphical Quarterly* 9, 200–6.

Solow, Robert. 1993a. 'The Economics of Resources or the Resources of Economics.' In Dorfman and Dorfman, eds. (1993), 162–78.

– 1993b. 'Sustainability: An Economist's Perspective.' In Dorfman and Dorfman, eds. (1993), 179–87.

Stanbury, W.T. 1986. *Business–Government Relations in Canada: Grappling with Leviathan.* Toronto: Methuen.
- 1989. 'Privatization in Canada: Ideology, Symbolism or Substance?' In Paul MacAvoy et al., eds., *Privatization and State-Owned Enterprises: Lessons from the United States, Great Britain and Canada,* chap. 5. Boston: Kluwer Academic Publishers.
- 1994. 'The Extent of Privatization in Canada, 1979–1994.' Paper prepared for presentation at the Canadian Law and Economics Association meetings, Faculty of Law, University of Toronto, 30 Sept.–1 Oct.

Standing Committee on Finance, Trade and Economic Affairs. 1982. *Report of the Sub-Committee to Promote Profit-Sharing by Employees in Business.* Ottawa, June.

Standing Committee on Human Resources Development. 1994. *Agenda: Jobs and Growth. Improving Social Security in Canada. A Discussion Paper.* Green Paper, Ottawa, Tabled 5 October.
- 1994b. *Concerns and Priorities Regarding the Modernization and Restructuring of Canada's Social Security System.* Interim Report. Ottawa. Tabled in March.
- 1995. *Security, Opportunity and Fairness: Canadians Renewing Their Social Programs.* Final Report. Tabled 6 February.

Stanford, Jim. 1996. 'Discipline, Insecurity and Productivity: The Economics behind Labour Market Flexibility.' In Pulkingham and Ternowetsky, eds., (1996), 130–50.
- 1996. 'Economic Dependency Profiles.' *Daily,* 17 July. Ottawa.
- Various years. *Annual Report of the Minister of Industry, Science, and Technology.* Ottawa.

Stein, Kenneth. 1988. 'Privatization: A Canadian Perspective.' In M.A. Walker, ed., *Privatization: Tactics and Techniques.* Vancouver: Fraser Institute.

Stevens, Garth. 1982. 'Property Rights Are Not Imperiled.' *Financial Post,* 8 May, 9.

Stevens, Joe B. 1993. *The Economics of Collective Choice.* Boulder, Col.: Westview Press.

Stevenson, Colin B. 1983. 'A New Perspective on Environmental Rights after the Charter.' *Osgoode Hall Law Journal* 21, no. 3, 390–421.

Stretton, Hugh, and Orchard, Lionel. 1994. *Public Goods, Public Enterprise, Public Choice.* New York: St Martin's Press.

Swaigen, J., and Woods, R. 1981. 'A Substantive Right to Environmental Quality.' In J. Swaigen, ed., *Environmental Rights,* 195–241, as cited in Schrecker (1992), 98.

Swimmer, Gene, ed. 1996. *How Ottawa Spends 1996–97, Life under the Knife.* Ottawa: Carleton University Press.

Taylor, F.W. 1911. *The Principles of Scientific Management.* New York: Harper.

Taylor, Malcolm. 1987. 'The Canadian Health Care Systen after Medicare.' In D.

Cobourn, ed., *Health and Canadian Society*, 2nd ed. Markham, Ont.: Fitzhenry and Whiteside.

Thomas, David, ed. 1993. *Canada and the United States: Differences That Count*. Peterborough, Ont.: Broadview Press.

Thomas, H., and Logan, C. 1982. *Mondragon: An Economic Analysis*. London: Allen and Unwin.

Tietenberg, Tom. 1994. *Environmental Economics and Policy*. New York: HarperCollins.

Toulin, Alan. 1995. 'Who Owns This Land of Ours?' *Financial Post*, 16 Sept., 7.

Traves, Tom. 1985. 'Business–Government Relations in Canadian History.' In K.J. Rea and Nelson Wiseman, eds., *Government and Enterprise in Canada*, 8–19. Toronto: Methuen.

Troughton, M.J. 1991. 'Agriculture and Rural Resources.' In Mitchell, ed. (1991), 54–84.

Tseo, George K.Y., and Ramos, Eduardo Lacerdo. 1995. 'Employee Empowerment: Solution to a Burgeoning Crisis?' *Challenge* (Sept.–Oct.), 25–31.

Tully, James. 1980. *A Discourse on Property: John Locke and His Adversaries*. Cambridge: Cambridge University Press.

Tupper, Allan, and Doern, G. Bruce. 1982. 'Understanding Public Corporations in Canada.' *Canadian Business Review* (autumn), 33–9.

– eds. 1989. *Privatization, Public Policy and Public Corporations in Canada*. Halifax: Institute for Research on Public Policy.

Turpel, Mary Ellen. 1989–90. 'Aboriginal Peoples and the Canadian Charter: Interpretive, Cultural Differences.' *Canadian Human Rights Yearbook*, no. 6, 3–45.

U.S. Department of Commerce and Labor. 1994. *Employee Participation and Labor–Management Cooperation in American Workplaces*. Washington, DC: Department of Commerce and Labor.

Usher, Peter J. 1992. 'Property as the Basis of Inuit Hunting Rights.' In Terry L. Anderson, ed., *Property Rights and Indian Economics*, 41–65. Lanham, Md.: Rowan and Littlefield.

Usher, Peter J., and Bankes, N.D. 1986. *Property: The Basis of Inuit Hunting Rights – a New Approach*. Ottawa: Inuit Committee on National Issues.

Van Doren, John W. 1985. 'Private Property: A Study in Incoherence.' *University of Detroit Law Review* 63, 683.

VanderZwaag, David, and Duncan, Linda. 1992. 'Canada and Environmental Protection: Confident Political Faces, Uncertain Legal Hands.' In Boardman, ed. (1992), 3–23.

Vanek, Jaroslav. 1970. *General Theory of Labour-Managed Market Economies*. Ithaca, NY: Cornell University Press.

Vaughan, E.J. 1976. 'Some Observations upon the Logic of Participative Management.' *Journal of Industrial Relations*, Sydney (Sept.) 220–8.
Vogt, Paul. 1985. 'Property Rights and the Canadian Charter.' MA thesis, Oxford University.
Vogt, Roy. 1981. 'Property Rights and Employee Decision Making in West Germany.' *Journal of Economic Issues* (June), 377–86.
Vosko, Leah F. 1996. 'Irregular Workers, New Involuntary Social Exiles and U.I. Reform.' In Pulkingham and Ternowetsky, eds. (1996), 256–72.
Waldron, Jeremy. 1985. 'What Is Private Property?' *Oxford Journal of Legal Studies* 5 no. 3, 313–45.
Walker, K.F. 1972. *Workers' Participation in Management: An International Perspective.* Geneva: International Institute for Labour Studies.
Ward, Benjamin N. 1958. 'The Firm in Illyria: Market Syndicalism.' *American Economic Review* 48 (Sept.), 373–86.
Waterman, Anthony. 1982. 'Property Rights in John Locke and in Christian Social Teaching.' *Review of Social Economy* 51 no. 2 (Oct.), 97–115.
Weinrib, Arnold S. 1988. 'Information and Property.' *University of Toronto Law Journal* 117–50.
Weitzman, Lenore, and Maclean, Mavis. 1992. *Economic Consequences of Divorce: The International Perspective.* Oxford: Clarendon Press.
Weitzman, Lenore J. 1992. 'Marital Property: Its Transformation and Division in the United States.' In Weitzman and Maclean, eds. (1992), 85–142.
Whitehorn, A. 1978. 'Workers' Self Management – A Blueprint for Industrial Democracy.' *Canadian Slavonic Papers*, Ottawa. (Sept.), 421–8.
Whyte, William, and Whyte, Kathleen. 1988. *Making Mondragon: The Growth and Dynamics of the Worker Cooperative Complex.* Ithaca, NY: ILR Press.
Wildsmith, Bruce H. 1985. 'Pre-Confederation Treaties.' In Morse, ed. (1985), 122–271.
Wiles, P.J.D. 1977. *Economic Institutions Compared.* Oxford: Basil Blackwell.
Williamson, Oliver. 1970. *Corporate Control and Business Behavior.* Englewood Cliffs, NJ: Prentice-Hall.
Wilson, H.P. 1974. *Democracy and the Work Place.* Montreal: Black Rose Books.
Wilson, Jeremy. 1992. 'Green Lobbies: Pressure Groups and Environmental Policy.' In Boardman, ed. (1992), 109–25.
Wiseman, John. 1996. 'National Social Policy in an Age of Global Power: Lessons from Canada and Australia.' In Pulkingham and Ternowetsky, eds. (1996b), 114–29.
Witte, John F. 1980. *Democracy, Authority, and Alienation in Work.* Chicago: University of Chicago Press.

World Bank. 1994. *World Development Report 1995*. Oxford: Oxford University Press.
World Commission on Environment and Development (Brudland Commission) 1987. *Our Common Future*. Oxford: Oxford University Press.
York, Geoffrey. 1989. *The Dispossessed: Life and Death in Native Canada*. Toronto: Lester & Orpen Dennys.
Zlotkin, Norman K. 1985. 'Post-Confederation Treaties.' In Morse, ed. (1985), 272–404.

Name Index

Abella, Rosalie Silberman, 81
Adelman, Jerry, 5
Aharoni, Yair, 58
Alchian, A., 157
Ambrose of Milan, 37
Anastassopoulos, Jean-Pierre, 58
Anton, Frank R., 155, 166
Aquinas, Thomas, 38, 39, 43
Aristotle, 41, 42
Armstrong, Christopher, 31, 32, 33
Asch, Michael, 94
Audet, Michel, 150, 167
Augustine of Hippo, 37
Avila, Charles, 37
Axworthy, Lloyd, 187, 191, 193

Baker, C. Edwin, 174, 177
Bakvis, Herman, 191–3
Bankes, N.D., 98
Banting, Keith, 185
Bartlett, Richard H., 90, 91
Barton, Stephen E., 42, 143, 156
Battle, Ken, 188, 190, 192
Bazelon, David, 14, 16, 17
Beck, Adam, 33, 44
Becker, Lawrence C., 38, 42
Becker, Rosa, 74

Belanger, Laurent, 150, 167
Belobaba, Edward, 109, 113–14
Bentham, Jeremy, 16
Berger, Thomas R., 99
Blair, Margaret M., 166
Bodin, Jean, 39
Boothman, Barry E.C., 58
Borins, Sanford F., 58
Bouchard, Lucien, 127
Boulding, Kenneth, 128
Bowles, Samuel, 6, 23, 42, 157–8, 162–3
Broadway, Robin, 185
Brooks, Stephen, 117, 124, 128, 131, 182, 184, 188–9
Brown, Lester R., 123–4
Brown, M. Paul, 126–7, 135, 138
Brubaker, Elizabeth, 132
Buchanan, James, 57, 63
Buchele, Robert, 171
Burke, Edmund, 114

Campbell, Kim, 190
Cardozo, Andrew, 203
Carnoy, Martin, 157
Carson, Rachel, 124
Chrétien, Jean, 191
Christiansen, Jens, 171

Name Index

Cobb, John B., Jr, 111–12, 113–14, 117–18, 134
Cohen, Henning, 99
Coleman, William, 131
Connaghan, C.J., 171
Cooper, F.D., 173
Corcoran, Terence, 121
Cornwallis, Colonel Edward, 87
Cote, Roy, 139
Courchene, Thomas, 57, 182, 189
Coval, Simon, 41
Craven, Paul, 148–9
Cribbet, J., 42
Cromwell, Oliver, 22–3
Cross, P.H., 54, 183
Cumming, Peter A., 100, 102
Cunningham, John, 23

Dahl, Robert A., 157–9
Dahlman, Carl J., 21
Dales, J.H., 119–20
Daly, Herman E., 111–14, 117–18, 134
Damsell, Keith, 93
Davidson, Greg, 197, 201
Davidson, Paul, 197, 201
DeAlessi, Louis, 35, 56
Demsetz, Harold, 26, 157
Dickson, Justice Brian, 74
Dietz, Gottfried, 39
Doern, G. Bruce, 49, 57–9, 131
Donahue, John D., 35, 59–61
Dorfman, Nancy, 110, 117, 120, 122
Dorfman, Robert, 110, 117, 120, 122
Drache, Daniel, 149
Dragun, A.K., 155
Dufour, Jules, 26, 28, 130–1
Duncan, Linda, 125–6, 128, 137–8
Durkheim, Emil, 41

Eichler, M., 81

Elden, J. Maxwell, 156
Ellerman, David P., 159
Elliott, David W., 18, 94–100, 102–4
Euken, Walter, 208
Evans, Patricia, 78–9
Evans, Robert, 186, 189

Farr, Eleanor, 75
Farr, Glen, 75
Ferguson, Howard, 33
Filyk, Gregor, 139
Fontaine, Phil, 106–7
Forsyth, Murray, 41
Fraser, Douglas, 15
Friedman, Milton, 4, 42
Friesen, Gerald, 99
Fusfeld, Daniel R., 160, 165, 169

Gall, Gerald L., 19, 25
Gardon, Garde, 51
Gillese, Eileen E., 20
Ginsberg, Morris, 37–8
Gintis, Herbert, 6, 23, 42, 157–8, 162–3
Glasbeek, Harry, 149
Glendon, Mary Ann, 68–9, 70, 80, 82
Gordon, H. Scott, 121
Gordon, Marsha, 105
Grant, George, 115
Green, T.H., 41
Greenberg, E.S., 155–6
Greenwood, John, 84, 93
Grunebaun, James O., 38–41, 198
Gustafsson, Bo, 157–8, 162–3
Gyllenhammar, P.G., 171

Hall, Justice Emmet, 99, 186
Hardin, Garrett, 56, 105, 117, 121–2
Harker, Paul, 26
Harris, R. Cote, 26–7
Hayek, Friedrich von, 42, 113

Name Index 233

Hegel, Georg W.F., 41
Heidenreich, C.E., 17
Held, Virginia, 23
Hill, Steven, 144
Hirsch, Fred, 114
Hobbes, Thomas, 42
Hobbs, Clem, 181
Hoggett, Brenda, 67, 70–1, 73
Honoré, A.M., 14
Hotelling, Harold, 123
Hume, David, 42

Iacocca, Lee, 15, 144
Ip, Greg, 67
Ireton, Henry, 23

Jay, Peter, 162
Jefferson, Thomas, 42, 197
Jessop, Bob, 195
Joyce, Greg, 98
Judson, Justice, 99, 103

Kant, Immanuel, 40–1
Kealey, Gregory, 146–8
Keet, Jean E., 71, 75
Keon, Jim, 155
King, William Lyon Mackenzie, 149
Kitchen, B., 79
Kitchen, Harry, 55, 59
Kopas, Paul, 131
Kreutzwisser, Reid D., 26, 130

Laflamme, Gilles, 150, 167
LaForest, Gerard V., 24–6, 28, 88–9, 102
Laux, Jeanne Kirk, 47–8, 61
Leatherdale, Barbara, 75
Lederer, Victor, 156
Lee, Ian, 181
Lenin, Vladimir Ilyich, 151, 198

Leo XIII, Pope, 39
Levernier, James, 99
Levine, Philip J., 175, 178
Lichtenstein, Peter M., 157
Little Bear, Leroy, 17
Locke, John, 16, 39–40, 42, 145–6, 152
Logan, C., 164
Low, Bobbi S., 135, 138
Lowe, Mick, 165
Lustig, Jeffery R., 153
Lyon, Noel, 101

McDavid, James, 55, 59
MacDonald, Grant, 147
McEachern, Allan, 97–8, 100, 102
McFetridge, D.G., 58
Mackenzie, William, 44
Maclean, John P., 74, 76
Maclean, Mavis, 77
MacLeod, J.T., 42, 46, 48
McMillan, Tom, 126–7
MacNeil, Michael, 175–80
Macpherson, C.B., 13, 23–4, 39, 41, 198
McQueen, Rod, 44–5
Mahoney, Justice, 96, 98
Malthus, Thomas, 43
Marshall, T.H., 111, 174
Martin, Paul, 191
Marx, Karl, 8, 40, 146, 150, 200
Maslove, Allan M., 185, 187, 193
Maslow, Abraham, 156
Mason, Greg, 119
Meadows, Dennis, et al., 124
Melnyk, George, 165, 168–9
Mercredi, Ovide, 83, 85–6, 89, 94–5, 101
Meredith, Thomas, 131, 139
Mickenberg, N.H., 100, 102
Mill, John Stuart, 200

Name Index

Mimoto, H., 54, 183
Mitchell, Bruce, 120, 139
Molot, Maureen, 47–8, 61
Monet, Don, 97–8
Morris, Alexander, 90
Morrison, Sir Herbert, 47
Morse, Bradford, 84, 92
Mossman, Mary Jane, 68–70, 72–3, 79, 81–2
Mulroney, Brian, 51, 181
Murdoch, Irene, 74
Myrdal, Alva, 82

Nankivell, Neville, 165
Nelles, H.V., 28, 29, 30–3
Nepon, M.B., 52
Nightingale, Donald V., 143, 155, 160–1
Niosi, Jorge, 44, 48
Norrie, Kenneth, 26, 27, 34
Noyes, C. Reinold, 20, 22, 24

O'Brien, George, 23, 37, 39
O'Connor, James, 53–4, 63
Oliverima, Karl, 39
Orchard, Lionel, 132, 136
Orwell, George, 151
Ostry, Sylvia, 34, 46
Owram, Douglas, 26–7, 34

Palmer, Bryan D., 147
Paquet, Gilles, 190
Parkin, Frank, 14, 16, 41
Payne, Julien D., 68–73, 75, 80–2
Pearse, Peter H., 26–9, 121
Pejovich, Svetozar, 56–7
Perry, David, 183, 186, 188
Pettkus, Lothar, 74
Phillips, Paul, 164
Plato, 41

Pulkingham, June, 187, 192

Quarter, Jack, 165, 168–9

Rainsborough, Thomas, 23
Ramos, Eduardo Lacerdo, 164
Rathwell, Helen, 74
Rawlick, Mr and Mrs, 76–7
Rawls, John, 134
Rea, K.J., 42, 46, 48
Reagan, Ronald, 49
Redbird, Duke, 94
Reeve, Andrew, 14
Reich, Charles, 69, 173–4
Reich, Robert, 114
Rice, James, 183
Riddell, Justice W.R., 32, 52
Ridley, Matt, 135, 138
Robinson, W.B., 89
Roodman, David Malin, 123
Rousseau, Jean-Jacques, 40, 42
Ruff, Larry E., 118, 120
Russell, Raymond, 145–6
Ryan, Alan, 38

Sax, Joseph, 3
Schellenberg, Grant, 194
Schmid, A. Allen, 3, 16
Schrecker, Ted, 125, 129–30, 132, 137
Schregle, J., 171
Schreimer, John, 97–8
Schuller, Tom, 157
Schwartz, Edward, 114–15
Schweikart, David, 162
Scott, Anthony, 56, 105
Self, Peter, 136, 138
Sen, Amartya, 133–4
Sharpe, M.E., 166
Shaw, D. Leslie, 130
Shearer, Derek, 157

Shepherd, Robert, 190
Shillington, Richard, 183
Silver, Susan, 185–6
Simon, Lord, 71, 75
Skanu'u (Ardythe Wilson), 97–8
Skogstad, Grace, 131
Smith, Adam, 39, 42, 44, 113, 117, 198–200
Smith, J.C., 41
Snare, Frank, 14
Solow, Robert, 109–11, 121–3
Stalin, Joseph, 151, 198
Stanbury, W.T., 46, 54–5, 61
Stanfield, Robert, 48–9
Stanford, Jim, 180–1
Stevens, Barbara J., 60
Stevenson, Colin B., 137
Stewart, Stan, 44
Stretton, Hugh, 132, 136

Tanner, John, 99
Taylor, F.W., 148
Taylor, Malcolm, 186
Ternowetsky, Gordon, 187, 192
Thatcher, Margaret, 49
Thomas, H., 164
Tietenberg, Tom, 119–20
Tocqueville, Alexis, 42
Torjman, Sherri, 188, 192
Toulin, Alan, 92–3
Traves, Tom, 34
Troughton, M.J., 17, 26–7, 122, 125
Tseo, George K., 164
Tully, James, 16, 39
Tupper, Allan, 49, 57–9
Turpel, Mary Ellen, 83, 85–7, 89, 94–5, 101

Usher, Peter J., 98–100, 102–5

Van Doren, John, 43
VanderZwaag, David, 125–6, 128, 137–8
Vanek, Jaroslav, 162
Vaughan, E.J., 171
Vogt, Paul, 38, 42
Vogt, Roy, 169–70
Vosko, Leah F., 181

Waldron, Jeremy, 36
Walker, Jeremy, 155
Ward, Benjamin N., 162
Warkentin, John, 26–7
Waterman, Anthony, 16, 38–9
Watson, Lord, 102
Weinrib, Arnold S., 152, 155
Weitzman, Lenore, 77–8
White, Jonathan R., 31
Whitehorn, A., 171
Whyte, Kathleen, 164
Whyte, William, 164
Wildsmith, Bruce H., 88
Wiles, P.J.D., 14
Williamson, Oliver, 56
Wilson, Justice Bertha, 81
Wilson, H.P., 159
Wilson, Jeremy, 133
Wiseman, John, 194
Witte, John F., 156
Wood, E.R., 32

York, Geoffrey, 87

Zlotkin, Norman K., 88–90

Subject Index

Aboriginal experience, 86–93, 198
Aboriginal peoples: Cree Nation, 93, 139; and Constitution Act, 84; Gitksan-Wet'suwet'en, 97, 100; Kanesatake Reserve, 83; legal definitions of, 84–6; Metis, 84; MicMac, 87; Mohawk, 83; Nisga'a, 96, 99, 106; Ojibwa, 89, 99; Plains, 17; population (1991 census), 84; Oka crisis, 83, 93; and property, 40; Royal Commission on Aboriginal Peoples (RCAP), 107; Shawnee, 99; Yukon Native Brotherhood, 18
Aboriginal property, 17–19, 40, 83–108; autonomy, 102–6; claims, 83, 92–3; claims, solutions to, 106–8; and common law, 95–100; communal rules, 105; compensation, 103; English River incident, 105; grievances, 205; historical background, 87, 93; ICC (Independent Claims Commission), 93; Indian Act, 1868, 85; Inuit rights, 102; pre-European settlement, 17; reserves, 87, 90–3; royal prerogative, 95; Royal Proclamation, 1763, 88, 96; scope and content of rights, 101–2; statues and constitutions, 100–1; *Tee-Hit-Ton* case, 1955, 103; Tungavik claim, 93
Aboriginal property, tests of legal status, 96–101; *Baker Lake*, 96, 98; *Calder v. Attorney General of BC*, 1973, 96–7, 103; *Delgamuukw et al. v. The Queen*, 97; Indian Act, 85; *St. Catharine's Milling and Lumber Co. v. The Queen*, 1889, 96; *Sparrow* case, 1989, 97
Aboriginal treaties, 89–91; land entitlement, prairies, 91; outstanding claims, 91; Treaties 1 to 7, 90; Treaties 3 to 11, 90; Robinson Treaties, 1850, 89

Bill of Rights, Canadian, 50
British North America Act, 1867. *See* Constitution Act, 1867
business behaviour: managerial school, 58
business theory: principal–agent problem, 56
Business Week, 113, 144

Canada: Parliament, 1981, 51
Canada Safeway, 115
Canadian Auto Workers Union, 181

238 Subject Index

Canadian Bar Association, 51
Charlottetown Accord, 51, 101
Charter of Rights, 49, 50, 101, 137
Chrysler Corporation, 15
citizen property rights, 109–42; assessing implementation, 127–32; assessing pollution damage, 129; citizen property, definition, 110; citizen rights, 111–12; community interests, protection of, 109–10; constitutional reform, 136; constraints on action, 125; consumer protection, 114; cost of pollution, 119; defining a healthy society, 133–4; environment and sustainability, 110; environmental policies, 126–7; environmental pollution, 11; externalities, 114, 117; individual transferable quotas (ITQS), 121; legal reform in, 134; market failure, technical and political imperatives, 117–32; negative externalities, 109–10, 129; policy making, participation in, 130–2; pollution permits, 119; pollution reduction, 120; protection of environment, 132; social citizenship, 111
Club of Rome, 124
common law: principle of constructive trust, 74, 76–7
common property, 36; fee simple interest, 18
Company of New France, 27
Constitution Act, 1867, 31, 85, 102; 1982, 84, 92, 100, 106, 137
Corn Laws, 199
Corporate Decision-Making in Canada, 58
crown corporations, 47

dams, 128

(Department of) Human Resources Development Canada (HRDC), 190–1
Divorce Act, 1968, 68–70, 72, 82
Domesday Book, 20
Dominion Lands Act, 1872, 100

Economic Council of Canada, 59
economics: property-rights school of, 55
Economist, 54, 131
economy, great and narrow, 134
economy, government involvement in, 34; family allowances, 34, 186; hospital care, 34, 186; (un)employment insurance, 34, 187, 194
environment: Brundtland Commission, 127; Earth Summit, 127; *Our Common Future*, 127; protecting, 132–3; *State of the World* report, 1996, 140; Toronto Conference on the Changing Atmosphere, 127; World Commission on Environment and Development, 127
environmental disasters, 124
environmental legislation: assessing implementation, 127; Canada Water Act, 126; Canadian Charter of Rights, 137; Canadian Environmental Protection Act (CEPA), 125–6; Clean Air Act, 126; Constitution Act, 137; constitutional reform, 136; Environmental Protection Act, 127; federal Fisheries Act, 125; legal reform, 134; Migratory Birds Protection Act, 125; Waters Protection Act, 125
environmental policies: Canadian Council of Resource and Environment Ministers (CCREM), 127;

Department of the Environment, creation of, 126; Green Plan, 127; National Task Force on Environment and Economy, 127; policy-making, participation, 10, 130; price on negative externalities, 129
environmental protection groups: Audubon Society, 124; Canadian Nature Federation, 133; Canadian Wildlife Federation, 128, 133; Energy Probe, 138; Friends of the Earth, 133; Greenpeace, 133; Pollution Probe, 133; Sierra Club, 124; Western Canadian Wilderness Committee, 133
European Union, 6

family law: inadequate support, 78; income support, 81; international trends in, 77; problems in, 78; recent legislation, 78; social assistance policy, 81
family property: asset ownership in marriage, 77; finite ownership, 77; long-term ownership, 77
family property legislation: Divorce Act, 1968, 72–3; Divorce Act, maintenance settlements, 73; *Farr v. Farr*, 75; federal v. provincial law, 73; indirect contribution of women to family property, 73; *Leatherdale v. Leatherdale*, 75; *Messier v. Delage*, 81; *Murdoch* case, 74; *Pettkus v. Becker*, 74; *Rathwell v. Rathwell*, 74–5
Financial Post, 51, 98
First Nations: definition, 85
Forbes magazine, 144

goods and services tax (GST), 52
government corporations: efficiency of, 58–60; empirical studies, 58; refuse collection, 59–60

independent land claims commission (ICC), 1990, 93
Indian Act: amendment to, 85
Inuit: definition, 84
Inuit rights, 102
Inuvaluit claim, 93

Knights of St Crispin, 147

law systems: '*lex loci*,' 99
The Limits to Growth, 124
Loyalists, 25

Macdonald Commission, 205
Maclean's, 173
Manitoba Act, 1870, 100
market failure: technical imperatives, 117–23; political imperatives, 123–5
Magna Carta, 22
Married Women's Property Act, Saskatchewan, 1907, 71
Metis: definition, 84

NAFTA, 45
National Council on Welfare, 189
new family: dependence of women in, 79; family property in, 79; poverty of divorced women, 80; remarriage in, 79
new family and social policy, 77–82
new property: accrued property rights, 174; definition, 69, 173; in health care and education, 185–8; in jobs, 175–82; limited access of women to, 80; new social policies, 188–91; social investments, 174; social safety net, 182–5

Subject Index 239

new property and health care legislation: Canada Health Act, 1986, 186; Federal-Provincial Fiscal Arrangements and Established Programs Act, 1997, 186; Health Services Review, 1980, 186; Hospital Insurance and Diagnostic Services Act, 1957, 185; Medical Care Act, 1966, 185

new property rights in the workplace: capitalist industrialization, 149; history, 145–51; workers' democracy, 164–71; workers' property rights, reasons for enlarging, 151–64; workers without property, emergence of, 145–51

New York Times, 144

private property: and attack on government, 49; growth of rights, 27; neoliberal movement, 49; rights to, 37

property creation in Canada, 25–34

property in labour, 152; intellectual property, 153–5

property law: in civil law, 19, 25–6; in common law, 19, 25–7; eminent domain, doctrine of, 24–5, 51

property law, history: evolution in the seventeenth century, 24; federal property rights, 19–22; medieval property, 19–22

property: nature of, 14

property rights: alienation, 22; ancient inheritance, 22; Canadian Bill of Rights, 1960, 50; Charter of Rights and Freedoms, 50; citizen rights, 203; common property, 16, 18; constitutional protection of, 50–3; crown grants, 27; crown rights of provinces, 28; Divorce Act, 68–70; employee property rights, 144; in the family, 67–82; fee simple, 30; fixed interest, 23; justification theories, 23; Married Women's Property Act, 1907, 71; new family law, recent changes, 67; ownership, 14, 21; ownership in business, 15; possessory rights, 20; private property, 15, 16; property position of female spouses, 71; seigneurial system, 26–7; shared property, 15–16; Statute of Quia Emptores, 22; unitary property, 15–16; workplace rights, 203

property rights and government: criticism of state sector, 54; 'downsizing' of government, 54; initiatives to reduce size and role of government, 53–4, 61; U.S. constitution, 14th Amendment, 31

property rights and settlement, 29

property-rights justification: acquisition theory, 38, 39; natural-rights theory, 38; utilitarian theory, 38, 40

property rights, restructuring: broader participation, 204; horizontal and vertical dimensions, 198–201; new property, 206; sharing property rights, 202; solutions, 201

property rights, types of: citizen rights, 202; disposal rights, 14, 21, 29, 92; income or enjoyment rights, 14, 29, 92, 102; shared rights, 21; tenant rights, 21; user rights, 14, 21, 29, 92, 102

property rights of workers, reasons for enlarging: economic reasons, 156–9; ethical-psychological reasons, 155–6; legal-philosophical reasons, 151–5; political reasons, 156–9; property in labour, 152

Subject Index 241

property theory: and attack on government, 55–62; Canadian multinational firms, 45; corporate forms of business, 44; crown corporations, 46; developments in Canada, 43; economies of scale, 43; foreign ownership, 45; growth of state enterprises in production, 46; increasing government involvement, 45–6; NAFTA, 45; natural-rights theory, 16; Royal Commission on the Economic Union, 46; state sector, 45
public and private property, 32–4

Quebec Act, 1774, 25

reserve: definition, 90
reserves: Canadian v. American system of, 90; current situation, 91–3; policy objectives, 90. *See also* Aboriginal property
resource rights: fisheries, 28; minerals, 29, 32; water (riparian) rights, 28–9, 32
resources: control of, 29–34; market failure, coping with, 117–25; market failure in, 112–17; non-renewable resources, 121; pollution costs, 119–23; renewable resources, 121. *See also* citizen property rights
Robinson Treaties, 1850, 89
Royal Commission on Aboriginal Peoples (RCAP), 107
Royal Commission on Corporate Concentration, 44
Royal Commission on the Economic Union, 1985, 46
Royal Proclamation, 1763, 88, 95–7

St. Catharine's Milling, 1889, 101–2

Silent Spring, 124
social safety net: basic social-resource program, 182; Canada Assistance Plan (CAP), 182, 187, 193, 194; Canada Health and Social Transfer (CHST), 193; Canada Pension Plan (CPP/QPP), 182, 187, 194; employment insurance (EI), 187, 194; Established Program Financing (EPF), 193; federal budget, 1995, 191; GIS, 187, 194; Government Action Plan, 191–3; hidden welfare system, 183; House of Commons Standing Committee on Human Resources Development, 191; Human Resources Investment Fund (HRIF), 193; income security system, 182; long-term problems in, 189; medicare, 182; protected society, 182; Social Security Review, 191; strategies to reform government social-benefit programs, 190; welfare state, 182
State of the World report, 123
state v. private property, 35–63; differences, 36; merits of, 36
Statistics Canada, 45, 54, 67, 175, 182, 187
subinfeudation, 20
Sun, 165
Supreme Court of Canada, 74–7, 81

treaties. *See* Aboriginal treaties
Treaty of Paris, 1763, 88

Universal Declaration of Human Rights, 1948, 50
United Steelworkers of America, 165
utilitarian theories: efficiency theory, 41–2; idealist theory, 41–2; republican theory, 41–2

Winnipeg Free Press, 4, 190
workplace: Brookings Institute, 166; Canadian Labour Code, 167; capitalist industrialization, 149; employee decision-making and involvement, 160–1; governance: agent–principal theory, 162, industrial democracy, 160; industrial forms of the producing enterprise: capitalist firms with collective bargaining, 161, firms with worker decision making, 161, labour-managed firms, 162, pure capitalist firms, 160; International Labour Organization (ILO), 165–6; job protection, devices for: collective bargaining, 178–9, contract law, 178, natural justice and fairness, 179–80, statutory protection, 178–9; labour-force insecurity, 180; management philosophy, 155; Mondragon, 164; participatory management, 155; U.S. Department of Commerce and Labor, 166; worker cooperatives: Algoma Steel, 165, Pine Falls Paper Company, 165, Spruce Falls Mill, 164–6, *Sun* newspaper, 165; worker-owned firms v. capitalist firms, 162, co-determination, 169–70, economic impact, 166, Employee Stock Ownership Plans (ESOPs), 168–9, quality circles, 167; workers' democracy, 164–71; workers' rights index, 171

workplace, West German experience: Co-Determination Act, 1976, 170; Works Constitution Act, 1972, 169

workplace and government: Royal Commission on Corporate Concentration, 1978, 168; Standing Committee on Finance, Trade and Economic Affairs, 1982, 168

workplace legislation: Canada Labour Code, 179; Public Services Employment Act, 179; Public Staff Relations Act, 179

World Bank, 134